Rick Steves' Postcards from Europe

25 Years of Travel Tales from America's Favorite Guidebook Writer

AVALON
TRAVEL

Other ATP travel guidebooks by Rick Steves
Rick Steves' Best of Europe
Rick Steves' Europe 101: History and Art for the Traveler (with Gene Openshaw)
Rick Steves' Europe Through the Back Door
Rick Steves' Mona Winks: Self-Guided Tours of Europe's Top Museums
    (with Gene Openshaw)
Rick Steves' France, Belgium & the Netherlands (with Steve Smith)
Rick Steves' Germany, Austria & Switzerland
Rick Steves' Great Britain
Rick Steves' Ireland (with Pat O'Connor)
Rick Steves' Italy
Rick Steves' Scandinavia
Rick Steves' Spain & Portugal
Rick Steves' Florence (with Gene Openshaw)
Rick Steves' London (with Gene Openshaw)
Rick Steves' Paris (with Steve Smith and Gene Openshaw)
Rick Steves' Rome (with Gene Openshaw)
Rick Steves' Venice (with Gene Openshaw)
Rick Steves' Phrase Books: German, Italian, French, Spanish/Portuguese, and
    French/Italian/German

Avalon Travel Publishing, 5855 Beaudry Street, Emeryville, CA 94608

Text copyright © 1999 by Rick Steves
Maps copyright © 1999 by Europe Through the Back Door. All rights reserved.

First edition. Fifth printing March 2002.
Printed in the United States of America by R.R. Donnelley

Library of Congress Cataloging-in-Publication Data
Steves, Rick, 1955—
    Rick Steves' Postcards from Europe: 25 years of travel tales from America's
    favorite guidebook writer / Rick Steves.
        p.   cm.
    ISBN: 1-56261-397-9
    1. Europe—Description and travel. 2. Steves, Rick, 1955—Journeys—Europe.
    1. Title: Postcards from Europe.
    D923 .S82   1999
    914.04'55—dc21

                                        98-45399
                                        CIP

Europe Through the Back Door Editor: Risa Laib
Avalon Travel Publishing editors: Dianna Delling, Krista Lyons-Gould, Elizabeth Wolf
Production: Janine Lehmann
Cover and Interior Design: Janine Lehmann
Typesetter: Kathleen Sparkes, White Hart Design
Map: David C. Hoerlein
Photography: Rick Steves, unless otherwise noted
Cover photo: Vernazza, Italy; copyright © Rick Steves

Distributed to the book trade by Publishers Group West, Berkeley, California

For the latest on Rick's lectures, guidebooks, tours, and public television series, contact
Europe Through the Back Door, Box 2009, Edmonds, WA 98020, tel. 425/771-8303,
fax 425/771-0833, Web site: www.ricksteves.com, or e-mail: rick@ricksteves.com.

While some names, characters, and situations are fictitious, this book is accurate in spirit.

Dedicated to:
My wife, Anne, and our children, Andy and Jackie.
Together, they make home my favorite destination.

TRIP ITINERARY

The STEVES
710 Brookmere Dr.
Edmonds, WASH.
98020
U.S.A.

ESPAÑA
15 PTAS
DRAGO
DRACAENA DRACO
CORREOS

DANCING WITH EUROPA

For two decades I've written guidebooks about eating, sleeping, and sightseeing. This book is about what comes next—when it's just you and Europa.

Good travel is like a dance. It's about people. I've enjoyed a twenty-five year dance with Europe. And while Europe's changed and I've changed too, we've never lost eye contact.

On a first trip tourists target the sights; people are incidental. On this trip the people are primary: The Swiss schoolteacher who risks my life to show me an edelweiss we can't pick. The Italian from Siena who still bears a medieval grudge against Florence. The Dutch men who become Dutch boys when the canals freeze over. The Parisian who takes a deep whiff of moldy cheese and sighs, "It smells like zee feet of angels."

Europe is where I'm from. Like a salmon homing in on its birthplace, I'm compelled to return. I haven't spent a quarter of my adult life in Europe for the gelato. I don't leave my wife and kids each summer for galleries of Madonnas and Children. And I don't travel for love or money. I'm on a quest for my roots.

I've tagged along with "roots seekers." Under Gore-tex hoods in a driving Norwegian rain they recite into mini–tape recorders the engravings on tombstones in a graveyard filled with possible ancestors. As if discovering the Dead Sea scrolls, they scan wide-eyed through Old World church records hoping to find their family name.

After years of paging through the yellowed records of European civilization—one pub, one church, one flea market at a time—I feel the same driving curiosity. But the roots I seek are not genetic but cultural.

I am European . . . born Christian, capitalist, and white. Now, I know Jesus wasn't white and he spoke English only as a second language. And I can't deny that one of the biggest and most sophisticated cities on earth in 1492 was Tenochtitlan, present-day Mexico City. But I am incurably European in my outlook. I stir at the thought of St. Brandon or Eric the Red or Columbus—or any European—"discovering" America.

After five years of traveling simply to feel the breeze of accelerated living, I spent two decades traveling as a tour guide and guidebook writer. This life-long affair with Europe has spawned my twenty-one guidebooks, thriving tour company, and the public television series *Travels in Europe with Rick Steves*. Now, with the help of thirty other travelers, I run Europe Through the Back Door, Inc.

This book will answer the question I'm asked most frequently: "How did you get started?" But I'm not writing it to provide a formula for turning travel into a business. My hope is that you'll distill out of my favorite European travel experiences a knack for enjoying Europe as I do.

Like postcards from Europe, this is my account of a recent trip to places both familiar and strange. Familiar because they're my old favorites, strange because they've changed and I've changed. They're more commercialized. And so am I—my travels have been complicated by the job aspects of being "Rick Steves the travel guy." I took this trip to sort out my ideal Europe from the sometimes bitter reality of the Continent today.

I like travel so much I started a monthly "World Travelers' Slide Club" and hosted it for ten years—just to have a regular gang of travelers to chat with. I used to talk travel with anyone, anywhere, anytime. Now, there's rarely time. For me, writing this book has been a return to those good old days.

So, let's consider this just me and you—two travelers, sharing a carafe of *vino rosso* at a canalside café in Venice—with plenty of time to talk.

CHAPTER ONE

AMSTERDAM

"In Holland, being ordinary is being prudent.
If you grow above the grain, you'll get your head cut
off. We don't have a Michael Jackson or Madonna.
Even our queen prefers to do her own shopping."

I'm flying Seattle to Amsterdam over the pole. No matter what concerns and troubles fill my workaday life, my plane leaves them grunting and tripping over each other on the hometown runway.

Already we're halfway there. I scan the horizon from my window seat, looking for the aurora borealis . . . elusive flaming dancers that hint of a great faraway party you have to travel to find. They danced for me on my first flight to Europe. In thirty over-the-pole flights since, I've searched the horizon and seen not even a flicker.

But I found my party. It's Europe.

Each summer I distill my material world into a carry-on-the-plane-size bag. I leave our brash young land of God-given and self-evident truths for a refresher course in good living. For me, good living is freedom. It's packing light with an open mind and an empty journal.

Usually I spend the flight reviewing the names and medical problems of my tour flock or organizing feedback I've received from guidebook readers into research notes. But this trip is different. No tour group to shepherd around. No guidebook research with days spent scrambling for budget hotels and museum tips. This trip will be a pirate's punch of travel memories, blending experiences past and present into one fiery brew—aquavit to ouzo chased by grappa.

Our lives are rainbows that we paint ourselves—and when I stop traveling I stop arcing upward. Someday I'll dream less of next year's trip and rely more on the slide carousels and journals of past adventures. But even though I'm older now, and more of a father figure than a travel buddy in youth hostels these days, I still have a need for empty passport pages.

Europe has also changed over the last twenty-five years. France and Britain now hold hands beneath the Channel. One-legged reminders of the Great War are forgotten. Old Nazis no longer spit *Sieg Heil* at tourists in Munich beerhalls. Mickey Mouse speaks French, and signs for McDonald's and sex shops share the same Copenhagen lamppost. With the breakup of Yugoslavia, lovers of Europe can no longer name all its capitals. And the acid that infiltrates Athens' air has chased the Parthenon statues indoors.

But it's the same Europe, as well. Dolphins playfully race Aegean ferries into the sunset. Oslo's fjord-weary fishermen still peddle tins of shrimp from their boats. Irish fiddlers stomp the paint off pub floors. And Italians still wave baby-style—seemingly at themselves—when they say "*ciao.*"

Of course, getting to the party still requires enduring a long flight. The man in front of me, in window seat 27A, slams his seat back as if trying to crunch my laptop screen off of its keyboard. The woman on my right, who has taped all my TV shows, spends most of Greenland trying to convince me we're all going to get sick from breathing the plane's recycled air. Struggling to face me in her too-tight middle seat, she says, "It's a cocktail of germs."

She rubs a fingerful of Vaseline around the inside of her nostrils with one hand, and offers me the jar with the other. "Germs settle on the tender skin in here," she says. "This gel blocks 'em out."

Even as the wet wind of a cough from the man behind me ruffles my hair, I politely refuse. All the way to Iceland, I wonder with each breath whose germs are becoming mine. The boy in 29C is lost in his headphones, sharing only the *tish tish* sound of tunes that would melt heavy metal. I look out the window, long-ing for those flaming dancers . . . or Europe.

Too tall for my seat, my head bent back like that of a wide-open Pez dispenser, I snooze through the movie. In the haze of sleep, my mind beats the plane to Europe. . . . A passenger's sneeze becomes the moist, salty breeze of a Greek island. No, it's the spray flying from an octopus being slapped over and over against a rock by a fisherman wearing a swimsuit the size of a rat's ham-mock. Now I take a seat in a beachside café and ponder a menu under a bare, dangling light bulb. I'm surrounded by the happy clicking of backgammon boards and leathery locals picking through fruits of the sea.

A woman wraps a steamy pita bread around my souvlaki. No . . . as I awaken I realize it's the flight attendant with a tray of hot towels. Smothering my face in steamy cotton, I savor that Greek moment while stretching the kinks out of my neck.

As nine hours creep by my toes swell up. After a couple of laps up and down the aisle they no longer rub. The good-time gang hangs out in the back next to the orange juice pitchers. The "occupied" sign on the toilet door always prompts the same ques-tion: "What is she *doing* in there?"

Finally, like the happy launch of a pinball, the "fasten seat belts" bell pings and the pilot announces that we're preparing to land. "Please return to your seats." Our descent begins with a stomach-elevating jolt that sends me hurrying home to my seat.

Reaching delicately under the woman next to me for the end of my seat belt, I snug myself down. I used to say a prayer for safety and remove the potentially deadly pen from my shirt pocket be-fore each landing. But flying no longer scares me. A particularly believable United Airlines pilot once told me he'd have bruises from his seat belt before turbulence would concern him. Offering further comfort, he explained that a plane doesn't land like a javelin. The pilot is still flying the plane even after touchdown. I told him I worried that a small skid or wiggle could cause the wing tip to graze the ground, sending this people-filled tube into a flam-ing tumble. "Not as long as the pilot is steady at the wheel," he assured me, explaining that slowly, and on his own terms, the pilot gives custody of the plane back to earth.

Minutes later, with my travel dreams raised and in their upright and locked positions, we rumble to a halt. The pilot, ever in control, takes the opportunity to say, "*Welkom in Amsterdam.*"

Haarlem before Nirvana

Amsterdam's Schiphol Airport offers a no-stress but sterile introduction to Europe. The seeds of cultural homogenization must come in by air, sprouting first in and around airports. Even communication problems are weeded out. Because in Dutch "a" is pronounced *ah*, "e" is *aye*, and "i" is *ee*, you won't find any gates identified by those potentially confusing letters.

In the scramble to turn airports into shopping malls, Schiphol is a prizewinner—voted "best in Europe" by businesspeople whose priorities matter most. Corporate banners—not windmills—blow in the Dutch breeze. The sandy, below-sea-level land still looks newly reclaimed. It's littered with sprawling rent-a-car lots and glassy office parks that missed the Houston exit.

Hoping to glean some new insight into the Dutch youth culture, I share a seat on the bus with a kid just getting off work at the airport. I say I'm from Seattle. A fan of the grunge band Nirvana, he's still mourning the death of its lead singer, Kurt Cobain. Any chance of a discussion of Dutch culture vanishes.

As we glide over and under huge freeways, I mourn the passing of a quaint, traditional Europe. We sit side by side in silence, each lamenting the loss of something entirely different. Then the bus dips under a sailboat navigating a canal-freeway overpass. Suddenly, our century is replaced by an earlier one, and we pull into the tidy market town of Haarlem.

A Dutch Masters kind of town, Haarlem is a good place to start a European trip. In small-town Holland cultural differences are obvious and travel is easy. Haarlem is a cultural wading pool that slopes gradually into the more challenging waters of central Europe.

I hop off the bus and set my sights on Haarlem's towering church spire. It is said a society builds its highest monuments to its greatest gods. But this spire towers over a community that worships trade.

Much of the architecture of today's "old Holland" is from the 1600s. That was Holland's golden age—when merchants ruled the waves, stockpiled profits, and hired Rembrandt to paint their portraits. While Haarlem has its fancy old guildhalls and business has reigned here for centuries, the town's strictly enforced building code assures that the church tower will always dominate the downtown.

After the futuristic Schiphol Airport, Haarlem's market square cheers me with a festival of flowers, bright bolts of cloth, evangelical cheese pushers, and warm, gooey *stroopwafels*. The carillon clangs with an out-of-tune sweetness only a medieval church clock tower can possess.

Savoring the cheery dissonance, a street vendor named Jos dishes up herring. The sign on his van reads "Jos Haring—Gezond en Lekkerrr" ("healthy and deeeeeelicious").

I order by pointing and ask, "*Gezond?*"

Jos hands me what looks more like bait than lunch and says, "*En lekkerrr.*"

I stand there—not sure what to do with my bait—apparently looking lost. Jos, a huge man who towers over his white fishy counter, mimes swallowing a sword and says, "I give you the herring Rotterdam style. You eat it like this. If I chop it up and give you these"—he points to the toothpicks—"this is Amsterdam style."

As I take a bite he asks, "You like it?"

Even with three "r"s on the delicious, "It's salty" is the only polite response I can muster.

"Yes. This is not raw. It is pickled in salt. Great in the hot weather. You sweat. You need salt. You eat my herring."

Taking tiny bites, I wander deeper into the market, happy that Jos is piling chopped onion on herring rather than dealing in Happy Meals.

Under high-stepping gables and yawning awnings, the square bustles expertly with the same commercial game it's practiced for centuries. In the town museum, 350-year-old paintings by hometown

boy Frans Hals show the same square, hotel buildings, market bus-
tle, and church.

A noisy traffic circle in the 1960s, the now car-free area has
become the town's social and psychological hub, the civic living
room. Dodging flower-laden one-speeds, I feel like part of the family here. America is gone. Schiphol is gone. I'm in Europe—with
raw herring breath.

Tent-like market stalls lead to red brick guildhalls. And above
it all rises the Grote Kerk (great church). The church, like all medieval churches, was built facing east to Jerusalem. But once inside, all eyes turn to the west wall, where its pipe organ, an Oz-like
tower of musical power, reaches nearly a hundred feet to the ceiling. Cupids swing from the largest of 5,000 pipes while gilded an-
gelic trumpeters seem stuck in an eighteenth-century game of
statue maker. Mozart trilled here.

The Dutch, among the least church-going people in Europe,
are mostly Protestant. While Catholics fill their churches with visual riches, the more puritan Protestants keep theirs plain. But the
irrepressible need to praise God with art vented itself in music.
After the Reformation, choir masters like Bach gained importance, and Protestant organs grew.

It's Frans, not Franz

Haarlem's Hotel Carillon overlooks the market square. In my tiny
room, under a slanted roof on the top floor, I open my window to
let the happy sound of the market in with the sunshine.

Hotel Carillon is named for the bells that pack the Grote Kerk
tower. They entertain through the day and, like friends who don't
know when to quit, keep sleepy tourists awake through the night.
Tossing my bag on the bed, I head down for a *jenever* with Frans.

Frans, who owns the hotel, artfully pours me a Dutch gin so
full I can't pick it up without spilling. Like the country in general,
Dutch gin glasses are small—only a skinny three inches tall—but
expertly filled.

I always feel like I could have been Frans. We're both forty-
two, both have a boy and a younger girl, both wear glasses—and

we even look alike. Frans, too, owns a business that gets too big a slice of his life, and he knows it.

Frans wears a weary businessman's face—full of ideals and a European self-confidence on how things should be—but worn down by the cumbersome regulations and tax burdens the small businesspeople of Europe must bear.

As is the trend throughout Europe, Frans has gone from "ye olde" to yuppie. He replaced the antique wood beams in his restaurant with chrome and ferns. But his ladder-steep stairs still lead to ramshackle rooms. I still have to prop open my window with a trash basket and level my bed on its medieval floor with tourist brochures.

As I sip the top off my drink, Frans puts his elbow on the table and his chin in one hand. He shakes a copy of my guidebook at me with the other hand and drills me with eye contact. "Rick," he says, "you spelled me Deutsche . . . *Franz*. I am Dutch—*Frans*—with an 's.'"

The Dutch live under a German shadow. While the Dutch rib the Germans good-naturedly, they rib them nevertheless and refer to them as "uninvited guests" when speaking of the Nazi occupation. The scars of World War II persist. Old bumper stickers said, "I want my grandfather's bike back." The new versions read, "You can keep the bike. I have a better one now."

Like others in Holland, Frans' family suffered under German occupation. Grandfathers starved so children could live. An entire generation of Dutch who grew up during the war and survived the "hunger winter of '44" are shorter than their countrymen.

Frans fetches a room key for a tourist heading upstairs, then sits back down. "The year 1944 was the last and hungriest year of the Nazi occupation," he says. "People ate the tulip bulbs only to have something in their stomachs. Today we eat well. Our youth are the tallest in the world."

"And no one invades anymore," I add cheerfully.

Frans, motioning to the outdoor tables filled with vacationers, corrects me. "No, Rick. Each summer, the Germans invade once again."

"They like the sandy beaches of Scheveningen."

I'm referring to the nearby resort and Frans agrees. "Scheveningen is filled with Germans. They plant a flag next to their beach blanket."

"As a kid," I say, "I visited Scheveningen for the Flintstones center on the amusement pier and to watch Dutch girls on the trampolines."

Frans smiles. I tell him how one night I got a history lesson, to boot. Hearing a German mispronounce her town's name, my waitress whispered, "It's *schchchchhave-uh-neeeng-un*. We Dutch used this word to test for German spies. If he could say it, he was Dutch. If not, he was a spy."

Pointing to a boisterous table of holiday-makers, Frans says, "Today, Germans get their Heineken either way."

Going Dutch

Frans is stuck behind his hotel desk. But I'm not. It's early afternoon and the merchants are packing up their stalls. I hike through the now-empty market across town to drop by the home of my friends, Hans and Marjet de Kiefte. They run what I consider to be the ideal B&B.

Hans, with a wiry forty-year-old body and a good-looking, toothy smile, has determined with German precision how to maintain the optimal pain/pleasure ratio. As if learning from Frans' failure, Hans has domesticated his work life. He's seen the world. Ever since Nepal, he's stowed his wrist watch. Now, having quit his desk job, Hans is in charge of injecting personality-plus into the family B&B.

Bouncy Marjet, with a head of wispy strawberry-blonde hair, red tennis shoes, and a knack for assembling a Salvation Army–chic outfit for under twenty dollars, is the sentimental half of this team. On each of my visits, my friends show me a new slice of Holland, and I renew my belief that the more you know about Europe, the more you'll uncover what's worth exploring.

Within minutes we've motored out of Haarlem and into polder country: vast tracts of reclaimed fertile land. It's early summer and the landscape is streaked with yellow and orange tulip fields. Windmills were used to pump the polders dry. Once the conquerors of the sea but now useless relics, they decorate the land like medallions on a war vet's chest.

Some Dutch think the name "Holland" comes from the German "Hell land." From an invader's point of view, the land was too marshy and the people too feisty. But my drive with Hans and Marjet reminds me that, from a tourist's point of view, Holland is precisely the opposite. If tourists are cultural beach-combers in search of clichés, Holland is a beach after a storm.

Hans points out another windmill.

"Every time I take a tour group through Holland's country-side," I say, "someone in the back of the bus marvels, 'Everything's so Dutch.'"

Hans then turns sharply, stopping at the gate of a large, fenced-in parking lot. There's a circular drive lined with covered bus stop–type benches painted pink. From there a lane leads to what looks like a twenty-stall drive-through car wash. The sign reads "Tippelzone. Geopend van 21:00 tot 3:00."

Hans looks at me like a professor about to make his point.

"Okay," I say, "what is *Tippel?*"

Hans tiptoes his fingers lightly across his dashboard by way of illustration. "*Tippel* is how a mouse walks . . . very soft," he ex-plains. "This is a drive-in red light district. Prostitutes. You say, 'Everything's so Dutch.' This is Dutch, too."

I imagine a busy Saturday night with women stationed at each pink bench, a bumper-to-bumper parade of shoppers, and cars privately rocking in the drive-through stalls. My treasured cozy images are under attack. I cling to memories of a time when morning rush hour in Holland featured intersections clogged with bikers—wooden shoes lashed to their handlebars—heading for the fields. Although wooden shoes still keep some feet dry in the boggy fields, these days a tourist will more likely see them used as flower pots nailed to souvenir shop windowsills. That Dutch boy of my travel dreams is off smoking somewhere with the Swiss Miss . . . or waiting for a 21:00 Tippel.

We move on, motoring past sprawling flower mogul mansions,

then through desolate dunes. The tiny road dwindles to a trail-head. Hans parks the car and we hike to a peaceful stretch of North Sea beach.

While Hans and I work up a sweat solving the world's problems during a blustery oceanfront walk, Marjet lags behind, collecting shells with the wide-eyed wonder of a ten-year-old.

"Cheap souvenirs," Hans says.

One cliché the Dutch don't dispute is their frugality. Hans quizzes me. "Who invented copper wire? Two Dutch boys fighting over a penny," he says. "And how do the Dutch take a census? We roll a guilder coin through each town and count the people who come running out."

While mythical locals may chase coins, the Dutch economy is strong. Throughout northern Europe, as populations age governments are tightening up on "cradle to grave" security. Although a bit more restrained than it used to be, the Dutch government's generosity survives. For instance, college used to be free, with living expenses included. Today, although it's still free for the poor, a university education costs most students $1,300 a year, plus room and board. Post-baby-boom Dutch, who foresee a Holland with half its population over sixty-five, expect to provide for their own retirement. Savings here are the highest in Europe. Despite the prostitutes lounging in windows and the sweet smell of pot filling many coffee shops, the Dutch are conservative people.

The same spirit that drove the Dutch to create their land drives them to creatively manage the life on it. Their "live and let live" attitude is actually a practical answer to many of their social problems.

Hans explains. "We subsidize our social problems to death. The government gives the Hell's Angels money for a clubhouse and a place to park their bikes, but only if they behave. We have a union for the unemployed. And for prostitutes having trouble with drugs and disease, there's even a hookers' union."

Referring to the government-sponsored "park and ride" program, Hans says, "Because of the AIDS problem, the Tippelzone comes with a clinic and comfortable lounge for the girls. These are street walkers—heroin girls—the most desperate kind of prostitute. They know the only place they're allowed to work with no trouble from the police is here. And in the lounge a social worker and a doctor gain their confidence. If they get AIDS, they go to a special home."

"That's expensive," I say.

"Not as expensive as having them roam the streets spreading their disease. Rotterdam keeps its prostitutes on a boat."

Hans moves from sex for sale to commerce in general. Pointing a stick of driftwood at a huge seagoing tanker, he says, "That ship's going to the big port at Rotterdam. We're clever at trade. We have to be. We're a small country."

Holland welcomes the world's business. And readily accepted immigrants have contributed to the rich Dutch economy for centuries. When the Jews—expelled from Spain and fleeing many parts of Europe—were welcomed in the sixteenth and seventeenth centuries, they brought trading connections and banking savvy along with them. Dutch trade boomed with Jewish help. This openness to immigrants has continued. Hungarians (who fled to Holland after their failed 1956 revolution), Spanish, and Portuguese have all found ways to weave their lives into the ever-colorful social tapestry of Holland.

But Holland is not designed for big-shots. Hans explains, "Being ordinary is being prudent. If you grow above the grains, you'll get your head cut off. We don't have a Michael Jackson or a Madonna. Even our queen prefers to do her own shopping."

"But Europe is uniting," I say. "Everything is becoming more aggressive . . . more American."

"Yes, we're Americanizing in some ways," he agrees. "But we will never allow bag ladies in our streets.

"Here in Europe we have kings and queens. But class differences are smaller than in the States. Our workers enjoy top job security, twenty-five days of paid vacation, and higher wages than yours."

"American politicians talk only of the middle class," I say, "not of the poor."

"Americans are 'the seeing blind' about understanding class differences," he replies.

"We have a fear of Marx," I say.

"Americans are so convinced Marx was wrong they can't see the growing gap between rich and poor. Business owners sell off the workers' pension plans and take the money. Nobody complains! Don't fear a race war. If you have a war, it will be a class war," Hans predicts.

"The American dream is of impossible wealth," I comment. I tell Hans of being stuck in traffic with a Chicago cabbie who was going nowhere in the land of promise. He drummed happily on the steering wheel of his ramshackle car, pointed to a flashing "Girls!" sign at a local bar, and declared, "America! Where else can women dance on tables and go home with five hundred dollars? And think of it, I could win the Lotto and become a millionaire."

Marjet scuffs through the sand, pockets full of seashells. Under big, romping white clouds, her scarf flapping in the wind like a jump rope, she's surrounded by Holland. As we wait for her to catch up, I scold myself for leaving my camera at the hotel.

Just when I'm about to tuck Marjet into my "sweet and meek kitten-lover" file, she backs me down to the surf, sticks an animal-rights flier in my pocket, and demands that I delete all mention of bullfighting from my Spain guidebook.

Flabbergasted in a B&B

Back in the de Kiefte's living room, we grab well-worn chairs in a room crowded with books, funky near-antiques, and an upright piano littered with tattered music.

Hans and Marjet live in three rooms and rent out five. Hans would like a little more living space but won't trade away his lush but pint-sized garden. Marjet sets a shell from our hike on the piano.

I point to a brass chandelier holding flowers rather than a candle in one of its holes. "If Rembrandt were here, he'd paint this," I say.

"And look at this," I say, walking over to the fireplace filled with dry flowers. "Your living room is a series of still lifes just waiting for a painter."

"Yes, but our guest rooms are plain," says Marjet.

Hans jumps in. "This is our latest discussion. I think tourists, after a long day of museums and sightseeing, want visual peace: plain rooms."

Moving the shell from the piano to the mantle, Marjet says, "Just a small painting on the wall or a bouquet in the window would make the rooms nicer."

"My wife and I have the same discussion," I say.

"It's a boy/girl thing," Hans says, pouring me a beer. "How long do you stay here this time?"

"Not long enough" is my regular response. I'm Hans' pet Yankee. He's on a personal crusade to get me to relax, to slow down. To Hans, I am the quintessential schedule-driven, goal-oriented American.

Running a B&B provides Hans and Marjet plenty of insights into the cultural differences of their guests. "We Dutch are in the middle," he says. "We are efficient like the Germans—that's why there are many American companies here in Holland. But we want to live like the French."

"And crack jokes like the English," adds Marjet. "Everybody here admires the British sense of humor. We watch BBC for the comedies."

Hans and Marjet see cultural differences in their guests' breakfast manners. Says Hans: "Americans like hard advice and to be directed. Europeans—especially the Germans—they know what they want. The French take three days to defrost. But Americans talk and make friends quickly. Europeans, even with no language differences, keep their private formal island at the breakfast table."

Pointing to their two kitchen tables, he continues. "If there are Germans sitting here and Americans there, I break the ice. Introducing the Americans to the Germans, I say, 'It's okay, they left their guns in the States.' We Dutch are like the Germans—but with a sense of humor."

Reaching for my Heineken, I notice it sits on a handbook the Dutch government produces to teach prostitutes about safe sex. I start to thumb through it. "It's both artistic and explicit," I tell Hans.

"Victoria without the secret," he whispers.

"Isn't this shocking to a lot of people?" I ask.

"Only to the English and the Americans," he replies. "Remember, this is Holland. Last night we saw a local TV documentary. It was about body piercing, in full graphic detail—tits, penises, everything. Last week there was a special on the Kama Sutra. Sexual gymnastics like I had never seen. To us Dutch, these were only two more documentaries . . . no big deal. Perhaps these would have been big hits on American TV."

"I don't know," I say, realizing that I was finding the handbook to be more interesting than Hans. "But you know what the most-visited file on my Web site is? A goofy little article comparing Amsterdam's two sex museums."

"Sex is not a taboo here in Holland," says Marjet. "But we are not reckless with sex, either. The Dutch teen pregnancy rate is one-half the American rate."

She turns to Hans. "Tell Rick the 'Dutch boys on the English beach' story. This body stuff may be stressful to Americans, but it sends the English under their pillows."

"As a schoolboy I traveled with a buddy to England," Hans begins. "We changed our pants on the beach without the towel hassle—no problem. We're good Dutch boys. As usual, the beach had an audience: benchloads of retired Brits enjoying the fresh air, suffering through their soggy sandwiches. When my friend began changing into his swimsuit, all the people turned their heads away. Amused by our power to move the English masses, we repeated the move. I pulled my trousers down and all the heads turned away again."

Marjet, laughing like she's hearing the story for the first time, says, "We don't see many English on our beaches."

"We get mostly Americans," says Hans.

"We'd be happy to fill our house with only Americans," says

Marjet. "Americans are easy to communicate with. They're open. They taught me to express myself, to say what I really think."

Hans breaks in with a Tony the Tiger tourist imitation, "Oh wwwow, this is grrreat! What a grrreat house you have here!"

"Americans get flabbergasted," Marjet adds.

"The English don't know how to be flabbergasted," says Hans.

"I think you nearly flabbergasted them on that beach," Marjet says. "When we visited Colorado, my trip went better when I learned to say 'wow' a couple of times a day."

Curling comfortably in the corner of the sofa, tucking her legs under her tiny body, Marjet explains, "When an American asks, 'How are you?' we say, 'Okay,' to mean 'good.' The American says, 'That doesn't sound very good.' We explain, 'We're European.'"

Hans says, "Then the American replies, 'Oh, yes—you're honest.'"

Fascinated by the smiley face-ism of America, Marjet says, "Even supermarket shopping bags have big 'smile and be a winner' signs."

"It's true," I agree. "Only in America could you find a bank that fines tellers if they don't tell every client to 'Have a nice day.'"

Hans says, "Did you know that the Dutch are the most wanted workers at Disneyland Paris? This is because most Dutch are open-minded. We can smile all day. And we speak our languages."

Marjet explains, "In Holland when someone asks, 'Do you speak your languages?' they mean do you speak French, German, and English along with Dutch."

Hans continues. "And for us, acting friendly is maybe less exhausting than for the French. Can you imagine a French person having to smile all day long?"

Hans tops off my Heineken. "God created all the world. It was marvelous. But France . . . it was just too perfect. So he put in the French to balance things out."

"And Canada could have had it all: British culture, French cuisine, American know-how," says Marjet. "But they messed up and got British food, French know-how, and American culture."

Blaming my yawns on jet lag, I thank my friends for a fine

afternoon and evening and head home. As I walk back to my hotel through sleepy time-warp streets, I ponder the American Dream, the Dutch Dream, freedom, and good living. By the end of my first day in Europe, it's clear my challenge during this trip will be to sort through and understand two Europes: the quaint, personable Europe full of Hanses and Marjets, which tourists seek, and the Europeans' Europe, a bold tomorrow of shopping mall airports with trade centers towering high above church spires.

Amster Amster Dam Dam Dam

A twenty-minute train ride takes me from cute Haarlem to big, bold Amsterdam, where the lions of the city seal atop the Amsterdam Centraal Station seem to roar, "Just do it."

Stepping from the train station, I look down Damrak, the main drag, which flushes visitors past cheers of commercial neon into the old center. It's always been this way. After all, long before there was a station, the Amstel River passed through the city here, following the route of today's Damrak.

Like no city in Europe, Amsterdam opens like a fan dance out of its train station. Breaking all rules of cartography, the map of Amsterdam is the only map in my guidebooks that has north on the bottom. Like a tree of life, it just seems right for a trading center to bloom from that lifeline to the world.

In the sixteenth century, Amsterdam was a fortified marina of 30,000 people—mostly merchants—who welcomed ships loaded with material delights from every corner of the trading world. Clever buoyant slings raised the most heavily laden ships enough to allow them to navigate the shallow waters. Ships would parade like pirates with plunder to the commercial altar of the town—the customs and weigh house next to the city hall on Dam Square, the main square, where they docked and unloaded.

Today the trade still comes, but to a different port: nearby Rotterdam, the biggest port in the world. The Dutch claim that money is made in Rotterdam (where shirts are sold with sleeves already rolled up), divided in Den Hague (where the government resides), and spent in Amsterdam.

Outside the station, trams glide and tourists huddle with room hustlers. Street people wearing stocking hats over matted hair, black boots, and heavy coats in the sun, choose the most public places in town to snooze. Children pedal to school as if in a small town and pairs of police add no stress to the laid-back scene. Tourists pop out of the station, eager to explore.

First-time sightseers leaving the station carry a predictable checklist of sights: the Anne Frank House is on the right, the red light district is on the left, and Damrak leads right through the middle toward two great museums. Filled with works by van Gogh and Rembrandt, they stand like cultural bulldogs on the opposite side of town.

Today my only agenda is to wander the streets—after a cup of coffee. As I stand for a moment on the breezy deck of a floating canalside café, assessing the seating choices, I find myself looking into the sad-dog eyes of an American girl. As if expecting me, she says, "Rick, I'm not doing so very well."

Enjoying the chance to be a two-bit Angel Gabriel, I sit down and assure her that it's natural for the fresh-off-the-plane tourist to feel overwhelmed. I look over her sightseeing plans and encourage her to take refuge in cozier Haarlem if necessary. I then direct her eyes above the trash-filled streets, past prowling men and scary-looking derelicts angry they have nothing left to pierce. "The best of Amsterdam is high," I tell her. "Pan up."

Our eyes rest for a fine, silent moment on bright white clouds blowing behind gables of a golden age.

As I settle into my trip notes, she surprises me with a local goodbye. With a confident "*Tot ziens*" and a smile she is on her way.

Because of my TV series, I'm better known among Americans in Europe than I am on the streets of my hometown. And while people apologize for invading my privacy, I enjoy meeting people—whether struggling or savvy—immersed in Europe.

In traditional Dutch coffeehouses, thick little rugs are draped over the tables and coffee is served with a classy little ginger cookie. On this visit I get the cookie but I miss the little rug—a victim of new hygiene laws.

As the coffee dissolves a nibble of ginger cookie, it occurs to me that, one by one, the fine points that distinguish different cultures are sadly giving way to prosperity, efficiency, and modern living. Each year more of my cultural fancies are driven into the theme parks and hotel fantasy rooms. That leaves me awkwardly craving tourist clichés and wondering if my image of Europe isn't just wishful thinking.

I leave the café and follow the crowds down Damrak. Today Damrak is about as traditionally Dutch as dancing the hora. Wooden shoes are crucified on a wall between a change bureau and the Sex Museum. The Venus Temple promises a look at "sex through the ages" that includes a "Sado Club," the Torture Tower, and the oldest sex shop in Amsterdam—all for 3.95 guilders. Visitors are stopped first by the poster of Marilyn Monroe fighting a randy gale, then lured in by a sultry mannequin wearing a provocative dress and a huge smile as she rides a bicycle with a single, hardworking piston.

The Damrak makes me feel moralistic. The neon "Change" sign in the bank window seems to preach a conversion that has little to do with money. The Damrak is why I sleep in small-town Haarlem.

Just past a gimmicky new torture museum and a thumping Hooters restaurant, the sound of an old-time barrel organ revives traditional Amsterdam and cheers me up. It's a two-man affair. While grandpa works the crowd, the boss is in the back spinning the wheel and feeding tunes punched into a scroll as if feeding bullets into a musical machine gun.

The street organ is a mini-carnival, painted in candy-colored pastels and peopled with busy figurines. Whittled ballerinas twitch to ring bells while Cracker Jack boys crash silver dollar–sized cymbals. Playing his coin-tin maracas and wearing a carved-on smile, the old man looks like an ornamental statue that has just leapt to life. While shoppers trudge by, two tourists break into a merry waltz. Another hugs a daybag between her knees and snaps a photo while her buddy winks into his camcorder.

Nearby, the Vlaamse Frites kiosk is painted with great art. This art has a purpose: to make you hungry for Flemish-style French fries. On one side of the kiosk God gives Adam the cone of fries (a variation on this decorates the Sistine Chapel). On the opposite side is van Gogh's famous "French Fried Potato Eaters." The peasants, for whom Vin-

God giving Adam the cone of fries

cent always had an affinity, are shown solemnly sitting down to a bountiful platter of bright yellow fries. All they need is the mayonnaise, the Flemish choice over ketchup.

I warm my hands around my cone of salty fries and continue to wander. In Amsterdam, cobbled roller-coaster roads connect a total of 1,300 bridges that cross seventy-five miles of peaceful green canals. Houses jostle for a canal view. As their foundations of pilings rot or settle, they lean on each other, looking as if someone has stolen their crutches. Reclaimed land and canals are tough to build on. In buildings throughout Holland, foundations account for about twenty percent of total building costs. Scanning a tipsy row of canal houses, I can tell who skimped on the foundation work.

Parking is tricky in downtown Amsterdam. Regulations are strictly enforced. Recently, the Amsterdam fire brigade had to push a car into the canal to get to a fire. Wheel clamps, a Dutch innovation, are a common sight along the canals.

Parking restrictions notwithstanding, Amsterdam means freedom—religious freedom, freedom to pierce your body, freedom to flash a tourist-laden sightseeing boat, freedom to roll with a prostitute or roll a joint. The pilgrims stopped here for a taste of religious freedom en route to the New Land. Nearly 400 years later, "newlanders" still see Amsterdam as a beacon of freedom.

The Dutch are a principled people and will fight small issues as if they were big ones. One wealthy Amsterdammer protested new parking restrictions by buying old cars and simply leaving

them around town to be impounded. When the government ini-
tiated a high-occupancy vehicle lane to lessen traffic congestion, a
local taxpayer contested the notion of a lane paid for by all but
open only to carpoolers—and won. The one law in Holland that
nobody contests: discrimination is wrong and all should be treated
as equals.

Rasta Colors and Red Lights

While Amsterdam has long been famous for its nicotine-stained
"brown cafés," these days "coffee shop" refers to a place where people gather to buy and smoke marijuana. While hard drugs are
strictly illegal, marijuana is sold openly in coffee shops throughout the Netherlands.

Every few blocks I pass a window full of plants and displaying a
red, yellow, and green Rastafarian flag—both indications that this
coffee shop doesn't sell much coffee. The one called Dark Side of
the Moon looks a little foreboding. A few blocks later, near the
Anne Frank House, I duck into the more inviting Grey Area Cafe.

I take a seat at the bar next to a leathery forty-something
biker and a Gen-X kid with two holes in his body for each one in
mine. I feel more like a tourist than I have all day. The bartender,
sporting a shaved head and a one-inch goatee, greets me in
English and passes me the menu.

I point to a clipped-on scrap of paper. "What's Aanbieding:
Swarte Marok?"

"Today's special is Black Moroccan," he says.

Swarte Marok, Blond Marok, White Widow, Northern Light,
Stonehedge, Grasstasy . . . so many choices, and that's just the *wiet*
(marijuana). Hashish selections fill the bottom of the menu.

Above me a tiny starship *Enterprise* dangles from a garland of
spiky leaves. And behind the bartender is a row of much-used and
apparently never-cleaned bongs, reminding me of the hubbly-
bubblies that litter Egyptian teahouses. With a flick of my finger, I
set the *Enterprise* rocking. The bartender says, "Access to the stars.
That's us."

I marvel out loud how open-minded the Dutch are.

"We're not open-minded, just tolerant," he explains. "There's a difference. *Wiet* is not legal . . . only tolerated.

"Does this kind of toleration cause a problem?" I ask.

Handing a two-foot-tall bong and a tiny baggie of leaves to a French girl, he says, "My grandmother has

Amsterdam "coffee shop"—
Smoke-in or take-out

a pipe rack. It has a sign: 'A satisfied smoker creates no problems.'"

"That was tobacco, wasn't it?"

"Yes, it's from the 1860s. But this still applies today."

I ask the guy with all the holes why he smokes here.

He speaks through the silver stud in his tongue. "Some young people hang out at Dutch coffee shops because their parents don't want them smoking pot at home," he says. "I smoke with my parents but come here for the coffee shop ambience."

The older guy in leather laughs. "Yeah, ambience with a shaved head," he says, as the bartender hands him his baggie-to-go.

Alone with the younger guy, I ask him about the sign with a delivery boy on it.

"In Holland we have pot delivery services," he explains, "like you have pizza delivery in America. Older people take out or have it delivered."

A middle-aged woman hurries in and says, "Yellow Club, please."

She presents the bartender with a small, stickered card. "Buy twelve, get one free," he explains to me, and hands her a baggie saying, "I cut you a fat bag."

With a "*Dank U wel*, Peter," she tosses it into her shopping tote and hurries out.

"This coffee shop would never be possible in the United States," I say.

"I know," Peter, the bartender, agrees. He shows me snapshots of Woody Harrelson and Willy Nelson, each in this obscure little coffee shop, and continues. "America's two most famous pot smokers told me all about America."

The kid chimes in. "Hollanders—even those who don't smoke—they believe soft drugs . . . you know, pot, hash . . . it shouldn't be a crime."

"What do your parents think?" I ask.

"They think the youth have a problem. My dad says, 'Holland will get the bill later on.'"

"And other countries . . . doesn't legal pot in Holland cause them a problem?" I ask.

"Actually, it's not legal here," he reminds me, "just tolerated. Officially, we can't legalize anything because of all these world treaties."

"The French complain about Holland's popularity with drug users, but they have a worse problem with illegal drugs," Peter adds. "In Holland, the police know just what's going on and where."

"But what about hard drugs?"

"These are the problem. Europe comes to Holland for more than the pot. Most Dutch agree that these hard drugs should be illegal. We Dutch—I think because pot is tolerated—handle our drugs better than the kids who travel here to get high. But, like everywhere, we have a hard drug problem."

Peter points to a chart on the wall that shows how to avoid bad XTC pills. "The police give us this chart. My English friends cannot believe our police help in this way. They call our Politie the 'polite-ies.'

"You don't see the Dutch dying from heroin overdoses," Peter continues. "But every time I read the newspaper it seems another German is found dead on the floor of a cheap Amsterdam hotel room.

"But pot . . ." he says, fingering a perfectly rolled joint, "this is not a problem."

"American prisons are filled with pot smokers," I say.

"Take your choice," he says. "Allow for alternative ways of living or build more prisons. Here in Holland, pot's like cigarettes. We smoke it. We pay taxes. We don't go to jail."

For years I've said that I prefer the Dutch approach to recreational drugs to the American war on drugs. The fact that in Holland there are fewer "heads" per capita than in America suggests that their approach is a winner. Recently, a sympathetic reader who described her job as "chief pee inspector" warned me that, since marijuana remains in your system and shows up on tests for forty-five days, my tips on "going local" while in Holland could cost people their jobs. She suggested people take seven-week vacations and start them in Amsterdam.

A round table at the front window is filled with a United Nations of tourists sharing travelers' tales stirred by swizzlesticks of smoke. The table is a clutter of teacups, maps, and guidebooks. From the looks of the ashtray, they've been here a while.

I squeeze a chair into their circle. When they learn I write guidebooks, the German with the brooding Trotsky brow under a black wool cap says, "With marijuana, I need no guidebook."

The entire table finds this very funny.

"What do you mean?" I ask.

He explains, "Today, for me, the people of Amsterdam were walking on tall sticks over the canals."

Like vagabond cardsharps, they begin trumping each other with favorite "stoned travel" moments in an effort to show the travel writer a Europe most never see.

The Canadian takes us through the van Gogh museum, where the "wind was actually blowing through the wheat fields of Vincent's canvas."

The newlywed Californians paddle us up a raging river of cobblestones to a Rhine castle for a "tacky, torch-lit tour that actually becomes spooky."

And traveling to Florence, we step into the Uffizi gallery, where "Botticelli maidens throw Renaissance confetti over the crowds."

With the Canadian we tumble out of a taxi on Rome's Campo dei Fiori and look sympathetically into the silent bronze eyes of the towering statue of Bruno, a fifteenth-century burned-at-the-stake heretic.

The German blows a long stairway of smoke and takes us wafting like incense through St. Peter's basilica. He explains how the altar is a cleat from which sunrays—like taut bowlines—seem to tie the good ship Earth to its heavenly dock.

Proposing a contest, the Canadian girl tries to get us all to take turns nibbling the same piece of bread into the recognizable shape of different European countries.

By this time I am about ready to trade the smoke for some fresh air. I say "*Tot ziens*" and hit the street.

The second of Amsterdam's touristic "oh, wows!" is prostitution. The city lines up its temptations conveniently. From the Dam Square, Damrak leads directly back to the train station. But with just a slight swing to the right, you walk past the most popular coffee shops and through Europe's most famous red light district.

Around De Oude Kerk, the oldest church in Amsterdam, practitioners of the world's oldest profession tempt souvenir-hunters. Bedrooms with big windows under red neon lights line the narrow alleys of Amsterdam's old sailors' quarter. As the steeple chimes, women from Jamaica holler, "Come on, dahling." Fifty guilders (thirty dollars) for fifteen minutes. Women who look like they might have diseases are marked down to thirty-five guilders.

Amsterdam seems to have taken everything sailors did, put it in a jar, and let it germinate for 200 years. Today that jar is open and browsers are welcome. But keep your camera stowed. Sneak a photo and you'll endure the humiliation of a line of angry prostitutes screaming obscenities at you and pelting you with fruit (or worse).

The red light district is Amsterdam's hard-core, nonstop, live-couples, first-floor-straight, second-floor-gay paseo. Americans who feel goofy gawking should remember that the area's streets are clogged with countless others—mostly from Asia and other parts of Europe—who feel just as wide-eyed as you do. The tour guide in me jumps at the opportunity to give a group such a unique memory as the Red Light Ramble. The kid in me delights in the spectacle. But the father in me cringes at the sight of a ten-year-old schoolgirl, bookbag on her back, studying a window full of vibrators, whips, and inflatable orifices.

I've never seen a prostitute in my hometown. But when a tourist is "on the road," that road is often "hooker row." And in the old town centers, the spectacle of women selling their bodies to men can be hard to avoid. I am fascinated by the drama of well-worn women in a male-dominated world humiliating lonely men in grotty little rooms by charging them a day's wage for ten minutes of sexual fun. Still not exactly clear on who the "victims" are, I can't resist swinging through the red light–illuminated streets that border many European train stations.

Prostitution is everywhere in Europe. It always has been. In London "models" keep the lanes of Soho crawling with men on the prowl. In Paris, Pigalle's impossibly friendly waitresses draw gawkers like rats to cheese into their velvety bars. Slipping in and out of toplessness, they look right into you, doing their best to make a bottle of cheap champagne worth a hundred bucks. Along Lisbon's Avenue Liberdad nubile girls compete coyly with Edith Bunkers wearing little more than a vest and panties. Oslo's prostitutes seem more drugged-out than most. They don't bother to cover up their needle marks, and their eyes have a hollow Viking-whore spaciness to them. Just off Barcelona's Ramblas, foul-mouthed ladies of the night fire off insults at gawkers. Just a condom shoot from the Columbus statue, they congregate around a statue honoring the inventor of penicillin. And Frankfurt's top-heavy towers of sexual power keep travelers—whether horny or just curious—with down-time between trains well entertained. Several six-story "eros towers" rattle with a commotion of men, parading like lusty chain gangs, up and down the fire escape–type stairs between corridors lined with women.

Rubbing shoulders with a hungry gaggle of Dutch boy regulars, I rubberneck my way to the most popular window on the street. There, framed in smoky red velvet, stands a sultry blonde. Her ability to flex and shake her backside brings the slow, gawking pedestrian flow to a stuttering stop. And it makes me just one of the faceless, rutting masses. I stand before an exotic woman wearing a black lace power-suit and enough lipstick to keep a third grader in crayons. Just making eye contact leaves me weak—and ready to rejoin the cute and quaint Holland back in the sunshine.

As I walk back to the Amsterdam station, I notice the carillon in the steeple of the old church is playing "All Through the Night."

Frozen Dutch Treat?

With all this tolerance, what's a Dutchman's favorite temptation?

Hans best enjoys his country on crisp February days, when he can skate the canals from town to town through Holland's farm country.

"Imagine this," he says. "Cold wind at your back, warm sun on your face. If the ice is good you have a smooth rhythm. I hold my hands behind my back and it is only me and our big, big sky.

"A trip of sixty kilometers (thirty-six miles) is a good afternoon. With bad luck, you could get way, way out and find your dream becomes a nightmare—snowfall means you walk home. Rainfall means you struggle home through the puddles missing holes marked with sticks and ducks.

"For me, a good day skating is better than skiing in the Alps. The world is still. It's quiet. The fields stretch and stretch. A church steeple marks the next town. Crossing under a bridge, you're in the town center. The pub invites you to come in and warm up. Rubber mats lead from the canal to its door. Inside we have a big fire and steamy windows. Lawyers, doctors, the farmers, and students. Everybody is together and warm. Cross-country skating, we are all equal—all just simple Dutch boys."

CHAPTER TWO

TO THE RHINE

*"Steiffs," she hiccups. "The Mercedes
of stuffed animals. My grandson had only
three stuffed animals. All Steiffs."*

Ready to wade deeper into Europe, I catch the train from
Amsterdam to Germany. Joyriding by train through Europe is
hardly slowing down to smell the roses, but a few petals do hit the
windshield. It's a kind of sightseeing—almost being there. Gazing
out the window, I catch whiffs of near misses.

We pass the town of Aalsmeer and I see what it calls "the
world's biggest building," filled with trainloads of fresh-cut flowers
and home to giant auction halls of international flower merchants.

An hour east of Amsterdam we approach the town of Ede.
Although I pass it nearly every year, I haven't stopped here since
my first trip to Europe in 1969. I was with my parents on a visit to
Ede's Rippen piano factory—my dad ran a piano store in Seattle
selling the finest European pianos. I was a fourteen-year-old kid with
greasy, combed-down hair and a turtleneck perpetually stretched out
by the school bully. I earned my souvenir money not by delivering
newspapers but by dusting pianos at Steves Sound of Music.

When I was a kid, travel was a local affair—we chose from
thirty-three flavors at the ice cream shop on the way to Anacortes,
where we'd crank our boat off its trailer and cruise the San Juan

Islands. The closest I ever thought I'd get to Europe was Victoria, British Columbia, where they had double-decker English buses and served fancy cream teas.

One day my parents excitedly announced we were going to Europe. My first thought was, "Why? They don't speak our language. I haven't even seen my own country yet." But my parents were not pro-choice when it came to family vacation plans. Those were the days when you dressed up to fly. Whether I liked it or not, I was collared in a necktie and we were Europe-bound.

As I settled into Ede, my distaste for foreign travel faded along with my first bout of jet lag. Dodging bulky one-speed bikes as they rattled over medieval cobbles, I wandered through a new world of entirely untested candies and soft drinks to the market square. Starstruck, then bewildered, by lanky Dutch women who revealed hairy armpits as they swallowed their pickled herring Rotterdam style, I decided travel might be more interesting than another day at home.

Visiting untouristy little Ede on this first trip whetted my appetite for offbeat Europe. It peeled history out of my school books and pasted it on real faces. Our Ede host, piano salesman John Konig, was a walking, talking scrapbook of World War II memories. As a Dutch resistance fighter, he was caught spying with a tiny camera in his shirt, then tortured by the Nazis and tossed into a concentration camp. Although balding and wearing lenses too thick for their delicate wire frames, he was thin, fit, and stood as straight as the stick he used as a kid to vault the polder canals.

I stared at Konig's mouth as he told his vivid stories. It looked much like it did the day he spit broken teeth at his interrogators. When he sunk his fingers deep into the keyboard to show off the latest Rippen piano, I couldn't take my eyes off the prisoner number still tattooed on his wrist. Faded, it slid in and out from under his jacket cuff as he played. It was his prize souvenir, a high-profile reminder he wore where the rest of us strap our watches.

Konig finally did get his revenge. In an industry long dominated by the many great German piano factories, his Dutch company had become Europe's biggest piano factory. He attributed the

rise of Rippen to Dutch hustle . . . aided by the strange destruc-
tion of most of their German competition. Back in the 1940s, the
Steinway family ran piano factories in New York and in Germany.
During World War II, all the great German piano factories were
bombed—all, that is, except the Steinway company in Hamburg.
Konig pointed out that a member of the Steinway family was in
the American bomber command. ("Very interesting," he noted, in
his best Nazi accent.)

Konig related to Americans as he thought he should: in su-
perlatives. As he guided us through Holland, wandering through
toy villages and climbing dikes with the pride of a mountain
climber, he kept nudging me and saying, "Fantastik, Reek." From
the summit of a dike, we surveyed the countryside. Konig—as if
he had personally done some of the digging—proclaimed, "God
made the world. But da Dutch, we made Holland."

To drive home that point, he showed off Flevoland, a region
entirely reclaimed from the Zuider Zee (sea). This new Dutch
state, defined by a sixty-mile-long rectangular dike and pumped
dry, looked like a lawn that had been rolled out in preparation for
our visit. Today the oldest things in Flevoland are some of its people. Trees and land date back only to the mid-1960s.

From Konig's car, we surveyed the tranquil countryside in this
most densely populated chunk of Europe. I remember rows of trans-
parent houses, huge windows front and back, lace-curtained to provide privacy but let in the sun. Holland is a compact and tidy
package. It comes in a miniature scale. Konig explained that Dutch
houses—too narrow to fit furniture up their steep stairs—lean out.

"This is on purpose," he said, pointing to a hoisting beam that
extended out from the gable. "You can haul your piano up. Then
you go in at the top, through those big double windows.

"And Dutch pianos," he continued, the salesman taking over
for the tour guide, "are the world's smallest. With full keyboard
and a sound so rich, yet they take only eleven inches of your floor."

Konig was old thirty years ago. But those early memories of
Europe are pressed into my brain like shiny good luck coins stuck
on the mossy ceiling of a wine cellar. I remember the things Konig

taught me about Holland. But most of all, I remember his pride in Dutch ways and the way he wore his tattoo. Travel is a crowbar and, already it was clear, this kid's hometown perspective was its target.

My train seems to speed up, whisking past tiny Ede as if trains never stop there anymore, hurtling east.

On that 1969 trip my parents and I rode this same train line to Vienna, where we visited the Bösendorfer piano factory. After dusting miles of Bösendorfers—the world's longest and most expensive pianos—I would now see them built.

We were in the care of flamboyant Dr. Radler. One of Vienna's piano aristocracy, he was the kind of guy you'd expect to wear an ascot and a monocle. Unlike Konig, Radler preferred his history pre-Hitler. With his leather gloves gripping the wheel of his luxury car, he bragged that he could zip through tiny farm towns with his eyes closed. We learned later he was terminally ill . . . bravado with little to lose.

Radler warmed us up with a tour of eastern Austria. We enjoyed Hungarian gypsy musicians performing just this side of Iron Curtain barbed wire, fine views from high atop the Vienna Woods, and a visit to Papa Haydn's house. Then Radler took us to the monastery where Bösendorfers were built.

This was the last piano factory in Vienna, a town once home to dozens of piano builders. At Bösendorfer, rather than assembly lines they had the industrial equivalent of maternity suites. Craftspeople lovingly birthed 200 pianos a year. Radler was fond of reminding us that in a factory of 200 workers, that's "one piano per man per year." Cranking up the harsh on his German accent, he compared his factory to the mega-factories of Japan, saying, "Yamaha produces more pianos in this month than we make since World War II."

If Steinway is a trumpet, Bösendorfer is a coronet—the mellowest of pianos. In an ideal world, I'd play Bach on a Steinway and Debussy on a Bösendorfer. Each Bösendorfer had its own personality. My dad was on a mission in Vienna: to find the right piano for a particular customer.

Dr. Radler lined up five grands. With my parents reflecting in the highly-polished, mirror-like finish of the music racks, I jumped from bench to bench, giving each piano a melodic test drive. We debated each instrument's personality, made the deal, and triumphantly jotted down the serial number of our musical catch.

Before leaving, Dr. Radler granted me the finest piano experience in Europe: ten minutes on the Imperial Grand, Bösendorfer's nine-foot, six-inch masterpiece. The next-longest piano was five inches shorter. The Imperial came with an extra octave in the bass. These eight notes—though not normally played—vibrated powerfully, providing the piano equivalent of a surround-sound woofer.

I sunk my fingers into those ivories and pulled out mighty chords, those fat, extra-long bass strings rumbling sympathetically. European life and culture had a certain richness and quality that— even as a gum-chewing schoolboy in a stretched-out turtleneck— I was growing to appreciate.

Our piano business finished, Dr. Radler piled us into his Mercedes for a Sunday morning victory spin. In the back seat, my mom and I hung from the leather grips to keep from slamming back and forth. We sped to a Danube village in time to see the entire population—kids in lederhosen, sturdy moms and dads, respected grandparents—tumbling out of the onion-domed church, across the square, and into the wine garden.

Many Americans snicker at the European habit of following a sip of wine at Mass with a glass of wine in a bar. Since that experience, I see no contradiction. Three generations enjoying a Sunday afternoon together with the fruits of their grape-picking labor is "family values" European style.

Dr. Radler, with his gawky American family in tow, sat down at the table marked "*Stammtisch*"—reserved for the most respected regular customers. Everyone in the village seemed to know him. Spreading gooey hunks of lard on coarse village bread, Radler was showing us a gritty slice of his culture. When I ordered two sausages and got four, he laughed at my surprise and explained, "Here in Austria, sausages come in pairs—like the lederhosen."

Under its exotic steeple and fortified towers, the town seemed marinated in history. To bring that history to life, Radler pulled up an extra chair, poured a glass of wine, and invited the oldest man in the village to sit next to me. Radler announced, "This man has seen with his own eyes the start of the Great

A gawky kid (far right), lucky to meet an eyewitness (far left) of the 1914 assassination

War . . . the assassination of the Archduke Ferdinand in 1914."

I thought Radler was being theatrical until the old man spoke. With two gray horsetails for a mustache and a droopy ivory pipe carved fine enough for a Hapsburg, he spoke in streaks, allowing Radler to translate.

"I saw the assassin Princip the Serb step out of a bar. Stopped at the corner was the Archduke Ferdinand in the back of his open car. Princip pulled out his gun, took two steps forward, and shot him in the head . . . dead."

Radler, delighted by my fascination with this eyewitness account of one of the defining moments of the twentieth century, asked the old man to back up a bit.

The man explained that Princip and his Serbian nationalist partners—upset with Hapsburg control—went to Sarajevo to kill Ferdinand, heir to the Hapsburg throne. They dropped a bomb on his parade from a bridge. But they miscalculated the speed of the entourage, and the bomb landed on the car behind Ferdinand. The assassins scattered.

Pausing as if to rewind the videotape of his life, the old man stared at his lard-covered bread. After twisting a pinch of salt on it with nicotine-stained fingers, he continued. "Princip went into a bar to hide . . . and have a schnapps. Later, as he left the bar he stood before his target."

Incredibly, the archduke—returning from the hospital where

he visited the man wounded by the earlier bombing—had stopped on the street in front of the demoralized assassin.

Leaning forward, as if we were the first to hear this part, the old man said, "Princip rubbed his eyes. How could this be true?"

My mom and dad and I leaned forward as well. Even Radler was on the edge of his chair. As we huddled together over our table, the translating continued. "The assassin pulled out his pistol. He shot both the archduke and his wife. And soon after this . . ."

He paused and I said, "World War One."

As Radler translated, the old man's eyes twinkled as if he understood that a seed was being planted in this wide-eyed American kid. That seed would grow to be a lifelong love of European history. It was people like Konig and Dr. Radler who first took me through Europe's "back door" and showed me the best of travel.

Baby in the Fountain

Babies, ancient astronomers, and Americans think the universe revolves around them. After two weeks in Europe, my fourteen-year-old pre-Copernican world was a shambles.

After the piano factories, we rode the train to Norway to visit relatives. In an Oslo park, I watched families at play. These Norwegians—tall, blond, and rich—seemed to have the world by the tail. As they doted over toddlers who frolicked naked under a fountain, I realized something powerful. Each of these parents loved their kids as much as my parents loved me.

Thomas Jefferson wrote, "Travel makes one wiser but less happy." Less happy because it can be sobering to discover that the world is more than a high school pep rally. Since that 1969 trip, patriotism has troubled me. It's a cheering squad that can buoy up one nation while submerging the people of another.

When the astronauts took that famous "one small step for man" on the moon, I was sitting on a living room floor in Norway. From their Apollo window, the crew saw an Earth with no borders. They saw, with unprecedented clarity, that we're all on this planet together. And even from my humbler vantage point—

a teenager on a Norwegian carpet having *"Ett lite skritt for et men-neske, ett stort skeitt menneskeheten"* translated for me by newfound relatives—I was warming to the notion that the best flag to wave is a global one.

When you come from a large and powerful country, it's easy to think your way is the norm. But with each visit, my Scandinavian relatives and their small-country perspectives challenge my persistent ethnocentrism. Recently, after I gloated over the performance of American Olympic athletes, my Uncle Thor pointed out, "Yes, America won the most medals, but Denmark—with six—earned far more per person."

I do what I can to bring this wider perspective home. To bruise my dad's ethnocentrism, I taught our three-year-old, Andy, to finish dinner prayers by waving his arms and saying, "Allah, Allah, Allah." The intensity of Grandpa's reaction was thought-provoking.

My passport—my key to the world—is nearly at the end of its ten-year lifespan. Having spent a quarter of that time strapped to my body, it's shaped like me. But as a schoolkid in Europe, it was zipped safely in my mom's purse and felt more like a leash.

In 1971 I was in the Copenhagen train station with my parents, sixteen years old and on my second trip to Europe. All around me, people—students, workers, soldiers, vagabonds—rattled in and out. The teasing, clicking, and flipping of the schedule board announced trains departing for Berlin, Frankfurt, Oslo, Amsterdam. I saw that kids just three or four years older than I were bounding off into Europe. The Continent was theirs to explore.

Then it hit me: I don't need my parents! I could come back with a rucksack and a railpass. I declared my freedom, vowing then and there that I would return to Europe every year for the rest of my life.

"I'd Kill for Your Job"

As the train pulls out of Zevenaar, the last stop in the Netherlands, a spunky young American tourist with a too-big bag shops her way down the aisle of the train car. She pokes her head into my compartment. "Rick Steves?" she says. "*The* Rick Steves?!" I detect a touch of mockery in her delight.

My bag reserves the window seat opposite mine for my feet. Saying "may I" without a hint of a question, she hefts my bag to the luggage rack above my head. The woman sits down across from me and pulls a copy of my guidebook from her daybag. As she matches my back-cover mug shot to my real-life face, the train reaches its cruising speed.

Without a sentence of small talk, she gets right to the point. "My name's Margo. I'm from Boston. I'd kill for your job. How did you get started anyway?" Without waiting for me to answer, she continues, "You wrote the book I should have written ages ago."

Intrigued by her energy and realizing we are stuck together on the train, I give her a more complete than normal answer to this frequently asked question.

"You can't just *want* to be a travel writer," I say. "You have to be a traveler first. I traveled for six summers purely for kicks. From the start, I had a passion for journal writing. I followed one strict rule: Never finish a day without writing it up."

I tell her that even as a kid, my prized souvenir was a box of postcards arranged chronologically, each carefully numbered and filled in with the day's weather and a "money spent/money left" chart. On later trips, I'd fill up 200-page "empty" books with fine-print accounts of my adventures. In Bulgaria during the Cold War, I'd protect my friends by writing my journal in cryptic notes to be deciphered and transcribed after crossing the border.

"But when did you actually become a travel writer—a professional travel writer?" Margo prompts.

"I was a teacher first," I say. "Even today, when I cross a border and the customs official asks my occupation, I say 'teacher.' I started teaching travel after I took a bad travel class at the university."

She crinkles her nose and looks up at me through a blonde tangle of too-moussed hair. "Explain," she demands.

I tell her that twenty years ago, in preparation for an overland trip from Europe to India, I took a class called "Istanbul to Katmandu: An Independent Traveler's Guide." It was part of the University of Washington's "Experimental College." When I signed up, I considered the class a godsend. But the teacher was unprepared, lazy, and disorganized. The room was filled with vagabonds about to embark on the trip of their lives. And the teacher didn't care. While he had the information we needed, he insulted us with pointless chatter. I learned nothing about travel to Katmandu, but the class taught me something far more important: I learned the value of well-presented travel information. And I realized that I could teach European travel.

As the train clangs and clatters on, we cross the border. The last Dutch windmill and the first German castle, standing like border guards, dutifully salute tourists leaving one country and entering another.

We hear a train door slam and the distant voice of a tired conductor chanting, "*Fahrkarten, bitte; billets, s'il vous plait;* tickets, please." Pulling the same type of moneybelt from her pants as I pull from mine, she says, "See, I bought your belt."

When the weary conductor reaches us, he stamps the date on our passes. As we tuck them away again he says, "*Gute fahrt,*" and slides the door shut.

"I just love the way they always say 'fart,'" says Margo.

I explain, "That means 'journey.' He wished us a good journey."

Many first-time visitors to Germany have a similar fascination with the *fahrts* of Deutschland. I don't tell Margo that between piano factory visits, my dad and I collected them. Driving down the Autobahn, counting *fahrt* signs was definitely more interesting than counting Volkswagen Beetles.

Autobahn exits are marked "Ausfahrt." (Some tourists actually wonder why so many towns in Germany are named Ausfahrt.) Beyond *ausfahrt* our collection included *gross fahrt* ("big trip"), *schnell fahrt* ("fast trip"), *zoofahrt* ("this way to the zoo"), *messerundfahrt* ("round-trip to the convention center"), and—our favorite—*panarama fahrt* ("scenic journey").

This sport worked north of Germany, too. In Denmark, "journey" is spelled *fart*. As we connected islands we read ferry schedules labeled "*fartplanner.*" And to hail elevators, I ran ahead of my parents . . . to push the button that read "*I fart.*" To this day my dad and I bid each other farewell as our German friends did, with a cheery, "Have a good *fahrt*."

Within minutes we are in the Ruhr Valley. Through the window, with a Teutonic lack of fanfare, stout and spartan cooling towers mark the eye of Germany's industrial storm.

"Are those nuclear?" Margo asks.

"Yeah. Germany's intense," I answer. "Imagine one-third the population and industrial capacity of the entire United States packed into a place the size of Montana."

Unimpressed, Margo steers the conversation back to my background. "So, after that lousy Katmandu class, you started teaching travel?"

"I signed up to teach my own Experimental College travel class," I tell her. "I called it 'European Travel—Cheap!' I thought maybe twenty or thirty college kids would sign up. But that first class was filled with a hundred *adults*—people my parents' age."

The class cost eight dollars. I'd bring a bundle of two-dollar bills and take home a bundle of tens. Walking quickly across a dark campus after those first classes with a bookbag full of money, I realized there was a business here. At first I was happy to earn enough to pay for my annual plane ticket. But as enrollment grew, I began making more teaching travel than I did teaching piano.

As my class evolved, so did my delivery. By responding to my audience and constantly experimenting, I learned what worked. To a group of decent people, the word "horny" was fun, but "pissed off" was offensive.

Over several years of lecturing, I developed a sixth sense of what people needed to know and what they didn't. By fielding thousands of questions, I learned which fears and apprehensions were most troubling as departure day neared.

"But when my aunt suggested I write a book about Europe, I thought she was crazy," I tell Margo. "I was a traveler with a bunch of slides, not a writer. Besides, I thought, why turn my play into work?"

Outside our train window, the burnt marshmallow–colored twin spires of Koln's cathedral salute a skyscraping "V" for victory.

They seem to celebrate that fact that, while Germany made the colossal mistake of following Hitler into all-out war and paid a colossal price, the cathedral survived. Margo doesn't notice.

"I'm taking a travel writing class," she says, looking at me as if I have a rucksack packed with extra credit.

"I never took a writing class," I say. "I learned to write by giving talks. Then I talk the same way to the page. I read one book— *On Writing Well* by William Zinsser. When I feel like I should read another book to fine-tune my writing, I read Zinsser again. And I travel. Travel writing means going to great places and taking your reader with you. You need to really be there."

"Sense of place," she says, as if on *Jeopardy*.

"Right." Pulling out one of my newsletters, I flip through the pages and say, "Read this paragraph out loud. Read it like you're a tour guide in wonderland."

With mock wide eyes, she whispers, "'You're walking along a ridge high in the Alps. On one side of you spreads the greatest Alpine panorama: the Eiger, Mönch, and Jungfrau. On the other, lakes stretch all the way to Germany. And ahead of you, the long legato tones of an alp horn announce that there's a helicopter-stocked mountain hut just around the corner . . . and the coffee schnapps is on.'"

"I like it," she says, slipping a bottle of wine and plastic glasses out of her daybag. "But," she persists, pouring me a glass, "how do you make money at travel?"

I haven't really considered my "formula" before. The wine is good, she's bubbly, and I feel a little flattered by her interest. So I take a long sip and, sounding both professorial and fatherly, trace the evolution of my writing career.

"I wrote my first book like I was giving my talk to the paper. I self-published it. Anyone with time and money can do that. I rented an IBM Selectric and got my girlfriend to help type my manuscript. My maps were ballpoint pen–crude. I pasted in sketches my college roommate drew of my favorite slides."

Coming up with a title was hard. Brainstorming, I collected a list: *Europe Yourself. Europe On Your Own. Go Local and European.*

Eurofiles. One day, as I reviewed the list and still found no winner, my dad asked, "What's the purpose of the book?"

I told him, "To give people the key to finding an informal and real Europe. So they can be friends with Europe."

He sipped his coffee and thought for a minute. "Europe Through the Back Door," he said simply.

I finished the book in 1980 and, with a check for $3,000, delivered 256 carefully assembled pages to the printer. Two weeks later I filled my station wagon with 2,500 copies of *Europe Through the Back Door*.

That first edition was a humble one. As if to sabotage my own work, I forgot to put on an ISBN number, which made it difficult for retailers to order the book. The first cover of the book was so basic that people in the media mistook it for a pre-publication edition. Holding my finished product, they'd ask, "And when will this be out?"

My first big break came when the travel editor of the *Seattle Post-Intelligencer*, Bob Davis, serialized my book. Given its focus on independent travel, this was a courageous move back then, one that offended advertisers and ultimately cost Davis his job.

I was honored and nervous when Mr. Davis took me to a French restaurant for lunch. I remember browsing through the menu and, not recognizing the word "quiche," asked, "What is quee-shee?"

My book sold only locally and in my classes. But after it came out, people saw me as an expert, even though I wasn't. Taking advantage of this momentum, I polished my teaching and built my business.

The train pulls into Bonn. Trying to redirect just a little of her attention from my job to Europe, I tell Margo how sleepy Bonn was a good choice for Germany's post-Hitler capital. "This was the home of Beethoven," I tell her. "It symbolized a peaceful and highly cultured Germany . . . a Germany without the goose-stepping."

Oblivious, Margo asks, "How can I make money traveling . . . like you?"

I launch into a pep talk: "There's a huge demand for practical, entertaining travel talks—libraries, schools, businesses, clubs, and universities. Be generous with your information. Give free talks. Get your teaching out there anyway you can. Let newspapers use your writing for free. Teach first. Sell second. But don't quit your day job."

As Margo considers allying herself with a travel agency, I interrupt. "Don't become a travel agent and don't expect help from the travel industry. You'll be considered dangerous competition. You are a teacher of travel, not a travel agent.

"Be passionate about the beauty of travel—a Johnny Appleseed of travel dreams. Cause people to marvel and ask, 'How do you make any money?' If you keep on teaching with a contagious enthusiasm for Europe, eventually you might make some money."

By now my enthusiasm is raging, but her once-eager eyes look weary as she slowly deflates. Squeezing the last of her wine into her glass, she says, "I could just come and work for you."

From the train window, we see the statue of Kaiser Wilhelm on a prancing horse that graces that piece of Koblenz real estate where the Rhine and Mosel Rivers meet.

Koblenz is Latin for "confluence." But for Margo and me it means exactly the opposite. I thank her for the wine and wish her well, then hop off the train.

The trackside schedule lists a train to my Rhine target in two minutes, and not another for two hours. A fine travel moment: I'm alone again, looking up at the schedule as the train pulls in. I put my hand on the train car door, frozen in thought. I was planning to catch the boat down the Rhine from here, but I don't know if or when the boat leaves. The conductor looks at me as if to ask, "Well, are you with us or not?" The whistle blows. Quickly reviewing my options, I follow that marvelous old traveler's axiom: a train at hand is worth jumping on.

Moments later, I'm rolling along the riverside track, alone with Europe—wind in my face and Rhine in my viewfinder.

Lady Loreley on the Rhine

My *milch*-run train stops at each village along the Rhine. But the villages turn their backs on the tracks and smile at the river. We pass a steamer, so I jump out in the town of Boppard. I have just enough time to hike from the train station to the boat dock and catch it.

As the sturdy white boat sidles up to the dock, dockhands lasso a huge cleat and lower the gangplank. Dozens of tour boats like this one cruise the Rhine River, stopping at all the villages and offering grand views of medieval castles.

This is the Romantic Rhine, a powerful stretch of the river slashing a deep and scenic gorge through western Germany from Koblenz to Mainz. When Hitler's inability to get along with his neighbors limited his people's vacation options, the Rhine was a leading German holiday destination. Even today, Germans feel drawn to their grand canyon. The sheer bulk of history that has poured through this craggy gorge rouses any romantic soul.

Jostling through crowds of Germans and tourists, I climb to the sun deck and grab a chair. With the last new passenger barely aboard, the gangplank is dragged in and the river pulls us away. My destination is the medieval village of Bacharach.

Parkas flap in the cool wind as the rugged hills gradually reveal castles both ruined and restored. The ridges of the gorge rise above us, unblemished by any modern building thanks to a strict code that holds the tide of contemporary Germany back, out of sight from this romantic river escape. Tortured green vineyards climb steep hillsides, and turreted towns grab friendly bits of shoreline. Trains streak like arrows along both shores. Bright green and red buoys battle the current, keeping the cautious parade of barges and sightseeing boats off the many reefs.

The Rhine starts from Swiss snowmelt and flows 800 miles to join the Atlantic at Rotterdam. Culturally, it's Europe's "Continental Divide." Once it divided ancient Rome from the barbarians; in later times it divided the Roman Catholic world (Bavaria, Belgium, and south) from Protestant Europe (northern Germany, the Netherlands, and north).

We pass ghostly Roman towers. Standing tall in spite of the ivy fingers trying to pull them to the ground, they mark the northern edge of what was once the Roman empire. To the north was the bar-bar-barbarian world, named for its crude-sounding, non-Latin way of talking. Anyone who didn't speak Latin or Greek back then was considered uncivilized. Barely human creatures who did more grunting than speaking, barbarians fell somewhere between animals and Romans.

Roman-style order, whether ancient or papal, came from the top and required conformity. Beyond Rome's reach, a kind of grassroots but chaotic freedom reigned. As I compare the go-by-the-book Catholic world and my free-as-the-wind Viking/Protestant heritage, it's hard to ignore contradictory images in Europe today. How can the jukebox orderliness of a planned Swedish suburb come out of barbarian chaos? And if the south is so inclined to embrace top-down-orderliness, why is there not a hint of the pope in Rome's chaotic traffic?

With a loud blast of its horn, our boat chugs to one of its many stops, dumping passengers as newcomers muscle for position. The configuration of tourists and deck chairs changes at every stop.

An American family gets on and settles in front of me. Mom flips open my Germany guidebook and plays tour guide with her family. She points as she reads from my self-guided tour of the Rhine, and her children squint at the castle crowning a hill directly above the boat.

So it would be easier to follow, I keyed my Rhine tour to the black and white kilometer signs along the shoreline. These bold, eight-foot-square billboards indicate the distance upstream to the Rhinefalls, where the river becomes navigable. While they were designed as ships' navigational aids, I joke in my book that I put them up myself as tourist aids . . . because I care so much.

The woman wonders out loud with her children, "I wonder how Rick managed to get all those signs up?"

People are inclined to like—and believe—their guidebook writer. I get several letters each year thanking me for these signs.

The river's historic strategic importance may be a subconscious attraction for the thousands who visit the region, but all along the Rhine romantic fairy tales fly like kites that got away in the breeze. Each castle and every rock comes with a story.

As the cliffs get steeper, the rocks darker, and the river faster,

the scenery becomes more
dramatic. With the boat's
sun deck filled mostly with
beer-sipping, ice cream-
licking Germans, the gen-
eral pulse quickens as we
approach the mythological
climax of this cruise. Over
the ship's blow horns comes
the story of Loreley—the
maiden who seduced sailors

The Loreley rock, the Rhine's bad-news corner

into shipwrecks—in three languages. The Germans know the story
by heart, but the story is repeated as a sort of national anthem.

The Loreley, a 400-foot-high black rock, shoves a zigzag into
the river. Like a slate lump in the throat of Germany, it stirs the
national soul. While the modern German state dates only from
1870, German culture is as old as Europe. It's as if the rich legends
and traditions of this gorge add to the legitimacy of the Johnny-
come-lately of European superpowers.

Germany's flag waves with pre–World War II pride from
Loreley's summit, and castles lurk as shadowy bodyguards checking
the traffic on either side. Our ship, slung low with tourists, plays a
lusty rendition of the Loreley song. And parents point to the rocky
bluff featured in the fairy-tale memory of every German schoolkid.

According to legend, a thousand years of skippers have
dreaded the Loreley. This is the bad news corner in what has always been Germany's major shipping river. The current speeds up
here as the gorge reaches its narrowest point, barely 150 feet
across. To make matters worse, a reef of seven rocks—named the
"Seven Maidens" by some medieval German misogynist—lies in
ambush just around the bend.

But it was the legendary *wunderbar fraulein* Loreley, her long
blonde hair almost covering her body, who lured boatloads of
drooling sailors to her river bed. Like a deadly wet dream, she held
the sailors' attention captive, letting go only after their ships were
dashed onto the rocks.

The legend recalls a count who sent his men to capture or kill Loreley after his son followed her to his death. When the soldiers cornered the nymph in her cave, she called her dad, Father Rhine, for help. Huge waves, the likes of which you'll never see today, rose from the river and carried her to safety. And she has never been seen since.

But alas, when the moon shines brightly and the wind is just right, a soft, playful Rhine whine can still be heard from the Loreley. As you pass, listen carefully. "*Sailors . . . sailors . . . over my bounding mane.*"

As late as the early 1900s, bells rang on ships reminding sailors that the Loreley was approaching and it was time to pray. Today, from a parking spot opposite the rock, tour guides shout across the river and the rock shouts back. Any medieval scholar will tell you these echoes are the ghostly voices of drowned sailors consumed by the lovely, lonely maiden who combed her hair and sang so seductively.

Battleground Bacharach

As the song of the Loreley fades, our boat docks at the half-timbered town of Bacharach and I jump out. Bacharach, wearing a castle hat and a vineyard cape, is a typical Rhine village. It lines the river and fills its tiny tributary valley with a history you can hook arms with in a noisy *weinstube.*

"Bacharach" means "altar to Bacchus." The town and its wine date from Celtic and Roman times. Local vintners brag that the medieval Pope Pius II preferred Bacharach wine and had it shipped to Rome by the cartload. Today tourists drink it on the spot.

Bacharach's honorary mayor is given the title of Bacchus. The last Bacchus, one of the best wine gods in memory, died a year ago. Posters left up as a memorial, it seems, show his pudgy highness riding a keg of Riesling, wearing a tunic, and crowned by grapes as the adoring villagers carry him on happy shoulders. Bacharach's annual wine fest is the first weekend of each October, just before the harvest. This is a wine fest with a reason: to empty the barrels and make room for the new wine—a chore locals take seriously.

The festival is months away, but the dank back alleys of Bacharach smell like the morning after. I drop my bag at Hotel Kranenturm, then head back to the boat dock. I've arranged a private walk through town with Herr Jung, Bacharach's retired schoolmaster.

The riverfront scene is local and laid-back. Retired German couples, thick after a lifetime of beer and potatoes, set the tempo at an easy stroll. I gaze across the Rhine. Lost in thoughts of Bacchus and Roman Bacharach, I'm in another age . . . until two castle-clipping WWIII fighters from a nearby American base drill through the silence.

The Rhine Valley is stained by war. While church bells play cheery ditties in Holland, on the Rhine they sound more like hammers on anvils. At bridges, road signs still indicate which lane is reinforced and able to support tanks. As the last of the World War II survivors pass on, memories fade. The war that ripped our grandparents' Europe in two will become like a black and white photo of a long-gone and never-known relative on the mantle.

I pause at Bacharach's old riverside war memorial. A big stone urn with a Maltese cross framed by two helmets, it seems pointedly ignored by holiday-makers. Erected to honor the dead of Bismarck's first war in 1864, it was designed with vision to accommodate the wars that followed: blank slabs became rolls of honor for the dead of 1866, 1870, and 1914–18. Compared to war's greedy toll, the Loreley seems as harmless as an over-sexed gnat.

Herr Jung arrives and I ask him to translate the words carved on the stone.

"To remember the hard but great time. . . ." he starts, then mutters, "Ahh, this is not important now."

Herr Jung explains, "We turn our backs to the monuments of old wars. We have one day in the year when we remember those who have died in the wars. Those who lost sons, fathers, and husbands have a monument in their heart. They don't need this old stone."

Rolf Jung is an ener-
getic gentleman whose
glasses seem to dance on
his nose as he weaves a
story. When meeting my
tour groups for guided
walks, he greets them as he
did his class of fifth-graders
thirty years ago, singing,
"Good morning, good

Herr Jung takes me through the back door.

morning, to you and you
and you. . . ." Like so many
Europeans, he has a knack for finding greatness in his work, no matter how grand or small the job. A walk with Herr Jung always makes
me feel good about Europe.

As I ponder the memorial, he quotes Bismarck: "Nobody wants
war, but everyone wants things they can't have without war."

Herr Jung seems dressed for remembering, wearing a white shirt
open at the collar under an old-time suit. He looks past the town's
castle where the ridge of the gorge meets the sky and says, "I remember the sky. It was a moving carpet of American bombers coming over that ridge. Mothers would run with their children. There
were no men left. In my class, forty-nine of the fifty-five boys lost
their fathers. My generation grew up with only mothers.

"I remember the bombings," he continues. "Lying in our cellar, praying with my mother. I was a furious deal-maker with God.
I can still hear the guns. Day after day we watched American and
Nazi airplanes fighting. We were boys. We'd jump on our bikes to
see the wreckage of killed planes. I was the neighborhood special-
ist on war planes. I could identify them by the sound.

"One day a huge plane was shot down. It had four engines. I
biked to the wreckage, and I couldn't believe my eyes. It was a
plane designed with a huge upright wing in the center. Then I realized this was only the tail section. The tail section was as big as
an entire plane. I knew then that we would lose this war."

The years after the war were hungry years. "I would wake in

middle of night and search the cupboards," he says. "There was no fat, no bread, no nothing. I licked spilled grain from the cupboard. We had friends from New York, and they sent coffee which we could trade with farmers for grain. For this I have always been thankful.

"When I think of what the Nazis did to Germany I remember a fine soup cooked by thirty people can be spoiled by one man with a handful of salt."

Herr Jung takes me on a historic ramble through the back lanes of Bacharach. Like any good small-town teacher, he's known and admired by everyone.

We climb through the vineyards above town to a bluff over-looking a six-mile stretch of Rhine. "I came here often as a boy to count the ships," he says. "I once saw fifty in the river in front of Bacharach."

We look out over the town's slate rooftops. Picking up a stone, he carves the letters "Rick" into a slate step and tells me, "Now you are here, carved in stone . . . until the next rain."

Ever a teacher, he explains, "Slate is very soft. The Rhine River found this and carved out this gorge. Soil made from slate absorbs the heat of sun. So our vines stay warm at night. We grow a fine wine here on the Rhine.

"Today the vineyards are going back to the wild. Germans won't work for eight marks [five dollars] per hour. The Polish come to do the work. During the Solidarity time I housed a guest worker. After eleven weeks in the fields, he drove home in a used Mercedes."

We pass under the fortified gate and walk back into town—cra-dled safely in half-timbered cuteness. My teacher can sense what I'm thinking: that Bacharach was never good for much more than in-spiring a poem, selling a cuckoo clock, or docking a Rhine boat. Propping his soft leather briefcase on his knee, he fingers through a file of visual aids, each carefully hand-colored and preserved in plas-tic for rainy walks. Herr Jung pulls out a sketch of Bacharach fortifi-cations intact and busy with trade to show how in its heyday—from 1300 to 1600—the town was rich and politically important.

"Medieval Bacharach had six thousand people—that was big

in the fifteenth century," he says. "But the plagues, fires, and religious wars of the seventeenth century ended our powerful days. Bacharach became empty. It was called 'the cuckoo town.' Other people moved in the way a cuckoo takes over an empty nest. For two hundred years now, our town is only a village of a thousand."

In the mid-nineteenth century, poets and painters like Victor Hugo were charmed by the Rhineland's romantic mix of past glory, present poverty, and rich legend. They put this part of the Rhine on the old "grand tour" map. And the tourists' "Romantic Rhine" was born.

A ruined fifteenth-century chapel hangs like a locket under the castle and over the town. In 1842 Victor Hugo stood where Herr Jung and I now stand. Looking at the chapel, he wrote, "No doors, no roof or windows, a magnificent skeleton puts its silhouette against the sky. Above it, the ivy-covered castle ruins provide a fitting crown. This is Bacharach, land of fairy tales, covered with legends and sagas."

As military jets soar, Roman towers crumble, and the Loreley sings, this land seems less like a fairy tale and more like a timeless battleground.

Earplugs, Not Chocolate

On early trips, I'd grab a bunk up at the youth hostel in the castle. Now I find ambience with comfort at Hotel Kranenturm, which fills Bacharach's medieval Kranenturm, or crane tower. Bacharach was located at a treacherous place along the Rhine where boats would have to lighten their loads to pass safely. Bacharach's cranes would hoist cargo—mostly kegs of wine—from boats to be portered downstream to a point where the river was easier to navigate. Dressed in slate, rough timbers, and pointy dormers, the crane tower's windows now give wives a powerful urge to play Rapunzel for camera-toting husbands out in the street.

The hotel is run by Herr and Frau Engel. Kurt Engel still looks like a ship's cook. During his merchant marine days he met and married Fatima in the Philippines. This hotel and restaurant on the Rhine is exactly what they dreamed of. Kurt and Fatima are a team. For ten years Kurt has whittled on his old building to meet the ever-increasing demands of the modern tourists. And for ten years Fatima has apologized for what Kurt has yet to whittle.

Here on the Rhine, you can't be on the river without being on the train tracks. In the 1800s, early tourists actually requested rooms with a "train view." Two trains—among the first in Europe—rolled by each day. And people traveled here just to watch them. Today trains rocket by every couple of minutes, and Rhineland hoteliers assure guests their bedrooms are equipped with special triple-pane windows to keep the noise out. But with earplugs instead of chocolates on the pillows, it's clear three panes aren't enough to silence the roar of modern Germany.

I have my customary pre-dinner glass of local wine on the Kranenturm terrace just to hear the still-schoolgirlish Fatima rhyme "drink wine on the Rhine." Thin and elegant Fatima, who looks like a Filipina Diana Ross with a toothy smile and boundless energy, plops down *"ein Viertel,"* a quarter-liter glass. Then she hands me the hotel's latest promotional postcard and gives me her annual "working too hard" line. This year it comes with a new twist: "I have only time to go to Mass in winter," she says. "When the priest comes to my restaurant, I remind him 'a work well done is a prayer itself.'"

Fatima turns so fast her long black hair flips out. It seems serving her customers keeps her young. Enjoying a slight buzz from my goblet of fruity white wine, I gaze peacefully past a bit of medieval wall fitted generously with hotel-terrace flower boxes. I look past four gleaming sets of rails, a two-lane highway, the Maltese cross war memorial—still ignored by strollers in the park—past the churning river, and up the vineyard-dotted distant hillside to another phantom castle. Then, *schwooooosh* . . . A train rockets by just a few feet away, shaking the terrace. I spin my head to read the destination plate on each car as it streaks by. Where are they speeding to? I can never tell.

At dinner, grape-bunch chandeliers shake from the ceiling and conversations pause as the blur of an express train fills the arched windows. Guests look at each other with frightened eyes, wondering in unison, "How will we sleep tonight?"

Kurt, with a beer belly begging for lederhosen but stuffed only into a greasy T-shirt and jeans, steps out of the kitchen to share his latest exasperation. After drawing himself a beer, he joins me at my table. The evening's cooking is done.

Looking exhausted and burned out, he says, "It's the new cook. He's always sick. A cook costs me four thousand deutsch marks [$2,500] a month. He gets one month paid vacation and up to six weeks paid sick time. Doctors say the best way for a German employee to stop being sick is to start his own business."

Sucking on his tired cigarette while his wife rushes by with a tray of glasses, he continues. "You cannot run a business this way. The only small business that can succeed is the family business. Family employees don't work the German system against you."

Thinking of the dedication to quality that I witnessed among workers in piano factories years before, I lament, "So the fine tradition of German craftsmanship is dying?"

Kurt fudges on the side of optimism. "Maybe in industries where you can see your final work it will survive. But for service industries such as tourism, things are very bad. Very bad."

An hour later, Kurt climbs down into the cellar, sheds ten years, and opens up his Tropical Tanz-Bar. Like an impish, balding, and German Alfred E. Neuman, he turns on the disco ball. Commanding his musical control panel as if driving a jet ski, he churns out schmaltzy German *schlager* and American pop. Lights flicker around the amazing room as tourists dance under medieval arches. Brown-and-white cowhides are draped over the seats, sombreros serve as light shades, and plastic palm trees camouflage the sewer pipes. A built-in tableau, like a museum display, features a tropical island nearly covered by a bigger-than-life turtle. On the dance floor, a fountain burbles in front of a wall-size beach mural. It's a bit of the Philippines with a splash of the Old West, right here on the Rhine. As Kurt's smile broadens, nearly completing the jolly circle his receding hair line starts, I realize how much happiness can hide behind old fortified walls.

I climb the stairs from the tropics back into medieval Germany and spiral up to my round tower room. My bathroom window overlooks the Rhine and what must be Germany's busiest train tracks. While most hotels post "no washing in the sink" signs, Fatima put her nervous stamp on the sign above my sink: "Washing of the clothes in room is extremely prohibited." The sign—which travelers intrepret as a warning not to let wet clothes drip on the floor or furniture—reminds me that I'm out of clean clothes.

I feel so domestic and responsible when I struggle with my filthy clothes. Having my hands wrist-deep in a sink full of murky gray water dissolves any twinge of guilt for ignoring Fatima's sign.

Even with triple panes bolted shut, the thunder of the train wakes me early. Giving up on sleep, I look across the tracks past that forgotten memorial to the still-misty river. Satisfied that there was a reason I was driven out of my sleep so early, I savor the view: huge barges rolling with the mist, one sporting a car on its bow like a hood ornament. Twentieth-century commerce under fifteenth-century castles.

A vivid memory of my first trip to Europe was the daily routine of Germans stepping sleepily into the breakfast room wishing each other a slow and pre-coffee-miserable *"Morgen"* for "Good morning." German businessmen do their *"Morgen"* very slow and very low.

In years past, Kranenturm's breakfast was always an occasion for a cheery *"Morgen."* Kurt's mother, my favorite *Grossmutter*, would scurry about, bent and secretive like a friendly sorcerer. She'd enter like a kettle boiling over with her bowl of *haus gemacht* (homemade) marmalade. With her Queen Mum smile, she'd explain that the dark red marmalade was a fruit cocktail of seven fruits but that the Johannisberry was the dominant fruit and overwhelmed the colors of the others.

Kurt's mom died last year and was replaced at breakfast by Fatima, whose nervous bubbliness is too intense for this early hour. Without grandma and her *haus gemacht* marmalade, the Kranenturm breakfast will never be quite right. *"Morgen."*

Giant Steins and Well-Hung Cuckoo Clocks

The town of St. Goar, nestled in the cliffs beneath the mighty Rheinfels Castle commands a visit. After a ten-minute train ride from Bacharach and a fifteen-minute climb, I find myself standing like a victorious mountain climber atop the highest tower of the castle, under the black, gold, and red stripes of a hard-flapping German flag. Far below me, cargo-laden barges dance their endless reels with the ferries and tour boats. The half-timbered dormers and steeples of St. Goar seem to tumble from the castle to the river.

St. Goar was established in pre-Roman times as a place where Celtic sailors would stop and give thanks to their gods after surviving that gurgling gauntlet of Loreley and the seven maidens. Today tour groups stop here, praying only for a good deal. They're cheered on by the flags of the biggest spenders: Americans, Japanese, Canadians, French, Germans, English, and Australians.

I hike down from the castle into St. Goar, landing right between the town's two biggest shops. A double-decker tour bus beats me by a minute, squirting its crowd directly into the clock shop. Heinz Mühl and his family run the shop with the world's largest free-hanging cuckoo clock. It's necessary to say "free-hanging" because there are actual cuckoo clock houses in Germany's Black Forest (reason enough to skip that area altogether). The shop across the street, run by Manfred Montag, his wife, Maria, and son Misha, boasts the world's biggest stein—a burly four-footer filling their front window.

Manfred has been my man on the Rhine for years. On each visit, my tour group drops by his shop to hear his talk about the local stein industry. Today Manfred greets me warmly and takes me across the street to see his friend Heinz. Heinz, whose shop wriggles with hyperactive time-keepers, takes me on a cuckoo clock tour. "Clocks with heavy pine cones mean you wind only once in eight days. Small pine cones must be wound every day."

"Every day?" I ask.

"When you brush your teeth, you wind your clock—no problem," says Heinz. "One cone controls the time. Clocks with two cones give you time and cuckoo. Three cones: time, cuckoo, and music."

With pride he pokes a tiny stick under the clock and adds,

"And now, we have this small lever. You can turn the cuckoo off and get some quiet at night."

"Probably by customer request," I say.

"Actually, people used to lock the cuckoo's door," Heinz explains, flipping a small wire latch to demonstrate. "But this was only good for transport. Each hour, the cuckoos would bounce against it and break their spring. So to save the cuckoos, we now have this lever instead."

"Aren't these clocks actually Swiss?" I ask.

Heinz grows suddenly tall and stern, with increased voltage in his eyes. As Heinz inhales deeply, Manfred jokes, "Now you get him going."

With an exasperated exhale, Heinz straightens me out. "Cuckoo clocks are German. Only one piece, the music roll, is Swiss-made. Tourists, they know Swiss watches and they think a watch is a clock. But the cuckoo clock, it is only German.

"The Swiss shops, they give tour guides bigger commissions. So tour guides say to their groups, 'Wait for the real thing in Switzerland.' Swiss shops stock only the 'little chalet' models. One tourist bought many cuckoo clocks in Switzerland. They ran out and had to have one clock shipped to her directly from the factory. When she received a package from Germany she sent it back to the Swiss shop with an angry note claiming she would accept only the 'genuine Swiss cuckoo clock.' It is amazing what tourists will believe."

Remembering the kilometer signposts I erected along the Rhine, I nod.

Brandishing a Swiss Army knife, Heinz says, "Would I tell people these are German?" Even though he seems a gentle sort, I figure I'm safest endorsing his disgust. I edge toward the door and return with Manfred back to his shop.

These merchant families get caught up in their own sales pitches. Stalking me as I browse, Maria Montag notices my attraction to the stuffed teddies. "Steiffs," she hiccups. "The Mercedes of stuffed animals. My grandson had only three stuffed animals. All Steiffs."

Like merchants throughout Europe, Herr Montag reads the world economic pulse via tourist trends. From the way he moans, you'd think the rise of the deutsche mark was giving him lederhosen wedgies.

Manfred says, "The Taiwanese are very good for us. But the Japanese, Chinese, and Koreans, they shop only at businesses owned by their tour companies. This hurts us."

"They follow the shopping advice of their guides," I say.

"And Japanese tourists don't just call their leaders *guide*," he says. "They call them *dai sensei* . . . that's 'honorable teacher.'"

"What about the English?" I ask.

"We get fewer English every year," he reports. "But they never buy nothing anyway. We had a group of forty in yesterday. Didn't sell one postcard. They buy no steins, only the beer."

The Rhine, once Europe's cultural divide, is now a thoroughfare for tourists. On this historic battleground—where Romans clobbered barbarians, Catholics butted Bibles with Protestants, and Allies met Nazis—today's battles are fought on a smaller, friendlier scale as family-run businesses compete for the tourist dollar.

In the heat of the summer, as Rhine boats are loaded with tourists and tour buses lumber like tanks down narrow roads, you can almost hear the Loreley singing, "*Tourists . . . tourists . . . I've got Steiffs and steins and kegs of white wine . . . .*"

CHAPTER THREE

CLUB ROTHENBURG

*"The tourists, they come like a big, one-
time-in-a-year flood. We Rothenburgers
sit and wait for you to float by."*

Changing trains on my way to Rothenburg, I have a few free minutes in Würzburg. As an experiment, I approach three different
lost-looking groups of tourists and ask, "Rothenburg?"

Each says, "Yes."

Like a caring traffic cop, I hold up fingers and say, "Track
number four, five minutes," and point them in the right direction.

This is a bad omen. Twenty years ago, I fell in love with a
Rothenburg in the rough. At that time, the town still fed a few
farm animals within its medieval walls. Today Rothenburg's barns
are hotels and its livestock are tourists. Once the premier stop on
a medieval trading route, Germany's best-preserved walled town
survives today as a popular stop along the tourist trail called the
Romantic Road. The English and German signs that long marked
the entire route have been replaced by new ones—still bilingual,
but in English and Japanese. And Mr. "Off the Beaten Path" is
right here with the camera-toting masses.

I walk from the Rothenburg train station through the plain,
modern neighborhood and step under the medieval gate into the
colorful old town. Short, squat shops with pastel sawtooth gables

line the narrow, always-clean lanes. Steps in the sidewalk are painted with stay-alert white lines to keep gawking visitors from tripping.

I climb Rothenburg's wall for the fifteen-minute stroll to my hotel. With medieval timbers and red tiles for a roof, a stone wall on the outside and a thin wooden railing on the inside, this elevated sidewalk arcs around the town as if bundling together a world of medieval cuteness. Even with a rucksack soaking up the sweat on my back, I choose this scenic hike over a quick and easy taxi ride. My mission: to find the ever-weaker pulse of medieval Rothenburg.

Peering through a narrow slit, I see the tour bus parking lot just outside the wall and three rows of empty tour buses. Fifty yards ahead of me a couple with a baby stroller approaches. By their trendy teal and evergreen parkas, I guess they're American tourists. As I get closer, the woman pulls out a camera, the man hums the theme song of my TV show. Now I *know* they're Americans. They're from Orange County. They saw the episode we shot with our kids—we filmed my daughter, Jackie, in her stroller on this same bit of town wall.

From this rampart perch, the city looks perfectly preserved. Row after row of higgledy-piggledy pointed roofs fill the skyline. Each roof is upholstered by red tiles patterned like fish scales. Romantic painters discovered Rothenburg in the 1880s. By about 1900, a society—the first of its kind—was created to preserve the town's physical character.

The wall is lined with memorial plaques, a reminder that no preservation society was a match for Hitler in the desperation of his last year. In the final phase of the war, in March 1945, Rothenburg was bombed. One-third of the old town burned. Overestimating the artistic conscience of all-out war, Nazis hid here. They thought the town was too cute for the Allies to target. Rothenburg was rebuilt with a fund-raising idea that was novel for its time. Donors who paid eighty deutsche marks for the restoration of one meter of town wall would be recognized by little plaques. Today all that is left of the war—other than these plaques—are the tired memories of Rothenburg's oldest citizens, who spend their afternoons gazing out second-story windows at waves of tourists sipping McMilchshakes.

Rothenburg is well on
its way to becoming a
theme park. Always anticipating a siege, the townspeople used to stock the
fountains with trout, fill
the lofts with corn, and
churn grain safely inside
the town walls at the
horse-powered mill. Today
the fountains are flower

Rothenburg under a modern-day siege

pots, the corn comes popped and candied, and the horse mill has
been turned into a youth hostel. The mighty cannons that were
used to defend the town are now aimed at playground crocodiles in
the park-filled moat. From ramparts where soldiers once splashed
hot oil onto screaming attackers, kids fly paper airplanes.

After I drop my bag at the Hotel Golden Rose, I realize I'm
angry. I'm angry at mobs of tour groups invading my medieval
playground. I'm mad at merchants selling their town's charms.
And I'm mad that by promoting this town in my guidebooks, I've
contributed to the prostitution of Rothenburg.

Hearing the spirited clip-clop of a horse pounding the cobbles, I look out my window. Coming through the gate is an old-
time carriage filled with tourists—in teal and evergreen. It rounds
the corner and the cobbles are quiet again.

I latch my window closed and remind myself that any original
Rothenburger would prefer the modern siege of tourism over the
meaner medieval sieges. I hang my room key on the rack behind the
postcards and powdered sugar *schneeballs* on the reception desk and
set out to take Rothenburg's touristic temperature.

Mele Kalikimaka from Kris Kringle

To see just how commercial Rothenburg has become, I make a re-
connaissance mission into the town's busiest place: Käthe
Wohlfahrt's Christmas shop.

A six-foot nutcracker—with a mouth big enough to crack a

camcorder—welcomes a steady stream of tourist shoppers. A spinning white-flocked Christmas tree is heavy with red and gold
bulbs. Serving as Santa's own turnstile, it whisks me into a land
of perpetual Christmas.

This ever-blinking, always-twinkling Kris Kringle market—
built on the notion that Christmas should last twelve months a
year—is the biggest consumer of electricity in Rothenburg. Deeper
and deeper past megawatt candles and chimes, into the grand
grotto of year-round Christmas I go.

The shop is oddly multicultural: Japanese salespeople sell
Chinese knickknacks as if they're German. A smiling monkey
cleans a chimney, Kermit der Frog hangs dirndls out to dry, and a
stern-faced teddy winds a cuckoo clock. Mossy manger scenes
come ready populated or a la carte. A toy medieval village street
shakes with autistic Steiffs—battery-powered teddies entertaining
a nonstop parade of tour groups.

Members of an East German group, sweaty after a long, hot
bus ride, clog the aisles. They come on twenty-deutsche-mark day
trips from Dresden and Leipzig with picnics from home and a lifetime backlog of curiosity. Pushing the East Germans deeper into
the store, an American group follows, chattering excitedly about
how they decorate their Christmas trees. The next group is
Japanese, snapping up souvenirs and shooting photos like
gunslingers. Old-time woven shopping baskets make impulse buying feel almost traditional.

I, too, have some Wohlfahrt souvenirs: a few shiny Christmas
tree ornaments and a letter from Wohlfahrt's lawyer. Displeased with
the favorable treatment my guidebook gives to a competing shop,
he warned me that it was "illegal" to favor one shop over another.

Ready to leave, a momentary panic hits me as false passage
after false passage leads me into more racks of trinkets. Finally,
dodging my way through steindorf and cuckooville, I roll past the
twelve zinging cash registers, out of December, and back into the
Rothenburg summer.

Annaliese (who runs the shop I do recommend in my guidebook) is sitting at a café across the street with a tall slender beer.

With "tsk tsk tsk" in her voice she says, "Oh, Rick. Rothenburg is becoming Wohlfahrtsburg. They got eight shops in Rothenburg now. What you do in there?"

"Just picking up my kickbacks," I joke.

She laughs and reminds me, "Tonight is the English Conversation Club. We save a place for you at our table."

The English Conversation Club

Several hours later, I meander deep into the pub through candlelit clouds of smoke. The *weinstube* shimmers with old-time ambience as locals enjoy their once-a-week excuse to get together, drink, and practice their fanciest English on each other and on visiting tourists.

I squeeze a three-legged stool up to a table already crowded with Annaliese, her family, and five or six other Rothenburg merchants.

"Did you like Las Vegas?" the man with the silent-movie mustache asks.

Crinkling her nose, the round woman with road map cheeks answers. "My daughter, she vin forty dollars in cents. Two bottles full. Then she lost every bit of it again. It is Lost Wages. Full power twenty-four hours."

Noticing me, the Lost Wages woman squints her eyes, rubs her temples, and says, "The beer in Vegas, it is not good. I had four days long a strong headache. No Weizen. I like our fizzy wheat beer better."

Tall glasses of beer multiply and tangle the table as Annaliese expertly networks. Introducing me to her son, Frankie, she says, "He was born in 1946. To celebrate the American army, I named him after Frank Sinatra. Frankie boy was on our radio all day long in 1946."

Another tourist wanders by and Annaliese pulls a *schneeball* (the local powdered doughnut-like "snowball") from a bag. She raises a cloud of powdered sugar as she pokes at the name on the now-empty bag. "Friedel is the bakery I explained you about," she says. "They make the best *schneeball*. I like it better than your American doughnut. Everyday, Frankie and I eat one. But only at this bakery."

She shoves a big doughy ball my way and asks, "You like to eat this?"

I break off a little chunk. "Only a teeny-weeny *bisschen*."

For four years, Annaliese has playfully tried to get me to write good things about *schneeballs*. I put *schneeballs* (which originated as a way to get more mileage out of leftover dough in a hungrier age) in that category of penitential foods—like *lutefisk*—whose only purpose is to help younger people remember the suffering of their parents. Nowadays these historic pastries are pitched to the tourists in caramel, chocolate, and flavors unknown in feudal times.

This "conversation club" is a traveler's jackpot—exactly what I seek out in writing my guidebooks. But even here, the business metabolism of Rothenburg is cranked up. With double the tourists but triple the shops, local businesspeople now trip over themselves to woo me.

Margarite, from the art shop on the market square, pulls out her old-time Rothenburg etchings. Dragging the top of her well-filled dirndl across the table to slip her business card under my mug of beer, she reminds me that tourists who drop in get a free shot of schnapps.

Rolf, a Friar Tuck of a man who runs the Peking Dragon restaurant with his petite Chinese wife, brings me another beer and says, "Our restaurant is just behind St. Jacob's church. You must come by tomorrow for lunch. For you, sir, it costs no money."

Getting this VIP treatment poisons my experience, making it different from that of my readers. It's bad for research. It seems the entire community of shopkeepers knows I'm in town. Ironically, as they scramble for a plug in my guidebook, they are souring me on a town I want to like. I need air.

"See you later, alligator," the merchants sing in unison as I pull on my coat.

"After a while, crocodile," I reply, forcing a grin. Leaving them belly-laughing as if they've never heard the phrase before, I hit the streets. I head away from the market square and find myself alone with Rothenburg.

The winds of history polish half-timbered gables. I follow the centuries-old grooves of horsecarts down to the castle garden. From a distance, the roars of laughter tumbling like waves out of *biergartens* and over the ramparts sound as medieval as they do modern.

Sitting in a mossy niche in the town wall, I finger the ancient stonework. I slowly pan across the town and survey the perfectly preserved, spiny rooftops. I aim my imaginary arrow into the dark forest that surrounds the city. Even today, it feels good to be within these protective walls.

Rothenburg is best at night, when the tour bus parking lot is empty. With the big tour groups gone, the locals—unless they're hitting up a travel writer—welcome the few independent travelers who remain as part of the party rather than part of the economy.

As nine o'clock approaches, I join a gang waiting on the town square for the night watchman's tour to begin. Half the group is carrying my guidebook. Fans of my TV show recognize me. As if hiding shy and self-conscious stalkers, video cameras catch me from an angle. Someone says, "So, he's a real person."

Suddenly I can empathize with my TV cameraman. He can't understand why people are so interested in him and his big camera when they are standing before some of the greatest sights of Europe. Surrounded by Europe's finest medieval walled city on a starry night, I don't want to be noticed.

Rothenburg has never depressed me until this visit. I love the place, but so does everybody else. Millions of people can love a TV show and not ruin it. But the charm of a small medieval wondertown is a consumable, and there's only so much to go around. My Rothenburg is being loved to death. But it's not "my" Rothenburg. And I'm part of the problem.

Tourists jostle to see the city hall's glockenspiel reenact Rothenburg's famous Thirty Years' War story. In 1631, the mayor drank three liters of wine in a single gulp to save the town from rape, pillage, and plunder. Deep down inside, tourists must know it's a lie. But they assemble here at nine each night and stare at the city hall. As the window overlooking the square pops open, so do the mouths of a hundred tourists. The wooden mayor slowly picks up the huge goblet, cocks his head back, and drinks.

So what? Of course, the big gulp is just a legend. But because I'm feeling wounded by the insincere friendliness of the merchants at the conversation club, I'm thinking hard about honesty. Around the floodlit market square, plaster is peeled back to reveal a humble half-timbered past. But the only thing old about Rothenburg's "oldest house" is its foundation. Fake and imported "rustic" Christmas knickknacks taunt more than twinkle. And Swiss Army knives on performance-enhancing electricity dance in shop windows.

I don't want to see traveling seekers, the last hurrah of the Romantic Age, become traveling shoppers.

The Night Watchman

But Rothenburg—even Club Rothenburg—still offers the best look possible at medieval Germany. And in this theme park, the best ride is the night watchman's historic town walk (presented in English at nine, in German at ten). With his eyebrows frozen in a raised position, he listens to the clock tower clang. When the wooden mayor puts down his goblet, the watchman winks, picks up his tall, pointed *hellebarde*, and lights his lantern. As he passes his three-cornered hat, we fill it with five-mark coins. Welcoming us into fifteenth-century Rothenburg, he looks believably medieval in his black robe, long hair, and scraggly beard. But the twinkle in his eyes admits, "I'm one of you."

With an insider's grin he begins: "It was a bad job, being medieval Rothenburg's night watchman—low esteem, low pay, dangerous work. Only two jobs were lower: the grave digger and the executioner. Yes, this was a dangerous job—all the good people were off the streets early. The watchman would sing the 'all's well' tune at the top of the hour through the night. You didn't want to hear him at three in the morning—but you were glad he was still alive.

"These days the job's more respectable: People take photos of me," he continues. "And it's no longer dangerous, because you're all coming with me." The night watchman's camera-toting flock of thirty tourists, already charmed, follow his bobbing lantern down the narrow cobbled lane.

Stopping under a sign announcing "Kriminal Museum," we watch the rusted old dunking cage swing in the breeze. The night watchman walks over to the stocks that stand empty next to the museum door and says, "If you know what's good for you, tomorrow you'll visit our Kriminal Museum."

He opens the top half of the stocks then slams it shut, saying, "A naughty boy might be put in the stocks. We rub salt on his soles and bring the goats. But inside, you'll learn about tools of torture and tools of humiliation."

Pausing to survey the group, he adds, "Like a metal gag for nags."

He scans the group again. His eyes stop on me and he asks, "Are you from Rothenburg?"

"*Nein,*" I say.

"Very good," he says. "Please come here."

As I move to the front he continues. "We were six thousand here in Rothenburg. In those days, around here, only Nürnburg and Augsburg were bigger. The Kaiser made us a free Imperial City. Such a city was given special privileges. The top privilege: We had our own court of justice. Rothenburg's citizens must be tried by their own court."

Shaking his head sadly, he puts his robed arm on my shoulder. "And you are not protected by our court," he announces. "We get a half day off when there's a hanging. Do you know anything about Herr Baumann's missing beehive?"

Again I say, "*Nein.*"

"You have no rights here, and we could use a half day off. You, my friend, have a problem. Local authorities might just allow a hanging."

In the light of his lantern, the swaying cage throws spidery shadows across the wall and faces of the group.

In the good old days, death sentences started with your basic execution and then got worse. The legal concept of "cumulation" meant a criminal's punishments would multiply with his crimes. While that petty bee thief might simply be hung, an adulterous bee-thieving murderer could be dragged to the place of execution with

painful stops along the way for
pinching with red-hot tongs. If he
were guilty of more crimes, he'd be
tied to stakes over timbers so a big
guy could bounce a wagon wheel on
his arms and legs, breaking all his
bones. Thoroughly "broken by the
wheel," he would then be woven
through the spokes of that wheel for
all to see. Hanging could be slow by
hoisting or fast by being pushed
from a ladder.

*Rothenburg's night watchman—
it's a dangerous job*

Sometimes even death wasn't
harsh enough. In cases when two
capital offenses were committed, a
criminal's corpse would be "quartered" by four horses heading out
in different directions.

A town's gallows, a medieval symbol of justice, were placed
high for all to see. Bodies of particularly dishonorable criminals
were left out to rot. The most important were hung on higher plat-
forms in anticipation of greater crowds. They were left in a cage so
birds and relatives couldn't get to the bodies.

Looking at me again, he says thoughtfully, "So, you're not
from Rothenburg." Then, turning abruptly, he walks down the
street. We follow.

He stops under an old-fashioned streetlight and says, "It was a
dirty time." Pointing with his boot to a gutter in the cobbles, he
continues, "All the garbage—from the people and from the animals, too—it went into the road. They had this ditch in the middle of the street. People tried to hit the ditch. This was not a good
system. Summer was stinking. The rich left for countryside homes.
Back then it wasn't the Romantic Road. It was the Filthy Road.
And this filth gave us the plague. In one terrible year, a third of
Rothenburg's population died."

We follow him farther to the ramparts at the edge of town.
Overlooking the valley, the watchman says, "Rothenburg was

never conquered until 1631. There was a siege. The armory, which was along this wall, blew up. Double disaster: We had a hole in the wall and no ammunition to make a defense. To be looted by forty thousand mercenaries was no fun. They were Catholics. So it was even worse.

"Our town was broken. And for the rest of the Thirty Years' War, Rothenburg lay wide open, undefended. We were sacked many times. Between lootings we suffered plagues."

Popping from an alley back onto the main square our hooded friend concludes, "From 1648—when the war and plagues stopped—time stood still in Rothenburg. Centuries of poverty . . . this was Rothenburg's cocoon. Now I must call the 'all's well.' You, my friends, should hurry home. Bed is the best place for good people at this hour."

Finishing his short song, he blows a long haunting tone on his horn. Then he steps quickly from medieval to modern, pulls a bundle from his smock, and adds, "Postcards, just one mark."

Asylum in Church

In the mood for a place that doesn't accept credit cards or display signs in three languages, I spend my Sunday morning in church. To give locals a little uninterrupted worshiping, churches in tourist towns post "no visits during Mass" signs.

I duck prayerfully past the sign and grab a well-worn pew among the most sizable gathering of Rothenburg residents I've seen. In Europe, congregations are dwarfed by their huge churches. With my feet resting on a floor paved with tombstones—lettering worn nearly smooth—I feel an old-time draftiness I don't feel in an American church.

Church-going in Europe comes with a language barrier. Not understanding a word of the service but having a general idea of the subject, I feel a bit like a medieval peasant must have felt. Back then the flock was mostly illiterate. And, to thwart the odd duck who could read the local language, the liturgy was done in Latin.

Apparently, the language barrier had a sedative effect on medieval church-goers, but sleeping in church was a great offense to God. Rather than doze off during a sermon, parishioners were instructed to stand up and listen. Today the only ones standing are the tourists lining the back wall and the upright tombstones that feature bigger-than-life medieval soldiers under the windows.

By going to church, the tourist rises above petty sightseeing endeavors much the way a peasant stepped above his futile existence in this same church 600 years ago. Even if he can't understand the language, an hour in church gives a peasant the chance to explore the notion that there's more to life than tilling the soil—or buying Hummels.

When everyone bows their heads and the pastor says, "*Deine Vater*," I start the same prayer with "Our Father." And as the congregation wraps things up with "*für immer und ewig, Amen*," I do, too, in English. Seeming to look right at me, the priest finishes the service with "*Gehet hin in Frieden*." "Go in peace."

Taiwanese Travels

As the congregation tumbles out of the church, I head to the market square, where the bright morning sunshine bounces merrily off the flower stalls, half-timbered gables, and blue-aproned merchants. It's still early and the town seems a little dazed—more playful than business-like.

Well-dressed locals stroll among tourists who sport camera bags and fannypacks. Children play around the fountain. Two boys with wooden swords chase each other in and out of the chunky columns decorating the portico of the city hall.

Three Taiwanese girls are camped out on the steps of the city hall, as should anyone who's looking for someone in Rothenburg. Sooner or later, everyone wanders by the market square. The one with the "American Girls" T-shirt approaches me and says, "Excuse me, Mr. Steves. This is a precious day to meet you, the man who wrote the book. Your book is very personable. It is popular in Taiwan. I had to use a library book."

I'm fascinated by the evolution of the Asian traveler in Europe. Watching Asian travelers grow in their traveling sophistication over the years has allowed me to retrace the learning curve American travelers embarked upon forty years ago. Like the Americans before them, the Japanese traveled first as rich individuals on the grand tour, then as middle-class, middle-aged mobs in tour groups, then as young individuals with guidebooks. Then, finally, older travelers got the confidence to travel independently. Twenty years ago a publisher in Tokyo politely rejected my suggestion that he translate and publish my guidebook *Europe Through the Back Door*. He said, "Too much information. Not enough photographs." Today Japanese travelers are armed with thick guidebooks packed with information (along with more than enough photos).

A Chinese edition of my book is now selling in Taiwan, but I'd never met anyone actually traveling with it. Imagining the serious culture shock they'd deal with traveling in Germany, I'm impressed by this hardy group of Taiwanese vagabonds.

Yun-Chen calls herself "Jenny" and Li-Shu is "Sue." The liveliest of the gang introduces herself as "Tina."

"Tina?" I question. "That's not very Chinese."

"Tina my English name," she tells me. "I like Tina Turner. She wild, strong, big inspiration for women. She energetic for her age. Husband beat her but now she successful. I took her name at time of *Private Dancer* movie."

Helping them finish a *schneeball*, I note they must be young—they look like students—and rich to be able to afford to travel to far.

"We're not students," says Tina. "We are schoolteachers. We save all year and spend it in one month here. Because our daily budget is thirty-six dollars each, we cook spaghetti in youth hostel."

Ever since a Japanese edition of *Europe Through the Back Door* by "Rick Steares" came out, I've cringed at the thought of some Asian translator slamming my work through his word mill. So when these girls say, "Your book is very personable," I'm encouraged.

I join my new friends on the city hall steps and ask them to help me spot-check the translation. Sue pulls a Chinese edition of my Scandinavia guide from her rucksack. In the English edition, I describe a waterfall as "an exciting time for drops and dribbles which came from miles around for the ultimate tumble into the fjord."

Tina's fingers move from wildly-hatched character to character as she reads from the Chinese edition. "Little drops come from many kilometers to join together to make the ride, bouncing happy into the sea." I'm satisfied.

"A precious day"

Jenny says, "We like the trees and rivers of Europe. And we like the quiet. But the people we like the best."

Sue adds, "In your book you say, 'Ask questions just to hear their voices.' We meet many old ladies this way. We ask questions and don't understand the answer, but we like to see her face, her attitude. To hear her voice and see the smile. It is attractive."

"Which people are most friendly?" I ask.

The three girls begin a medley of comparisons. Sue observes, "The Germans are like the Taiwanese. . . ."

"Social formality," they giggle in unison.

"The French are the least friendly, especially in Paris," says Jenny.

Sue agrees, searching the sky for just the right word. "The Paris people are . . . indifferent."

"Spain people are the best," Tina says. "They like to talk. They don't speak English, but we understand their body language."

"What's your favorite country?" I ask.

"Spain is passionate. We talk of Spain all year long."

"Where do the boys give you the most attention?"

"Spain."

"So you like *passionate* Spain!"

"Trick!" Tina declares.

The market square glockenspiel finishes its top-of-the-hour show, setting a mob of tourists free. Four more Taiwanese girls join us on the already crowded steps. "Where are the Taiwanese boys?" I ask.

"Military service," Sue says. "Boys regard duty more. Boys save money for future family. To get a house. With no money and no house he will find no good wife."

Tina adds, "Boys in Taiwan are not romantic enough. Single girls travel now because after we marry there is no time to travel. I will be very devoted to my family."

"Do German people think you are Japanese?" I ask.

"Every day!"

"What do you think about that?"

"Well, when we're doing something bad we don't mind."

Golden Rose After-Hours

I spend my Sunday afternoon on a rental bike, exploring the Tauber River Valley one ruddy village at a time. Cheered by the realization that Rothenburg's walls keep modern tourism in as effectively as they were designed to keep medieval armies out, I pedal back to town and turn in the bike. Like an illiterate peasant, I hike down cobbled Spitalgasse looking for the shiny metal "golden rose" that swings in the sun above the flower boxes, marking my hotel's doorway.

Throughout my early visits to Rothenburg—even with my tour groups—I slept at the youth hostel. My first tour bus driver, a Belgian named Guido, thought I treated my groups rudely by making them stay at the hostel.

One night I met Guido in the hallway outside my dorm room. Carrying bedding over his shoulder, overwhelmed by German teenagers on a field trip, he declared, "I sleep on me bus." Later that year, Guido found a more comfortable escape just down the street: the Hotel Golden Rose. Eventually, as we all grew older, softer, and richer, we followed Guido.

The Golden Rose is run by the Favetta family: Guerrino, Finni, and their daughters. While Rino, an Italian, met and married Finni in the 1960s, her family goes way back in Rothenburg. As he does during each year's visit, Rino shows me the new streak of gray in his beard and explains it's because he's surrounded by women.

Rino says his wife talks too much. Because she speaks no Italian, Rino jokes that they holiday in Italy. "*Tranquillo*," he sighs. Daughter Fernanda knew at age five that she would be a gardener, and that's what she does today. Stately Henni grew up in the hotel and knew from the start that she would someday run the place.

While half-Italian, Henni is beautiful in a German way— tall, direct, blonde, with piercing eyes. Causing male tourists to dream in German, she gives dignity to the job of head waitress in a small hotel.

While Henni is the queen of the house, tiny scurrying Karin is the workhorse. Always wearing her white smock and always smiling under her thick Prince Valiant mop of black hair and scrub-brush eyebrows, her life is this hotel. It's Karin who percolates the breakfast coffee. And it's Karin, in her sturdy black waitress boots, who serves the last beer.

In Europe the best social moments combust after a long day of work, and after the normal guests say "*ciao*." It happens in a pub after hours in Galway when the door is locked and the musicians play on. It's on the Italian Riviera when the anchovies are eaten, the dishes are washed, and the guitars come out. And it's here in Germany when a family and the hired help stow their workplace hierarchy with their aprons and take out a special bottle of wine.

For ten years of annual visits, I've sat down hurriedly at a Golden Rose restaurant table to update my guidebook listing, then dashed. Tonight I sit down to simply relax with the Favetta family. Except for our candlelit table, the once noisy restaurant is now empty and dark. We gather around the *stammtisch*. A good goal for a traveler is to be invited to the *stammtisch*—the table you'll find in most German bars and restaurants reserved for family, staff, and regulars.

Well into our second glass of wine, Henni makes horns with her fingers atop her head and says, "I think you are the steer— Taurus. Were you born in May?"

"May 10," I say.

Everyone delights in the opportunity to shine some attention on their loyal little helper. "That's Karin's birthday, too," they say.

The mention of birthdays makes Rino cringe and rub his salt-and-pepper beard. I say, "But we're all getting older."

This reminds Henni to request a change in my guidebook. Pointing to her hotel's write-up, she says, "Please, take out 'Henni causes American tourists to dream in German.' I have two kids now. Soon tourists will come to me and ask, 'Where's Henni?'"

I assure Henni that she still contributes to tourists' dreams.

She flips through the dictionary that sits like a referee on the *stammtisch* muttering, "How do you say this . . . *Alptraum*." Finding her word, she says, "Yes, soon you can make this dream a nightmare."

Under romantic etchings of Rothenburg, we indulge in the sport many in the tourist business enjoy—cultural puzzles. Henni asks, "Why can't Americans eat with a knife? You cut things with your fork."

I confess I know nothing about holding silverware. Editors of my TV show edit out scenes of me with forks in nice restaurants.

And just to hit a Yankee when he's down, she adds, "And you people love to drink plain water—we call this water the American Champagne. But you never eat liver or blood sausage. The Japanese love these."

A crystal bowl of *schneeballs* sits on our table like an inedible centerpiece. Ringing the bowl with my finger, I say, "Each culture has its treats. I'm just happy we have a choice."

I ask Henni if it's not dangerous to make generalizations about other cultures. She says, "Even deaf people generalize."

"What?" I say.

She explains with the help of her hands. "In international sign language 'Germany' is my finger pointing up from my head." She makes a fist-and-finger Prussian helmet.

"'France' is this wavy little mustache," she continues, wiggling a finger across her upper lip. "And 'Russia' is the Cossack dancer." Henni bounces on her chair while her fingers do a tiny cancan dance from her hips.

"And what's the sign for America?" I ask.

"The fat cat," she says, propping up a rotund belly with her arms.

Rino, whose English is worse than my German, struggles to keep up with me and his family. Whenever the conversation reaches a spirited tempo, he jumps in, brings it to a screeching halt, and sends it in a completely new direction. Pretending to add to Henni's thoughts, he leans over to me. Stopping in mid-sentence, I look to him.

As if a magician sharing a secret, he holds his hand palm down in front of my face. Stretching his thumb high and out, he forms a small bay in the top of his hand. Peppering in a little snuff tobacco, he announces, "Snoof tobak."

With Henni's help, Rino clarifies it, saying, "the anatomical snuffbox," and snorts. I try it and it works.

As noses wiggle, I ask Henni if living in a tourist fantasy-town gets old. "I will live and die in Rothenburg," she answers. "Teenagers here dream of leaving Rothenburg. One by one they try the big city—München or Nürnburg—and they come home. Summer is action time. Winter is quiet. The tourists, they come like a big one-time-in-a-year flood. We Rothenburgers sit and wait for you to float by."

"Like barnacles," I add cheerfully, even though I figure that word is not in Henni's English vocabulary.

Henni looks at me like I just burped. "People who live here have magic vision," she says. "If we want to, we can see no tourists and only local people. Rothenburg is a village. We know everyone."

Still scratching her nose after an encounter with the snuff, Karin urges Henni to tell the story of the Americans who took the *"Zimmer Frei"* vacancy sign literally.

Henni recalls, "One American family paid for their dinner. But thinking '*Zimmer Frei*' meant 'room free,' they nearly walked out after breakfast as if the room cost no money. And one time an East German couple left without paying. On their bed we found a note saying, 'For forty years you have had the good life. Now it is our time.'"

Henni's sister Fernanda bops in wearing fine new American hightops. Since she once had an American soldier for a boyfriend, her English is American.

"American people want Birkenstocks," she announces. "German people want American tennis shoes. We steal everything American: We have our own *Baywatch*, *Jeopardy*, *Wheel of Fortune*, even trash talk shows."

"So you want to *dress* American?" I ask.

"Americans are getting fashion," she says. "But your really fat women wear shorts. I saw the biggest people in my life in the States."

As the family agrees, Henni says, "And they wear tight T-shirts!"

Rino empties his tall glass of beer, licks his foamy upper lip, and adds, "The big German women wear the *ein man Zelt*."

I look to Henni, who translates, "One-man tent."

When I counter, "But fat German men have skinny legs," the entire family laughs.

"Beer bellies," Henni says. "German men say a man without a belly isn't a man. A German saying is, 'Better to have a big belly from drinking than a broken back from working.' In Rothenburg, even today, if workers aren't given free beer while they build a house, they mortar a mug into the wall to show how cheap the owner is."

Thanking them for their hospitality, I get up to leave. As he does after each visit, Rino offers me a squat gift bottle of Franconian wine. After my traditional, "*Danke nein*, I'm packing light," he sends me out of the door with a smile.

After my *stammtisch* evening at the Golden Rose, I add a new item to my wish list: the ability to make good things happen after closing—European style—in the United States.

Lately, with my public role as TV travel guy, I've been in polite-laugh situations more than ever. I've learned that when I laugh with a snort, it's heartfelt. Enjoying the Favetta family after hours, I snorted three times—bringing my total for the day to . . . three.

The midnight streets of Rothenburg are deserted. The sounds

of my footsteps bounce with the floodlights off fifteenth-century buildings while cobbles glisten after a hard but short rain.

Sitting down next to an old fountain, I slide the medieval spout—a six-foot-long pivoting tin gutter—over to divert the water and watch it splash into the street. Two hundred years ago, I'd be a peasant filling a needy bucket. Last year, I demonstrated this neat trick to my tour group like a proud father showing his children his long forgotten hometown. Tonight I'm just a mixed-up romantic sorting out my mood swings.

Yesterday I took a gulp from the wrong pool. Today I felt joy after communion—at church, with the Taiwanese girls, and with the Favetta family. I've seen the buildings and I've heard the legends. Only people have a gift for making you feel at home.

More drunk than sleepy, I know that alone on the ramparts, not alone in bed, is the place for me right now. Once again, notching my imaginary crossbow, I climb onto the town wall. On the ramparts after dark, I look over a choppy sea of red-tiled roofs to the murky and mysterious moat beyond the wall. The cannons are loaded. Torches illuminate the gory heads of bad guys on pikes that greet visitors at the city gates. With a dash of moonlight and a splash of wine, Rothenburg once again is a crossroads where modern-day travelers meet medieval wayfarers.

CHAPTER FOUR

MUNICH

*The beermaid puts her face—red after a
lifetime of grimacing—close to mine and says,
"Drink a beer and you worry no more."*

A three-hour train ride takes me from cute Rothenburg to mighty
Munich by mid-morning. After my stay in a peaceful small town,
Munich's train station roars like a soccer stadium. Great European
train stations stir my wanderlust.

I never enter a city until I've planned my exit. Stepping off the
train, I stand under the station's towering steel and glass rooftop
and study the big black schedule board crowned by the station
clock. It lists two dozen departures. Every few minutes, the letters
and numbers on each line spin and tumble as one by one cities and
departure times work their way to the top and flutter away.

Surrounded by Germany on the move, I notice businessmen
in tight neckties, giddy teenage girls, speedy handcarts, and a
Marx-like bum leaning on a *bierstube* counter. The fast and the
slow, the young and the old, we're all working our way up life's departure board.

Like a kid playing "spin the globe," I study the board, imagining all the places I could visit. Tonight, between ten and midnight, overnight trains depart for every corner of Europe. I can
have a full day in Munich capped by a beerhall evening, then

hop—or stagger—onto a train and be in Copenhagen, Berlin, Zagreb, Budapest, Amsterdam, or Venice for breakfast. I'm a sucker for Venice.

My decision to head to Italy isn't quite final when I grab a spot at the rear of the shortest ticket line. My love of simply being on the road sometimes surpasses my interest in the places I'm actually visiting. I just arrived in Munich, with a full plate of plans for the day, but eager thoughts of Venice are already tugging me over the Alps.

Making an itinerary decision is fast but train station ticket lines aren't. At the head of a long ticket line, otherwise sullen people suddenly become animated conversationalists. Having the ticket agent all to oneself while the line waits is strangely exhilarating.

Both nervous and impatient, I wonder if my line—leading to the "*Fahrscheine*" window—is the place to reserve a bed on the train. As the traveler's fear of being in the wrong line climbs up my spine, I consider leaping to a newly opened but mysteriously unpopular window. Playing it safe, I stay put.

The challenge of sleeping well for free on a train has become less appealing. In fact, tonight I want no challenge at all. Just my own bed on the train. For twenty dollars I'll have it . . . unless "*Fahrscheine*" means "lost and found."

The boy in front of me with a black cap reading "no logo" assures me I'm in the right line. He's taking the train to Frankfurt for a flight to the United States. It's a young German's dream come true: nineteen-year-old Florian is flying to California for snowboarding, rollerblading, and mountain biking.

"We go to the United States for action and for nature," Florian says. "I love the cars. In America, you have V-8 engines. The V-8 sound makes you a very cool person. With a V-8 you are not driving—you are cruising."

I counter, "But I thought Germans had it good behind the wheel: BMWs . . . Mercedes. . . ."

"Yeah, I drive a BMW. But it's like a computer. No soul. My friend just bought a Chevy Caprice Classic: V-8, 5.6 liters, 340 cubic inches. He will pay very bad taxes for such an engine and even more because it has no catalytic converter. But it is worth it."

You can learn something of a country by how it levies its road taxes. The practical Dutch pay by weight of car. Money-minded Americans are taxed according to the cost of the car. The German government goes right for the thrill-seeking jugular vein, levying road taxes according to the power of a car's engine.

But this power tax buys BMW, Audi, and Mercedes owners their own lane on the Autobahn—the notorious fast lane—and the right to speed with no limits. The "no speed limit" policy is as precious to most Germans as the right to bear arms is to many Americans. The American driver learns one lesson quickly when on the super-freeways of Germany: Don't cruise in the passing lane.

The relative speed difference is fun to illustrate. When my tour groups became accustomed to Autobahn driving, I'd slow our minibus down to fifty-five miles per hour. Passengers threatened to get out and jog.

Tickets and reservations in hand, Florian and I go off to pursue our separate dreams.

Das Deutsches Hollywood

Munich is at once Germany's Hollywood, Silicon Valley, most livable place, and university town. While Munich prides itself as a capital of the easy-going good life, the ever-present jackhammer staccato in the background urges a faster tempo.

And my tempo here is fast indeed: one day to enjoy downtown Munich, make a side trip to Dachau, and join an American expatriate for a beerhall dinner. Then I'll catch the night train to Venice.

As if playing a game of luggage locker roulette, I choose a spot to leave my pack in the station. Even though I've never been ripped off, for twenty-five years I've had to talk myself into relaxing as I trade all my luggage for one tiny easy-for-a-thief-to-copy key. Zipping that key into my moneybelt, I set off to enjoy Munich.

I cross under a busy street through a "medieval" arch younger than I am. Medieval Munich was bombed flat in World War II. As in many medieval towns, the protective walls are long gone but the gates remain as decoration. They mark the entrances to pedestrian shopping centers and remind twentieth-century residents and visitors alike that there were shoppers before them.

Munich's gates are landmarks. Called *"tors,"* they stand like bookends defining the town center. Rebuilt after the war when reconstruction money for such frills was very tight, they feel cheap—freshly poured, as if built for a fair.

I stroll down Munich's main pedestrian boulevard. The sound of traffic is erased by the refreshing rush of a fountain, which is then replaced by the sound of playful families and street singers.

In Munich—as in most of Europe these days—senior citizens do not look like the thick, bent, and bristly elders of twenty-five years ago. Today the retired women of Munich seem to be out en masse. They are fit and tan with good teeth and designer glasses. Their hair is carefully tinted and coiffed. Dodging shopping bags, I can feel the prosperity.

Central Munich has more pedestrian and bike lanes than roads. The main drag used to be choked in traffic. Now this nearly mile-long browse is a glassy arcade—one of Europe's most entertaining busker zones.

Street entertainers of all stripes gather huge crowds or are ignored. Two Croat folk singers with pom-poms and accordions bellow into each other's faces, unnoticed by the crowd. They announce a loud sarcastic *"danke"* after each tune. A short old man wearing baggy genie pants and sitting next to a board full of nails relaxes between acts. A guitar duo with a squirt gun routine for each chorus strikes a chord with its huge audience. A bronze-painted woman—her breasts covered by two just-large-enough scallop shells—takes a revealing bow with each coin that enters her hat. And gathering a different crowd, "Charlie Chaplin," with a new frozen look of surprise for each clink in his pot, has parents digging for coins and sending their delighted kids on a mission.

Postcard racks show the typical mix of rude and goofy. Produce stands tempt but "Nix Grabsch" signs keep hungry fingers off the apricots.

Tourists are marked by the map or guidebook in their hands.

Italians tote guidebooks on Monaco. ("Monaco di Bavaria" is the Italian name for this city.)

The Church of Our Lady, or Frauenkirche—her twin domes a symbol of Munich—was destroyed by World War II bombs. Today small bits of the church's heritage survive, plastered into its sleek modern shell. From the top of its lofty onion domes you can see the Alps in the distance and Mary's Place below.

Munich church bells—like the domes that contain them—now have a hint of the south. On sunny days, their joyful ring seems to say, "Celebrate life, especially life in Bavaria."

Mary's Place

The pedestrian mall dumps me with the crowds onto a busy but peaceful square the size of a football field. This is Marienplatz—Mary's Place. The lacy, neo-Gothic "new city hall" takes center stage while the smaller "old city hall" sits quietly to the right. Six-story Lego-simple buildings complete the rectangle. The center of the square is filled with people loitering and a tall stone column crowned by a gilded Mary. Around its flowery base are four bronze-helmeted angels fighting dragons with swords and spears. Cafés and beer gardens spill tables—festively decorated in the blue and white of the Bavarian flag—onto the square.

It's a scene of a contented Germany, not the scene of fascist mayhem I remember from photos in my history books. But I'm confused because the square is bounded by the new town hall and the old town hall, and I'm not sure which is which.

In Europe "new" often means "first," which is the oldest. Twenty-five hundred years ago, Naples was "Neapolis," Greek for "new city." Paris' Pont Neuf ("new bridge") is the oldest bridge in town. Thanks to World War II bombs, Munich's old town hall—called the new town hall—actually *is* new. Its ornate spires were rebuilt after the war.

The new town hall's "medieval" dancers attract crowds who wait for the dull show at the top of the hour. I enjoy the figurines mostly for their ability to attract a fun-to-watch crowd. Today an Italian couple who didn't read their Monaco guidebook wait at the wrong hour for the dance. I tell them, "There is no dance until the next hour."

The husband entertains his wife by doing a mock German toy soldier dance. Italians are a movable party. They can make a traffic jam fun. Although tempers may flare, they are just as likely to pull the car

Mary's Place, a trendy festival of good living

over, set up a card table, and share a bottle of wine with perfect strangers.

"In Munich the streets are great entertainment," I say. "Wonderful people-watching."

"Maybe, yes," the husband says. "But in Rome, the *passeggiata* is more lively."

"I'll be in Rome next week," I say, "I will compare."

Jotting his phone number on a scrap of paper, he tells me, "My name is Stefano. When you come to Rome, you telephone us. Paola and I will show you the best street life in all of Europe."

Promising to call them, I say "*Ciao*" and head on my way.

Dachau

En route to Dachau's infamous concentration camp, I sit next to an old German woman on the bus. I smile at her weakly as if to say, "I don't hold your people's genocidal atrocities against you."

She glances at me and sneers down at my camera. Suddenly, surprising me with her crusty but fluent English, she rips into me. "You tourists come here not to learn but to hate," she seethes.

Pulling the loose skin down from a long ago strong upper arm she shows me a two-sided scar. "When I was a girl, a bullet cut straight through my arm," she says. "Another bullet killed my father. The war took many good people. My father ran a *Grüss Gott* shop."

I'm stunned by her rage. But I sense a desperation on her part to simply unload her story on one of the hordes of tourists who tramp daily through her town to ogle at an icon of the Holocaust.

I ask, "What do you mean, a *Grüss Gott* shop?"

She explains that in Bavaria shopkeepers greet customers with a "*Grüss Gott*" ("praise God"). During the Third Reich it was safer to change the greeting to "*Sieg Heil.*" It was a hard choice. Each shopkeeper had to make it. Everyone in Dachau knew which shops were *Grüss Gott* shops and which were *Sieg Heil* shops. Pausing, as if mustering the energy for one last sentence, she stands up and says, "My father's shop was a *Grüss Gott* shop," then steps off the bus.

By the end of the line there are only tourists and pilgrims on the bus. Together, in silence, we walk into the concentration camp.

Dachau, founded in 1933, was the first concentration camp, a model camp, a training ground for wannabe camp commandants who studied such subjects as crowd control and torture. The camp at Dachau was built to hold 5,000, but on Liberation Day 30,000 were found packed inside its walls. Some 3,000 were so sick that they died after liberation. The number of Dachau deaths is estimated at 40,000, but the total will never be known. Thousands of Russian soldiers were brought here as prisoners. Not even registered, they were simply taken into the field and shot for target practice.

Since many Holocaust survivors refuse to enter Germany, the Dachau memorial headquarters is in Brussels. Some make the pilgrimage against the wishes of their parents. Others, refusing to spend a night in Germany, come after sunrise and leave before sunset.

I shuffle into the camp's memorial theater. It's filled with 500 people, mostly tourists who are pilgrims for the morning. They sit in silence, looking at black and white film clips of tangled bodies and the faces of the dead. As the camera pans silently across the corpses, gasps emanate from the audience. A frothing Hitler stands high, his hand waving furiously at the adoring masses. Even on the scratchy newsreel clips, he seems strangely charismatic, not dead but only hiding.

After leaving the theater, I wander through the museum. It shows how, under Hitler, Germany's prison system overflowed. A

network of concentration camps provided a solution. Standing before the chart of the camp system network, I see an integrated cir-
cuit of misery. When you arrived, you passed under the *"Arbeit
macht frei"* ("Work liberates you") sign. You traded your property,
rights, and human dignity for a number—tattooed on your wrist.

No one had the right even to hope. During sick parade, the ill
and infirm were beaten and ridiculed in public each evening. A
photo shows a Jewish violinist forced to serenade the execution
cart as his friend was paraded to his death. The eyes of the
German guards are scratched out.

When one inmate escaped, all would suffer. For instance, after
a successful escape one freezing February, the entire camp was
forced to endure an all-night roll call. Inmates stood naked, at attention in long lines. Guards doused them with cold water.
Catching a cold routinely led to death by pneumonia. Nazis could
kill you without even touching you.

After the costly battle of Stalingrad, the struggling German
war machine pulled out all the stops. Able-bodied inmates were
fed enough to provide slave labor to keep Germany's war machine
in armaments.

Toward the end of the war, inmates could hear the noise of
the battlefront as the Allies closed in. The inmate community's
drive to survive took a deep breath. On the eve of liberation,
5,000 of the inmates who had survived the longest—considered
the most damaging potential witnesses in war crimes trials—were
marched out with the retreating soldiers. Nearly half of these
dropped from exhaustion and were killed on the roadside.

The American soldiers found train cars filled with dead bodies. In the chaos of those last days, new arrivals to Dachau simply
weren't unloaded. At the sight of this misery, battle-hardened
American soldiers broke down and wept.

Wandering angrily through a gallery of inmate art leaves me
with a jumbled collage of images: A sky filled with *Sieg Heil* arms
mimics a field filled with tombstones. A bald man in rags stands at
attention facing a brick wall. Behind the wall a man in shorts,
shivering in a cell, pulls his knees tight to his chest in search of

warmth. Outside, a skeleton bangs the drum he sits upon while barking God-and-country slogans at a field of raised hands. And in the forest of howling wolves a man in white—eyes wide with terror—kneels on skulls and howls along. He figures it's that or death. In the distance, a bent old man paints a sea of crosses . . . anticipating many deaths.

Dachau is an eternal flame, memories in a barbed wire box. The sound of hushed voices and sad feet on the pebbled walk seem to promise remembrance. The breeze whispers "never again" through trees on the parade ground where inmates once stood. A statue, as big as the train cars that brought in the inmates, stands in the middle of the camp. It's a black steel tangle of bodies—like the real ones found woven together at the gas chamber door. At its base, in French, English, German, Russian, and Hebrew, is the wish of those victims: Forgive, but never forget.

A Secret Beerhall

Dachau is a common stop for travelers exploring the Romantic Road through Germany on their way to Munich. One year, my Germany guidebook came out with a regrettable chapter head: "The Romantic Road to Dachau."

Thoughtfully fitting a pilgrimage to Dachau between cheery half-timbered Bavarian villages and Munich beerhalls is tricky. On a fast tour, it's hard not to follow an afternoon at Dachau with a wild night at a Munich beerhall. It makes me think of Munich locals who, during the Nazi rule, managed not to know there was a concentration camp in their suburb.

Tonight's my one night in Munich and I'm beerhall-bound with Alan Wissenberg. On each trip to Munich, I drop in at my friend's office. Alan, who was meant to be a German, was accidentally born in the United States to American parents. He's done his best to correct this, marrying a German woman, living in a small Bavarian town without a hint of tourism, and working for the German National Railway in the Munich train station.

A boyish forty with more than his share of floppy brown hair, Alan runs the EurAide office designed to help foreign (mostly

American) train travelers get around on Germany's train system. Like a Lilliputian doing a jig on Gulliver, he thrives on making the lumbering German bureaucracy work for us little tourists.

"Germans thrive on bureaucracy," he jokes as we leave his small but efficient trackside office. "Even the toilet paper here comes in triplicate."

Like a kid excited about a new tongue-twister, Alan can talk train fare and schedule strategies until your Eurailpass expires. And he's my man when it comes to updating that part of my guidebook.

Alan offers to take me to his favorite beerhall—right at a subway station, not listed in any guidebooks, filled with a cool German crowd, decent prices, traditional food, great beer, and dripping with ambience—on one condition: that I never write it up.

A frustrating thing about "making it" as a travel writer is that local friends take me to their best places—only if I promise not to put them in my books.

At a lecture I once heard Arthur Frommer describe his favorite little ivy-covered Roman pension—where the bath was down the hall but your landlord gave you a lavish, oversized robe and drew your bath for you. The entire audience was poised with pencils and notepads, all ready for the tip. Then he boasted that he keeps it a secret so he'll have the place all to himself when he's in Rome.

I could only think, "Great, the place is a secret for three hundred sixty-five days a year so Arthur can have it to himself for two or three."

Frommer's lecture was twenty-four hours after Anne, my wife, had given birth to our boy. Only a chance to hear the father of modern budget travel could have taken me away. If I hadn't had to rush back, I would have told Frommer my view that gathering travel information is more than a job, it's a service. I must shout from the mountaintops about any great place I discover in my travels.

I promise Alan I'll tell no one. But my up-till-now favorite beerhall has a date with the wrecking ball this winter, a Planet Hollywood just went in across the street from the Hofbrauhaus, and this particular promise pains me greatly.

Jackie O: The Bavarian Statue of Liberty

As we grab a table, I note, "Hitler would have loved this crowd—it's perfectly German."

Alan, who talks as if he's reading from a thesis, says, "In Germany, *multicultural* is a negative thing to anyone on the right. It's a buzz word for 'easy on immigrants . . . no pride in your nation.'

"This crowd is Bavarian first . . . German second. Bavarians are considered bumpkins to other Germans but are proud themselves. Now that Germany is united, Bavaria seems relatively less important," he continues. "But Bavaria has the sophisticated national culture. People here consider Germany an upstart nation."

As I set down my beer, the coaster catches my eye. A scene decked out in Bavarian majesty stars a Jackie Onassis look-alike riding a keg. With her long black dress and orange shawl blowing in the wind and a come-hither smile, she hoists two steins into the setting sun. "This coaster is enthusiastically Bavarian," I observe.

Alan breaks a pretzel the size of a TV dinner in half and says, "In some ways Germany is strong. But it's also a vanquished nation. Seventy percent of Germans don't know the words to their national anthem."

A beermaid—who clearly wasn't the model for the coaster art—plops our dinners before us and garnishes them with two mustard packets pulled from her cleavage. I look over at Alan. Finishing a giant swig from his giant beer and licking the foam from his upper lip, he says, "Only in Bavaria."

In some cases, patriotism is charming. It's heartwarming to see kids in pewter buckles on Norway's independence day filling Oslo's main drag all the way to the royal palace. And to hear Spaniards on gondolas in Venice filling the evening air with rousing choruses of "Viva d'España" makes you want to blow kisses and holler, "Oil of Olay." But German patriotism makes many nervous.

Alan rips open a mustard packet and lays a fine yellow slalom course on his bratwurst. "There's a disturbing aspect to German patriotism," he admits. "Locals still feel this. You don't see Germans waving their flag. But this is changing. The scars of World War II are fading. Germany has been stable for fifty years. That's rare. Germany is even getting along with its neighbors. Not since the reign of Karl the Gross have Germany and France had such a cozy relationship."

"Karl the Gross?" I ask.

"You would call him Charlemagne."

I tuck a few Jackie O coasters in my pocket and empty my beer. Alan makes me repeat my oath of secrecy. I admit it was enjoyable to eat dinner without a hint of tourism. And we step back into the subway.

I'm on the road and Alan's not. He's headed home to his wife and kids while I head to a beerhall that is absolutely no secret at all . . . Mathauser's.

Put Me in a Beer Stein and Roll Me Home

A night in a Bavarian beerhall before an overnight train to Italy always puts me in a fine mood. I follow the messy noise of a thousand people—eating, drinking, yelling, and laughing—down a long corridor to the huge hall. I take a seat leaning against a thick wooden pillar facing the band and surrounded by a good mix of Germans and tourists well on their way to a great evening. The crowd seems to sense that the wrecking ball is parked out back.

Mathauser's beerhall is a house for serious drinking—the largest, by its measure, in Germany. Scowling beermaids waddle down aisles rolling carts jangling with frothy beers. Lowenbrau comes in regular "*Mass*" (full-liter) mugs and petite half-liter mugs. Tour groups turn the area below the stage into an oompah mosh pit while locals observe from the rear. In the men's room a congested line of twenty urinals leads to a vomitorium—a chest-high porcelain funnel with two handhold bars.

The boys in the band nurse their mugs. Their shiny lederhosen accentuate huge bellies, which accentuate bird-like legs. With knowing smirks, they conduct a musical liturgy from their high altar. Without even having to say, "Please rise," the band gets the crowd on its feet for the beerhall anthem, "*Eins, zwei, zuffa.*" ("One, two, drink.") This is followed by a ritual of clinking and drinking. In this cathedral of gaiety, "*Ein Mass*" is the cry for more beer.

A beermaid scrubs the ashtray on my table with something resembling an ivory-handled shaving brush. I point to a line of faded Bavarian script on the ceiling and shrug my shoulders. She reads it out loud: "*Durst ist schlimmer als Heimweh.*" Sliding a clean ashtray across the table, she translates: "Thirst is worse than homesickness."

I still look puzzled. The beermaid puts her face—red after a lifetime of grimacing—close to mine and says, "Drink a beer and you worry no more." Then she walks on to the next ashtray.

Apart from the "under thirty-five" party tour groups, it's a three-generations-together scene. Kids build houses out of beer coasters while moms sip Radlers, a nearly dainty mix of beer and lemonade. The hefty glass mugs clink solidly, encouraging that very Teutonic sport of toasting.

But Mathauser's is also a place begging for a brawl. Once while I was here with a tour group, two brawlers rolled like drunk tumbleweeds into my section and actually onto the table of two older group members. I leapt to my feet (after carefully putting down my beer), ran over, and heaved them across the room away from my group. As they flip-flopped away, I stood tall, clapped the dust off my hands, and looked for the pride on my wife's face. Anne was in the restroom and never believed the stories told.

But while Bavarian lions still climb the walls, Mathauser's beerhall traditions have been watered down. Waiters pull beer from computerized stainless steel beer dispensers. The old wooden keg sits like a relic next to a photo showing how it was used. The only people in lederhosen are members of the band and the guy who snaps tourists with his Polaroid and comes back later for the sale. A whiff of oldtime German militarism persists. A few pickled octogenarians still show snappy salutes as tour groups march in and out. But goosestepping grandpas have been replaced by bunny-hopping Aussies.

Next year, a cinema will serve Coke and popcorn where Mathauser's now serves beer. I'll get over it. But what about the brawling beermaids who spent the best forty years of their lives wheeling carts of beer, pretzels, and carved radishes, loading the loaded, and overcharging drunk tourists? I like to think that some- where in a small town just outside of Munich—maybe where Alan lives—there'll be a retirement home where surly old beermaids still pull condiments from their dirndls.

But Mathauser's booms tonight. Contemplating beerstained memories and enjoying that small feeling you get when struggling with a giant pretzel and a glass beermug the size of a State-side pitcher, I'm entertained by Trafalgar tour #6421. Fifty-strong, the group stands on their chairs and bellows this year's beerhall pop anthem: "*Alice? Alice? Who the f— is Alice?*" Pretty soon, the entire hall, intrigued by the opportunity to yell such a rude word, is roar- ing along.

Beerhalls are great. If you don't have a partner, you can talk to yourself. One guy, a Jackie Gleason type, tries doggedly to hold his head up. His neighbor peers down at his spiral-carved radish as if he dropped a thought into it. Another man, with a mouthful of pretzel, really believes he's conducting the band. A young New Jersey cou- ple, who spent tomorrow's lunch money on the extra beer tonight, are sheepishly feeding their leftover *kraut* and *weisswurst* into a zip- lock baggie. They have one-upped me in the cheap tricks category and, looking as sober as possible, I nod my sage approval.

On the next table a balding guy with sleepy turtle eyes and perfectly parallel forehead wrinkles gives me a coaster from a com- peting beerhall. I rub my eyes (the way I think Princip must have when he stepped out of the Sarajevo pub only to see Ferdinand). There she is again . . . Jackie O, still riding that keg with her "this one's on me" smile.

In a booming baritone, he says, "*Für Bier in München, das ist das beste.*" Holding the coaster and thinking of that wrecking ball, my promise to Alan of keeping his favorite beerhall a secret takes another big hit.

Suddenly, another coaster, launched like a Frisbee from a faraway table, bounces off my mug—like it did in my old minibus tour days.

SingaSongaSongaEurope

A travel writer alone with his notepad in a Munich beerhall is like a music lover sitting in the middle of an orchestra. The sounds and sights of Germany and travel swirl everywhere: Old Bavarians cling to the past, tour guides hawk clichés, hormones rage far from home, and even the shy shout brassy anthems to drinking. As Cosmos tours march in and out following the raised umbrella of their guides, I remember my years of tour-guiding fun.

Each spring through my college years I bought my plane ticket before I knew how I'd pay for the trip. Loans from my parents—who got me hooked on Europe in the first place—allowed me to deficit-finance those early journeys. I worked the debt off by teaching piano. For several years, I earned a free airplane ticket by escorting groups of travelers from Seattle on Cosmos tours.

With the sponsorship of Dale Torgrimson, a travel agent friend, I'd choose a basic three-week Europe tour. When I sold twenty seats during my travel lectures, I earned a free flight and tour. The tour came with an official guide; I was the "escort" for my group—generally half the tour—and a wannabe guide for the entire busload.

While most of my travel time was still spent exploring Europe without groups, for several years mass tourism was my free plane ride. The joy of independent travel mixed with the ugliness of group travel helped strengthen my desire to teach *smart* travel.

On my last Cosmos tour, my group and I tumbled off the boat in Belgium in search of bus #4816. Packing onto #4816, we met our harried guide. Monica, a German, picked up the microphone and said, "I was to be finished for the season today. Finally going home. Yesterday I said goodbye to my last group. It was a difficult group. I am ready to go home. Then I receive a message that I must do you."

She was a hardened, chain-smoking woman in her fifties who plotted potty breaks as if on a military campaign. She could sense the pain in your bladder even before you got the nerve to raise your hand. Clenching the mic, she'd splice in a terse "cross your legs" midway through a lecture on Mad King Ludwig.

There were forty-nine tourists on this forty-nine-seat bus. Everyone rotated, moving up one seat each day—except for a chubby little New Zealander who wore kiwi T-shirts and stayed in the middle of the five-seat back row. Every time I'd look at him he'd make a strange but polite squawk. His accent was so heavy that over three weeks I never understood a sentence he uttered.

I remember three retired Belgian brothers, slow-moving shoppers in dapper little hats. There was a gentle old guy from San Mateo who had an embarrassing crush on a petite Japanese girl. An Indian engineer who worked in Saudi Arabia explained that his wife packed twenty-four saris, one for each day of their trip—for better scrapbook photos. And I remember a lawyer's wife with tight lips, frizzy hair, and a son who was so excited he had to blow on his hands to keep them cool.

Scott, a childish twenty whose parents sent him on the tour to grow up and get a little culture, was less thrilled. He packed Gatorade from home. Staying on the bus during most stops—for his own safety—he wondered out loud why they just don't tear down the old buildings and make modern, efficient ones.

Marv was newly retired and also on his first trip. Figuring a bribe was the standard best way to ensure a great time, he tucked a $100 bill into my shirt pocket on day one. That was a lot of money to me then—enough for five days of travel. I tried . . . weakly . . . to give it back. I failed. But moving that bill from my pocket into my wallet, I was determined not to let this get Marv a better trip. But the money made it clear: This trip was important not only to Marv but to each person on that bus. To give him a good return on his investment, I decided to give every person in my group 110 percent.

My frustration with big-bus travel grew as the trip dragged on. Waiting for the bus to pull out was the exasperating norm. Pressing my nose against the window, I scanned the parking lot ten minutes past departure time. Cliques of tourists passed the time merrily complaining about last night's hotel. Disgruntled husbands—who would prefer that the European experience be distilled neatly into a large park in California—compared things to "back home."

Squawking at my Kiwi friend and waiting for the Belgian gentlemen to finish their shopping, I'd stew and develop both a passion for tour group punctuality and tricks to enforce it. And jamming a pillow against the speaker to muffle Monica's harsh voice, I developed an appreciation of tour guide charm.

I learned about expensive sightseeing "options" on those Cosmos tours. My mission as group escort was to spare my group the extra expense but not the experience. After reviewing with my group which sightseeing options were worth taking, Monica's sales pitch went over like a bathless double.

As I left the hotel with my hearty splinter group, Monica said, "Really, you will see nothing in town without taking my 'Munich by Night' option."

With a battle cry of "Double the oompah for half the deutsche marks!" I led my group of renegades into the tram and on to the beerhall.

Mathauser's wasn't overrun with tour groups back then. With a little organizing of chairs we sat directly under the band—three tables closer than where I sit now.

To meet the neighbors, we'd fly a coaster like a Frisbee into a happy gang at the next table. With glasses raised in our direction, they'd roar a lusty welcome. The happy sound of my tourists clinking mugs with new German friends fired my determination to save tourists from the greedy grip of European guides.

Guides like Monica hate guidebooks. On a bus, guides know good travel information spreads like a cancer and pretty soon, no one's taking their optional sightseeing excursions.

I saw the greedy dance of tour guide and merchant as Monica prepped us for cuckoo clocks, dazzled us with a merchant's demo, and gave us twenty minutes to buy. While shoppers compared newly purchased treasures back on the bus, Monica shared a cigarette with the owner of the shop and picked up her fifteen percent.

As we traveled through Europe, our group hardly realized it was one tiny link in a steady chain gang of groups going from tour-friendly hotel to restaurant to shop. The only locals we encountered were vendors who slapped on a smile with the arrival of our bus and expertly put up with us for their livelihood.

On the last day of the tour, Monica, wearing her payday smile, gave an inspirational plea for big tips. We'd long remember Monica. But on the keyboard of a jaded tour guide's memory, goodbye and delete are the same key.

Merchants appreciate the business but marvel at blitz tour itineraries. Any bus driver can rattle off the basic route:

Day one: Wake up in Amsterdam; morning at Anne Frank's, the Diamond polishers and Rijksmuseum; noon to seven o'clock drive to the Rhine hotel, wine tasting, sleep.

Day two: 7:00 to 7:30 breakfast, 7:30 to 8:00 Stein talk and shopping, 8:15 depart to Dachau, Olympic Stadium, and the beerhall in Munich.

Day three: Drive to Venice with a quick stop in Innsbruck to see the Golden Roof.

And so on.

Bus drivers call these "pajama tours" because the tour members might as well stay in their pajamas.

On the Road is the tour industry magazine. It's distributed free at better kilt, stein, Swiss clock, crystal, wooden shoe, and *stocknegel* dealerships. *On the Road* is a tour guide's grapevine filled with news and warnings: "Due to staff shortages, Pompeii will close on Sundays." "Buses are no longer allowed into central Florence." "Non-local guides risk stiff fines and expulsion in Venice." "In Rome, bus drivers who don't park in the 'mafia lot' behind the Colosseum can buy back their tires at the Porta Portese flea market." "The British Tourist Board is now accepting nominations for its annual 'Loo of the Year' award."

On the Road reports on the best commissions (Bucherer in Lucerne for Swiss clocks), clever ways to sell optional tours ("sell Paris tours after the champagne tasting at Reims when everyone's in a bubbly mood"), and even tips on getting a break from your tour members (crank up the heat on the bus after lunch to put everyone to sleep).

And when groups aren't sleepy, they need games. *On the Road* suggests awarding a bottle of Chianti to the tourist who correctly guesses the number of tunnels the bus goes through between Florence and Orvieto. It even lists handy tour guide trivia: Did you know that Churchill's statue is wired with a weak current of electricity to keep pigeons from mistaking his bald head for a potty stop?

The folks at *On the Road* also produce a cassette with all the necessary tunes to fit your tour route—from the Blue Danube waltz to "Climb Every Mountain" to "Arrivederci Roma." Their "Super SingaSongaSongaEurope" tape is packed "with favorites from Europe and around the world that your clients will hear at folklore shows, banquets, and gala evenings. Plus three songs written all about taking coach tours!"

Imagine being stalled in an Autobahn traffic jam with your endlessly energetic tour guide leading you in the SingaSonga-SongaEurope theme ditty:

Up with the lark each morning,
On the bus by eight o'clock,
Our driver loads the baggage,
Our leader counts his flock.
Take a seat by the window,
Remember we have to rotate,
Rest stops are twenty minutes,
Hurry back 'cause the bus won't wait!"

In 1978, after three years of escorting Cosmos tours, I was more adamant than ever about the importance of teaching independent travel. After one of my travel lectures at the University of Washington, a family friend, Patty Price, took me out for pizza. She had an agenda: to convince me to organize, sell, and lead a tour. Flattered by Patty's vision but already sure my answer would be "no," I nevertheless heard her out.

I was a content and satisfied twenty-two-year-old piano teacher who did enough lecturing on the side to pay for my annual European vacations. My life was extremely simple: teach twelve piano lessons in six hours and call it a good day's work. My girlfriend—also a piano teacher—and I were going to marry, move our grand pianos in together, and play duets. While I sensed that there was more of a limit to teaching piano than teaching travel, I was satisfied with my life.

The major ideas in my career—writing a guidebook, leading tours, and producing a TV series—were the brainstorms of friends and family. I rarely took such suggestions seriously. But a good idea keeps knocking.

Looking back, becoming a tour organizer shouldn't have surprised me. When traveling with college friends, I was the self-appointed tour guide eager to park my travel partner with the bags while I ran around to find a hotel or line up a bus connection. Even back then, I'd assemble impromptu groups of English-speaking tourists to get a group discount or merit an English guided tour. And several times, when indecision slowed our momentum or I felt unappreciated for my tour-guiding services, I'd go on strike. By pouting on the curb and letting my travel partner figure out our next move, I immaturely hoped to demonstrate the indispensability of my hard work.

In other words, getting me to organize a tour was easy. By the time Patty and I finished our pizza, we had a complete itinerary scribbled on a napkin.

We concocted an easy plan that I recommend to anyone trying to build a tour business: start small—eight in a minibus. Charge only enough to cover expenses. With a small group and small expectations, I could experiment. With experience, I gained confidence—and promotional photos of me happily sharing Europe with my traveling customers.

That first tour—so cheap it sold itself—was a commune on wheels. Wanting hearty travel mates, I actually auditioned customers for those first seats. There was no itinerary. Each participant signed a form that promised, "I understand that on some nights we may find no accommodations. If we need to sleep in the van, I will do so without complaint."

Tour Number One was me and eight women (which I don't think had anything to do with the audition). Each day was filled with experiences no tour organizer could reserve in advance. We picked up a hitchhiker in Switzerland's remote Engadine on the condition that he'd teach us to yodel. We tied our belts together to lower the frightened ones down a tough part of the Schilthorn. We dropped by Oberammergau's Passion Play and snared tickets at the door. For super-scenic stretches—under Admiral Nelson oak trees and past Cotswold sheep—we'd take turns riding on the rooftop luggage rack. And we'd ponder our place in creation with Sunday morning fellowships.

Parking on market squares of towns that had never seen a tour bus, we looked at each other for a group "thumbs up" or "thumbs down" and either explore it or head on. If confronted by a hill town with a locked tower, we'd sweet-talk the barber with the key into closing his shop just long enough for a private tour. We brought tourism to virgin hill towns, climbed crumbling castles, and paddled fantasy canoes down sweet brown rivers at Swiss chocolate factories. And to overcome tension within our traveling family, whenever necessary we'd unload for a group hug.

Driving was my "alone time." Leaning over the steering wheel, I'd crank up my Walkman. With the one boy on board wrapped in earphones, it became a girls' bus. I learned a lot about the feminine side of crudeness—puns, songs, and jokes not meant for male ears. Driving out of Amsterdam's red light district, the conversation floated from comparing lace souvenirs to a lilting chorus of "How much is that dildo in the window?"

Each day at about mid-afternoon, I'd hit a phone booth and find beds. Occasionally I failed and we'd pull into a new town roomless. Parking on the main square, I'd give the order to "Fan out, search for rooms, and meet back here in twenty minutes to compare notes."

Getting rooms on the fly honed my room-finding tricks. I didn't realize it, but I was also finding key listings for future guidebooks.

For several years, I did tours with no reservations—free to meet nightly with my group and explore tomorrow's options. Spreading out the map, we'd discuss and debate which of Europe's treats to sample next. Like settling into an ultimately comfortable spot on a rocky beach, eventually this itinerary experimentation left me with winning routes for future books and tours.

But finding comfortable routes had nothing to do with comfortable beds. Back then I had a personal crusade to put "soft" Americans into miserable hotel rooms, forcing them to experience the ugly side of being on the road . . . if only to understand how comfortable they had it back home.

When Americans complain of hardships on the road, I crank up the voice of my grandmother telling stories of her immigration from Norway to Canada. The boat ride was miserable. The only thing she could keep down was beer. She's been a teetotaler since the day she saw the Statue of Liberty. Having entered America like a bad traveler—not speaking the language, packing too much luggage and not enough money—she navigated the immigrants' road to Edmonton, Alberta, where she eventually met her Norwegian husband. The physical hardship, uncertainty, and risk my grandparents endured became the foundation for a big, happy, typically American family.

Two generations later, I'm safe and comfortable. But I regret that my life will never know this adventure and struggle. For me, raw travel provides constructive hardship. Maybe that helps explain my sadistic tendencies as a rookie tour guide.

My determination to help travelers realize rich experiences from hard times also came out of my own vagabond experiences. I'd suffer through an all-night stint on the blistered black vinyl floor of a Yugoslavian train—farmers bouncing bags of potatoes, peppers, and chickens over my hostel sleep sack—in order to wake up in Sofia. I'd stumble out of the Sofia station into a blue new Bulgarian day. Dragging the sleep from my eyes, I'd consider my options for the day. Just being off the train made Sofia a thrilling destination. Travel is best with a few rough edges.

Seeing fear in the eyes of my group after telling them, "I'm not sure where we're sleeping tonight, but, hey, let's have dinner," drew from me an irrepressible giggle. The sight of a culture-shocked tour member lying in the middle of a lumpy bed above a rude pub in an Italian port town was a triumph. If she was afraid of bugs it was even better. My goal: to forcefeed a global perspective on my suburban American tour groups. My first aid kit: a baggie of Valium.

Back then, we'd spend our Munich evenings here at Mathauser's beerhall. Then, bellowing German drinking songs out open windows and slap-dancing in our seats, we'd follow the tracks of tram #17 out to "the Tent," Munich's giant circus tent crashpad.

I didn't know how to drive there because, without a group, I'd only been there by trolley. So, year after year, we'd follow the tram tracks through midnight Munich to the huge park at the edge of town. Picking up our blankets and mattresses, we'd stake out a corner to call home for the night. With 400 roommates under the big canvas, the Tent was a cross between Woodstock and a slumber party.

Those minibus groups were a small family—intense socially. With nine travelers slumming through Europe together, either you got along or you didn't. There was no escape. It was three weeks in a petri dish of love and hate.

One group was particularly intense. It featured Arlene, who gave me tension headaches; Gloria, who caused perfect strangers to hum the "Wicked Witch of the West" theme song; Lorraine, a psychologist who pushed people's buttons for sport; Tammy, a slut in hot pants who couldn't understand why the local guys were tripping over themselves to be alone with her; and Lana.

Lana talked nearly as fast as I can think. She loved history much the way a little kid loves putting black olives on her fingers. She likened her sense of fashion to a troglodyte's but had a figure that hardly needed clothes. While older than I, Lana had had a child young and raised him alone. Lana was just now discovering the world. She embraced the romance of Europe and I managed to be in between.

Any tour guide knows the danger of mixing work and romance. You cannot favor one person romantically without causing major problems with the rest of the group. Many guides have tried. None have succeeded. Even the sleaziest bus company on the road—Top Deck—tells its guides, "If you sleep with one, you gotta sleep with them all."

We were in yodelin'
good moods after our beerhall evening. Somehow we
managed to get the mini-
bus to the Tent and park.
We were issued our mat-
tresses and blankets and
staked out places under
the big top. Managing to
cross paths behind our bus,
Lana bellied up to her tour
guide and said, "Hold me."

*I believe I'm the only tour organizer
who ever opted for The Tent.*

I did.

She was a head shorter than me and as we hugged, I gazed out
into the lantern-lit crowd of vagabonds. There in the distance, by
the ping pong table, I saw the Wicked Witch of the West. She had
spied us. That tune sprung, fast and fortissimo, into my head as she
ran to the group.

That night our group lay in a corral of mattresses. Lana and I
got as close as we dared . . . together in a sea of roommates with
the sound of drunk Australians rutting in the corner. I believe I'm
the only tour organizer who ever opted for the Tent. Our group survived. But Lana's and my love lasted only until the end of the tour.

Several tours later—long after Lana, but in the same tent—I
woke up to the amorous grunting of a nearby couple. Next to me
was one of my tour members, sitting up, shaking, and silently sob-
bing. Sounding as if she feared disappointing me she admitted,
"Rick, I don't think I can take this anymore."

I realized then that sharing a tent with 400 rutting roommates
was not really a prerequisite to a broader perspective. As she swallowed the last of my Valium, I decided it was time to find a gentler
way to introduce Americans to Europe. From that point on, I up-
graded our accommodations.

The psychological makeup of my tour groups was changing. As
tour prices went up, the carefree gangs of friends who left the wor-
rying to me were replaced by customers—the kind who couldn't

concentrate on the sightseeing if we didn't have hotel rooms reserved by mid-afternoon.

There is a delightful irony about tourists from a country that leads the rich world in homelessness, being so nervous about the remote possibility of a single bedless night. Only my growing business sense prompted me to make hotel reservations part of my fledgling tour business.

A summer's tour calendar was nonstop: typically a total of forty-eight people on six three-week laps around Europe. Successive groups passed me like a baton between relay runners.

One year this exchange took place in a London theater. To save time and get discounted big-group tickets, I'd finish one group and start the next at the same play. After our tour-ending group hug, I'd step into the theater as the guide of one group. Two hours later, I'd walk out leading the next.

I learned I could handle anyone for three weeks. The first week we were all fresh and new to each other. Through the second week we were a comfortable family. By the end of the third week, our once-charming idiosyncracies began to wear on each other—but not enough to get in the way of a great last supper.

One year, the most difficult tourist happened to take two different tours back to back—forty-four days rather than twenty-two. I learned a valuable lesson: Be in charge of one individual's travel happiness for a maximum of three weeks.

Studying two groups in the same circumstance—one happy and the next miserable—taught me the importance of attitude. To one group, the arrival of a noisy group of students in a youth hostel robbed them of much-needed peace and quiet. To the next, it was an opportunity to make friends with a local teacher and learn about another country's school system. My challenge was to connect groups with the positive in whatever experience Europe doled out.

Willing to take risks for any powerful travel experience, I deposited one group without warning in the French monastery of Taize, south of Dijon. Taize offered a chance to experience modern European monasticism. The icon-oriented meditation that dominated the Mass was an exciting opportunity to grapple with the

American fear of silence. And the silence was particularly pro-
found when sandwiched between the easy-to-love music of Taize.
But what my group experienced most vividly were the crude dorm
beds and meals of thin soup and thick bread. Taize taught me the
essential tour-guiding skill of preparing a group for the rugged experiences well in advance.

By experimenting with group after group to find the best hill
town, castle, and Madonna and Child, I was managing time as
well as money. Eventually, my tour handbooks became guidebooks
so people could do our tours on their own.

These books were originally designed only as tour handbooks.
I left them laying around at my lectures (hoping to interest people
in my tours). Students began stealing these books. No one had ever
stolen from me in classes before. It was clear: These tour handbooks
were driving decent people to theft. They needed to be available
for sale. I self-published the first *22 Days in Europe* guidebook.
Then came *22 Days in Britain.* Eventually my publisher ran with
the concept and the books spawned an entire line of guidebooks.

These "22 days" books focused on getting the most out of your
vacation time. Back in the 1960s, Arthur Frommer's ground-
breaking "Europe on $5 a Day" series stretched the vacation dollar
of the generation that survived the Great Depression. My guidebooks addressed the needs of a new "time-is-money" generation.

Confident I could help Americans enjoy Europe, I let my
piano students go, turned my recital hall into a travel classroom,
and started Europe Through the Back Door, Inc.

Our key to enjoying Europe—whether through guidebooks or
on tours—was connecting with its people. And many of our travelers managed to do this particularly well. My memories of one 1984
tour are dominated by the love story of Colleen and the driver, Jan.

Jan was a Belgian man born to romance. Well-dressed, with
movie-star gray hair and Old World manners, he was always the
best dancer on board. Jan was a romantic whose personal hardships somehow made him even more lovable. It took nearly everything Jan earned to cover the costs of his reckless son's legal
problems and a ruined first marriage.

Jan's Belgian girlfriend, Huguette, was planning a romantic mid-tour rendezvous with him on the Italian Riviera. But by Venice, Jan was hopelessly in love with a stately Seattle blonde named Colleen.

Colleen, straitlaced into a predictable suburban life with a flat marriage, was traveling to explore her options. Tall as Jan but twenty years younger, she saw in him the finer points of European life.

As we neared the Riviera, the entire group was buzzing with speculation. At the last freeway rest stop, Jan climbed wearily down from the bus. Amazed at his tragic predicament, he said, "Rick, I don't know what I gonna do."

Huguette met us at the Riviera hotel. The group was wild about Jan. The anticipation was electric. Not wanting to take sides but being the all-powerful room assigner, I went person by person through the rooming list. When I said, "In room twenty-four, Colleen and . . . Huguette," twenty-four tourists gasped. For some reason, it seemed right to me.

Colleen went home, got a divorce, sold her house, and moved to Belgium. Today she speaks Flemish and lives happily with the bus driver of her dreams.

A big part of my early tours was introducing American friends to European friends. One year I'd visit Herr and Frau Moser, the Swiss parents of my sister's ski teacher. The next year I'd drop by with a busload of tourists. The Mosers would take us on a tour of their mandatory bomb shelter. Then, slicing hard, sharp, and curly pieces from an ancient brick of alpine cheese, they'd tell tales of Swiss military readiness: hidden jets ready to rip out of mountains like airborne Batmobiles, bridges designed with self-destruct explosives, and loaves of bomb shelter bread so hard they doubled as weapons. We'd conquer Alpine ridges with the Moser children, romping like mountain goats up one side to glissade down the loose shale slopes of the other. Landing on the doorstep of an uncle's lonely high meadow hut, we'd ring the bovine bell choir hung from his eaves before playing spoons and drinking schnapps at his hearth.

Much of my Europe was like the Mosers—a place I discovered alone that can be shared in small groups. But as groups grew, the experience inevitably drifted from a friendly show-and-tell to canned culture on stage. Sadly, my visits to the Mosers became a Swiss folk show as our groups grew from eight to sixteen, eighteen, twenty-one, then finally twenty-five. Now I tell stories of the Mosers from my bus microphone as we zip by their town on the Autobahn. While I still lead an occasional tour, most of the 3,000 people who take a Europe Through the Back Door tour each year never meet me. And our first aid kits come with everything you'd expect . . . and no Valium.

A happy ending is that my biggest tour group of all, the viewers of my TV series, can still fit through the "back door." My couch potato travel partners have joined me thumping empty wine kegs in Etruscan cellars, gambling at the dog races in Belfast, and celebrating five-year-old Ibrahim's circumcision in Cappadocia. And, thanks to our PBS camera crew, which travels where a tour group can't, countless Americans know my friends the Mosers. They're right there with us carving the cheese, visiting the bomb shelter, even seeing the grandkid pull out his tooth and put it in the oven (where the Swiss tooth fairy looks). And as TV brings European lives into American living rooms, I hope it inspires a few Americans to be their own tour guide.

Another beer coaster Frisbee bounces off my empty stein. It's a random hit—maybe a reminder that it's time for Italy. I finish a postcard to my wife by pasting a tiny bit of sauerkraut under the air mail sticker (she loves the Bavarian stuff). I'm sending her cards from each country and this is the final call for the last of my German stamps. Grabbing my pretzel and tucking Jackie O into my bag, I head for the train station.

Scusi, How's Your Bag Attached?

Sleeping on a train far from home where no one knows who or where I am replaces my confidence with anxiety. Will I find a place? Will I get any sleep? If I do, will I wake up with my valuables intact? Do bandits still gas trains in Italy? What if I get thirsty? Who are my compartment mates?

I become methodical as an overnight train ride approaches.

Before any overnight train ride, I give myself my ritual treat—a good dinner. I buy the latest *Herald Tribune*.

Knowing that the moment I step onto that Italy-bound train, my German coins—which can be worth several dollars each—become pricey souvenirs, I graze the kiosks with a goal rare to shoestring travelers: blow the money, and fast.

On board, I meet my compartment mates, prepare my bunk, arrange my luggage, and settle in mentally. Stowing today's travel information and reviewing tomorrow's, I'm already in Italy mentally.

The Irishman on the top bunk opposite mine notices me busily reading my Italy guidebook. "You look like a student preparing for a test," he says.

"I'm cramming for Italy," I reply. "I love Italy."

"What's so good about Italy?" he asks.

"Italy's the closest thing in Europe to India," I answer.

The beauties and horrors of India always prompt a fine conversation among travelers. India rearranges my cultural furniture. India is 800 million people who understand God, pain, music, food, and time completely differently than I do. I grew up thinking Indian music was tribal noise and then learned it's as sophisticated as Beethoven.

"India reshuffles my God-given truths," I say.

"How?"

"To find a land where time is not money," I explain. "To consider the sum total of joy and happiness in a land with nearly a billion people rather than the pain of a particular individual. To sit in a restaurant and be joined by a proud professor who pointedly illustrates to the Westerner how a highly educated and cultured person can eat with his fingers. This is how India reshuffles my God-given truths. That's why I like the India of Europe—Italy."

Trying my bunk on for size, I stretch out. At over six feet tall, I can do this only if I park my feet in opposite corners. I requested an upper bunk for the privacy, head room, and a safe zone behind my head and over the aisle to stow my bag. But hot air rises and it gets stuffy. And the ceiling curves, cramping my toes.

Every train comes with a thief—union rules. They case out the train and choose the bag they want. When the train enters a tunnel, everything goes black. They reach in and grab the bag. Even on short trips, I clip my bag to the luggage rack above the seat. Then when we enter the tunnel and the thief grabs my bag, it doesn't go. He's not going to ask, "Scusi, how's your bag attached?"

In my lectures I set my "beware of thieves" lessons in Italy. This offends honest Italians. Italy is travel with abandon, the place you're most likely to fall in love and the place you're most likely to be robbed. Of course hearts and wallets can be stolen anywhere. You don't even need a passport. But when it comes to nearly any activity, I'd just as soon do it or have it done to me in Italy.

I slip a film canister under the handle on our door so it can't be jimmied from outside.

"Clever trick," says the Irishman. "Where'd you learn that?"

"Russia," I say.

Russia, dangerous even when you're awake, is notorious for nighttime train robberies. On my last visit, the St. Petersburg newspaper ran a story on mafia thieves gassing compartments on night trains and robbing passengers. The "midnight express" from St. Petersburg to Moscow, which was most popular with Western tourists, was noted as the train most likely to be targeted.

With rumors flying everywhere, travelers gathered at the St. Petersburg youth hostel to trade misinformation and form partnerships. I teamed up with an unlikely couple: Dave, whose year on the road made him look and act like some shaggy mountain man, and petite, demure Mary Pat, his girlfriend, who had just flown in to see him. Seeing them together, I kept expecting her to say in a damsel-in-distress voice, "But I *can't* pay the rent." For safety, we rented an entire four-bed compartment for the three of us.

On board, a spooky-looking conductor welcomed us. (In our mental state, any stranger looked spooky.) He poked his head into our compartment and lifted up the bench-like seat revealing a big tin bin. He said, "There are thieves on this train. Mafia. Put everything you like to keep in here and sleep on top of it."

Naturally, after he left, Dave and I got down on our knees to scour the bin, convinced there was a hidden trap door somewhere in it. We declared it safe. Dave "locked" the door with a film canister. For good measure he lashed it shut. I opened the window enough to keep a steady breeze flowing so we couldn't be gassed from under the door. Mary Pat cheered from her top bunk.

Where Mary Pat cheered, the Irishman on tonight's train to Venice now snores. The train exhales, stopping at the summit where Austria meets Italy. A noisy Italian crew boards and we roll out of the Alps. Lying on my back, I'm comforted by the weight of my moneybelt sitting on my stomach. As the train picks up speed, I drift away clutching nagging thoughts of theft.

We hurtle through the Italian darkness like a roller coaster on a straight stretch. Sweating, I crack open the window. Now passing trains sound like they're in the compartment. But with the noisy rush of wind comes air. The night passes in a sleepy medley of me, desperate for air, waking up to crack open the window and bottom bunkers, desperate for peace, closing it.

The attendant flips the lights on and announces "Venezia, *trenti minuti* . . . Venice, thirty minutes." He returns my passport and railpass. Warm and still sleepy, I feel smug about having slept and traveled at the same time. I hold the documents with groggy fingers while grabbing a few more miles of sleep.

The train jolts to a stop and I snap awake. Wading quickly through my marshmallow mind, I momentarily forget where we're going. Panicking, I lean to look out the window. The sign on the platform says "Mestre"—we're still ten minutes from Venice.

I zip up my bag, climb out of my bunk, and position myself in the aisle in anticipation of Venice.

The platform is filled with tourists leaving the train here in Mestre. They've read about the terrible crowds and smell of Venice. I feel like yelling, "Don't go yet. You're making a big mistake. To experience Venice you must sleep there and wake up in it!"

Mestre is the real world with cars, jobs, and big industry. It's the placenta of Venice. I'd bury it.

Slowly, my train leaves the mainland.

CHAPTER FIVE

VENICE

"I am Venetian in my blood. Not Italian. Venice is
boring for young people—no disco, no nightlife. It is
only beautiful. Venice. It is a philosophy to live here
. . . the philosophy of beauty."

Suddenly there's water on both sides of my train. I lean out the
train window in anticipation of Venice and take a deep whiff of
tangy lagoon air. I never miss this approach to Venice. The mucky,
marshy last bits of the Italian mainland give way to the island's
umbilical causeway: train tracks and a highway. The huge industrial center just to the south waves a real world farewell. Ahead in the
hazy distance, tilting bell towers wink their welcome.

St. Mark's distinctive bell tower, the city's grandest, is on the
opposite side of the island. But even from the train, it seems close
by. This is a small town on a small island. The morning sun sprin-
kles diamonds on the Adriatic promising visitors they're in for a
rich experience. Organizing my luggage, I stow the sweater I
needed daily in Germany. We're in Italy—half past eight and it's
already hot.

Bold, plain, and white, the Venice train station stands like a
fascist bulldog facing the fanciful Grand Canal. The station's broad
steps are still lazy with backpackers who called it home for the night.

As I survey the vagabonds, I grow nostalgic for the days when
I traveled simply for fun. As a piano teacher, I'd learned the futility

of trying to get students to practice from June to September. Summering in Europe made more sense. Now my travel experiences are a business expense: the research and development program that fuels my business. Frustrated with my need to always be productive, it hits me that when you let your time become money you cheapen your life.

One measure of a culture is its treatment of time. In the United States time is money: we save it, spend it, invest it, and waste it. Not so in traditional Italy. Here life is rich and savored slowly. In Italy—like in India—time is more like chewing gum. You munch on it and play with it . . . as if it will be there forever.

For new arrivals to Venice, the steps of the train station provide a starting block from which to dive into a different world. A hard-working *vaporetto*—one of the big floating buses that serve as public transportation on Venice's canals—glides by. I hop on and struggle past clots of Italians deep in conversation, gesturing intensely into the stylish black of each other's sunglasses. Gradually, I make my way to the front of the boat. My ritual entry into Europe's best preserved big city is from the front seat of a *vaporetto*. I wind down the Grand Canal from the train station through the heart of town to the center at Piazza San Marco. Somewhere along the way I stand up, just to hear the captain yell, "Sit down!" It's great to be in Italy.

This boat ride settles me into Venetian time. Clock towers, which chime lazily somewhere near the top of each hour, set the pace. The best way to become lonely in Venice is to expect punctuality from your Italian friends. When mine show up late, they shrug and say, "Venetian time." Even the giant fancy clock on the main square—famous as the world's first "digital" clock—has a carved "minute block" that displays time no more accurately than in five-minute chunks.

Maybe a city which has been on the decline for several centuries is in no hurry for a good reason. Venice is expertly rundown. With 300 years of practice and a steadily declining population, it should be.

The Grand Canal, choppy with small-time commerce, winds through the heart of town. Its mouth receives the food that fuels

Venice. Cars, trucks, buses, and trains unload here. Riding like an ornament on the bow of the *vaporetto*, I snap photos I know I've already taken. Venice—so old and decrepit—always feels new to me.

It's rush hour and the canal is a two-way highway busy with *vaporettos* gracefully dodging each other. In Venice the hotels are full but the houses are empty. The wind whistles through vacant buildings while the *vaporettos* ride low—packed mostly with sightseers gawking at this soggy, depopulated commotion of beauty.

After a thousand years of treehouse-type expansion, buildings here have grown together, turning lanes into tunnels and leaving only rooftops for gardens. The city is like a massive coral reef filled with people and shops that have no memory of their original builders. Exteriors are haphazard, some finely painted stucco, others stucco-crusted red brick with elegant windows cut in. The whole place is rotting—kept together by iron supports and petrifying resin.

Leaping from boat to dock, I'm a stagehand in the open air theater of Italy: Porters sing happily while wheeling their carts. Cooing pigeons, jostling lanes, inky forgotten canals, ritual cafés, *piazza* schoolyards—there are pastel views in every direction. All of Venice is a bridge of sighs.

Alternative Venice

Reaching the big black door of my hotel, I push a bronze lion's nose. This security buzzer brings Piero to the second-floor window. He welcomes me with a "*Ciao*, Reek!" and buzzes the door open. I climb the steps eager to settle in.

Piero, who runs the Venetian hotel I call home, shaved his head five years ago. His girlfriend wanted him to look like Michael Jordan. With his operatic voice, he reminds me more of Yul Brynner. Though not a performer, he says, "My voice is guilty of my love for opera."

Proud of the improvements in his place since my last visit, Piero shows me around. While remodeling the hotel, he discovered seventeenth-century frescoes on the walls of several rooms. The place was a convent back then. An antique wooden prayer kneeler, found in the attic and unused for generations, decorates a

corner of my room. The whitewash is partially peeled away, revealing peaceful aqua, ochre, and lavender floral patterns. In
Venice, behind the old, the really old peeks through.

The breakfast room is decorated in traditional Venetian—
green and red decorative glass, prints of Venice canal scenes, and
sequined masks reminiscent of Carnival indiscretions. The room is
strewn with antiques. Everything is old. "It's kitsch," Piero admits,
"but only the best kitsch." I sit down. As Piero brings me a red orange juice—made from blood oranges—he reports on his work
and the latest Venice news. While the sounds of Don Giovanni
fill the air, guests prepare for the day.

When Piero's cellular phone rings, he apologizes with operatic eyes. "In Italy, this is prestige." He talks on the phone as if
overwhelmed with work: "*Si, si, si, va bene* ["that's fine"], *va bene,
va bene, certo* ["exactly"], *certo, bello, bello, bello, bello, bello*
["beautiful," in descending pitch], *si, si, okay, va bene, va bene,
okay, okay, okay, ciao, ciao, ciao, ciao, ciao, ciao.*" He hangs up and
explains, "That was the night manager. Always problems. I call
him my nightmare manager."

In my early travels, hotel night managers were a sorry lot.
Generally unable to speak anything but the local language, they
worked at night when the most complicated guest problems hit.
When a tourist in a bind came to them, things just got worse. On
a good night, they'd spend their time carefully ripping the paper
napkins so they'd go twice as far at the breakfast table.

Opera continues to fill the air as Piero dashes to help some
French guests heading out for the day. He pours coffee for both of us,
then sits back down and says, "In hotel all the people are different.
French don't use the shower. Young Americans are most messy but
use the shower very much. I don't understand this. Americans ask,
'What is this bidet for?' I cannot tell them. It is for washing more
than the feet. In it we wash the parts . . . which rub together when
you walk. The Japanese think the bidet is very funny."

I say sadly, "The tourists have taken over your city."

Walking me to the window and tossing open the decrepit
blind, Piero says, "But Venice survives."

Piero, girl watcher and mama's boy, is pure Venetian.

As my gaze moves from the red-tiled roofs to the marketplace commotion filling the street below, I see his point. Tourists cannot take over Venice.

"Venice is a little city," he says. "Only a village, really. About seventy thousand people live on this island. I am Venetian in my blood. Not Italian. We are just one century Italian. Our language is different. The life here is another thing. It is with no cars . . . only boats. I cannot work in another town. Venice is boring for young people— no disco, no nightlife. It is only beautiful. Venetian people are travelers. Remember Marco Polo? But when we come home we know this place is the most beautiful. Venice. It is a philosophy to live here . . . the philosophy of beauty.

"To live properly in Venice you must have a boat. When you walk, you walk with the tourists. With a boat you live Venice in another dimension—with no tourists. You cruise under bridges and see the tourists walking in their dimension but you are in the Venice of no tourists. Next year I buy a boat. Now I almost live in the boat of my friend. The boat is my alternative Venice."

Piazza San Marco

Piero and I agree to meet back at the hotel later for dinner. I grab my day bag and walk to the square Napoleon called "Europe's finest drawing room," Piazza San Marco.

The exotic basilica of St. Mark's overlooks the huge square. On the cathedral, the saint's symbol, the winged lion, regally paws the Bible. A hierarchy of gilded and marble saints and angels culminates in the haloed head of St. Mark himself blessing the square full of tourists.

The cathedral, a richly decorated mess of mosaics, domes,

mismatched columns, and proud Catholic statuary, seems more ornate compared to the orderly buildings that define the square. Simple neoclassical halls stand like stern school mistresses overseeing a vast playground filled with people and pigeons. Marble columns, arches, and porticos fill three sides of the square as flat and predictable as if assembled from a book of black and white clip art. The bell tower is a pointed red brick skyscraper. As if Venice were still powerful, it stands three times as tall as the otherwise grand buildings on the square.

When I'm on tour, I walk my groups to Piazza San Marco approaching through tiny alleys. I pop the charms of the square on them like the sudden burst of a champagne cork. The sight of their tired faces lighting up is my tip for a good day's work. I'll never forget one woman who broke into tears. Her husband had dreamed of seeing this with her but died a year too soon. Now, she said, she was here for both of them.

Today, I'm alone, kicking at pigeons like a carefree kid kicks October leaves. A 1,500-lire bag of seed must be the most entertaining dollar you can spend here. Surrounded by historic and cultural wonders scholars would kill to see, today's tourists seem to see only what the locals call "rats with wings."

Unlike the great art that fills Venice's museums, the pigeons are interactive. Lovers sprinkle seeds in each other's hair. A crying little girl, overwhelmed by a feeding frenzy as she spills a sack, is rescued by a laughing mom. A dog swoops in and the air is suddenly filled with feathers. But the dog's task is hopeless and, within seconds, the pigeons are back in full force. Kids join in, flapping imaginary wings.

These pigeons are a problem. The locals are tired of putting out laundry wet and clean only to pull it in dry and covered with pigeon droppings. Apparently the birth control chemicals the city mixes into the seed don't work. Early in the morning, local crews shoot nets over the square catching piles of these birds. (I've often wondered why Chicken McNuggets are so cheap in Venice.)

As if to corral the entire scene—birds, dueling café orchestras, and dancing children—arches hold hands around the *piazza*.

Two café orchestras wage a musical tug-of-war to entice strollers to sit down and order a drink. It's Paganini, Mazurkas, and Gershwin versus Gypsy violin serenades, Sinatra, and Manilow.

Above the door to the church, a mosaic celebrates the great day when Venice made it onto the religious map of Europe. Venice got its start as a kind of refugee camp. Fifth-century farmers from the mainland, sick and tired of being overrun by barbarians, got together and—hoping the Huns didn't like water—moved into the lagoon.

Nothing of religious importance happened in the pre-Venice lagoon. But in the days of relics, Venice had become a wealthy superpower and it wasn't that tough for a city of its stature to acquire some first-class bones.

The bones of St. Mark were "rescued" (as local historians put it) from Egypt and buried under Venice's cathedral. In the mosaic, saints carry Mark's coffin into the cathedral, already glittering well beyond its importance. Propped on his elbow, a grumpy Mark glares out at the noisy line of tourists waiting to get into his church.

While a quarter of that mob will be turned away for wearing shorts, I scoot right by the decency guards. Inside, I climb a straight flight of stone steps to the loggia of the basilica, high above the square. It's a long view balcony with a pitted pink marble banister held in place by rusty iron support rods. Four huge and regal horses stand in the middle, as if enjoying this grandest of Venetian views.

From this peaceful perch I find my own zone. While not quite the private Venice of the pigeons or Piero in his boat, it's a place where I can be alone in the greatness of Venice. I close my eyes and ponder the crowds filling Piazza San Marco. The café orchestra stops and all I hear is a white noise of people. With no cars, this audio mash is broken only by the rare whistle, sneeze, or cry of a baby.

Piazza San Marco is the lowest part of Venice. From atop the church, I spot small puddles—flood buds—forming around drainage holes in the paving stones. When wind and tide combine to drive maximum water into this northern end of the Adriatic Sea, the *aqua alta* (high water) hits.

About thirty times a year, mostly in the winter, Venice floods. Squares sprout elevated wooden walkways, locals pull on their boots, and life goes on. Today's puddles will recede almost unnoticed. And most visitors assume the bits of walkway are convenient picnic benches.

A young man lifts his sweetheart onto the banister between me and the bronze horses. As they hug, I turn away and scan the people-filled square. Only the merchants and stray tour guides are jaded. The emphasis is on togetherness. Nearly all the people are with someone. Like rocks in a river, every once in a while pairs of lovers interrupt the flow of people. Wrapped in a deep embrace and knee-deep in their own love, they savor their own private Venice. Venice is difficult alone.

When I'm lonely, my thoughts are louder. I fight the loneliness with thoughts of old friends and travels, and the good life at home with Anne—my rucksack empty on the floor of our closet.

At the top of the hour, bells ring everywhere: overwhelming the café orchestras, filling the square like droning Buddhist gongs. Across the *piazza*, from atop the clock tower, two bronze Moors stand like blacksmiths at an anvil whacking out the hours as they have for centuries.

The tower used to be open to tourists. It's closed now but I always remember it being open.

As a college kid I fell for a Japanese girl named Emi in Venice. We climbed up to the Moors tower. We were all alone, high above the *piazza*. The Moors had just swung their clappers, and our ears were still ringing. We were drenched in Venice. The moment screamed *bacio*! Determined to be a gentleman, I asked Emi if I could kiss her. She burst out laughing. (I think it was a cultural thing.) When she regained control, we tapped into that shadow Venice.

Having sailed the world romantically, I ended up permanently moored right back at home, marrying Anne Jenkins. My forever travel partner is not only from my own culture . . . but from Omaha, America's heartland.

I met Anne in one of my travel classes at the University of

Washington's experimental college. To entertain myself during these eight-hour Saturday slideshow/lectures, I'd play with my delivery and roam the classroom with my eyes.

Anne, a nurse who had given up waiting for her friends to join her on a European trip, took the class in preparation for a solo trip. By the end of the day, without having spoken a word to each other, Anne and I were already traveling.

The class cleared out. And while my tired projector bulb cooled, Anne and I hugged. I was heading off on a three-month trip in two days, but we had time for one date.

Our relationship enjoyed a novel early growth period . . . three months of short phone calls and long letters shuttled over by fellow tour guides carrying chocolate chip cookie care packages. Anne gave me a warm homecoming at the airport. And within six months we had married our dream trips together.

Today this globetrotter is married to the same wonderful woman from hometown America. I look out my office window and see my junior high school and count Iowa's Lake Okoboji as a favorite place to vacation.

Exploring the world is most enjoyable when done from a solid home base. After allowing myself a few moments of homesickness with that thought, I climb down from the loggia and plunge into the Piazza San Marco crowds.

. . . and a Free Glass 'Orse

Glass merchants troll the *piazza* for shoppers. I wander unnoticed by a glass merchant. On my last visit, group in tow, the same guy grabbed my elbow and said, "Bring your groups here. We give the guide twenty percent back and a free glass 'orse." The shops behind the San Marco orchestras, their windows sparkling with the glass equivalent of Rossini, compete fiercely for the tour group business.

Whenever possible, I do non-touristy things in touristy towns. Rather than visit a glassblower, I visit a barber. Today I'm shaggy enough for a visit to Alessandro, my long-time Venetian barber. He runs his shop on a peaceful lane hiding out a few blocks from San Marco. Singing and serving his customers champagne, he wields his scissors with an artist's flair. For ten years, he's been my connection to behind-the-scenes Venice.

Hopping onto the old-time barber's chair, I marvel that I don't need an appointment for such a fine barber. Alessandro wears a white smock, a smirk, and a bushy head of curly black hair. He's short and pudgy and needs a haircut more than any of his customers. Holding his scissors in one hand and a glass of champagne in the other, it's hard to take him too seriously. But he always has something interesting to say.

When I mention the empty buildings lining the Grand Canal, he says, "Venice is not sinking. It is shrinking. In 1960 we have two hundred fifty thousand people. Today, only one quarter that."

"Who stays?" I ask.

"Mostly the rich," he answers. "You must have money to live on the island. It is very expensive. Only the top class stays. The old rich are the people of nobility. They must do everything correctly. The women, they cannot step outside without their hair and their clothes perfect. Remember there are no cars to hide in. We are a village. You step outside and everybody see you. The new rich, they have only money . . . without the nobility."

"Who are the new rich?"

"The people who work with the tourists. They own the hotels, the restaurants, glass factories, and the gondolas."

"Gondoliers are rich?" I ask.

"My god," says Alessandro, "they can make one million a day [$600]. And this is clean money . . . no tax."

As tufts of hair litter my cape, I sip a tall cool glass of bubbly and ask Alessandro how the old-time art of Venetian glassblowing survives.

Like a painter studying his canvas, Alessandro sizes me up in the mirror. Then, as if he dipped his scissors into just the right corner of his palette, he attacks my hair. "Glassblowing is like a mafia," he explains. "Ten years ago the business was very lucky. Rich Japanese, Americans, and Arabian sheiks made this industry big in Venice. We Venetians like glass, but not those red, green, and blue gilded baroque teacups.

"We like a simple, elegant, very light glass." He stops to take a floating-pinky sip from a sleek champagne glass. "This feels light. It is very nice. In Venice you can count the masters on one hand. All the other glass people, they are sharks."

Like so many tourist purchases, glass may look sumptuous in Venice, but get it home and it fits only in a box in the attic. But tourists love Venetian glass.

Alessandro snaps the cape in the air, sending my cut hair flying as I put my glasses back on and check his work.

As is our routine after each haircut, he says, "Ahhh, I make you Casanova."

And I agree, saying, "*Grazie*, Michelangelo."

Walking back to St. Mark's, I see a tour group funneling into a glass showroom. The routine is entirely predictable. They will climb a hot and sweaty staircase to a small cramped workshop. As they grab seats on crude bleachers that face the furnace, their guide gives his business card to an attendant. As city maps become fans, the salesman introduces the glassblower as some kind of Houdini. "For twenty-one years, this master apprenticed on the island of Murano. Now, ladies and gentlemen, he will make a horse from glass in only one minute."

Fanning harder, the crowd leans forward as the glassblower pulls a blob of red glass on a stick out of the oven. Expertly wielding his pincers, he pulls out four prancing legs, models a head complete with enraged nostrils and hair flying in the wind, and adjusts the tail to finish the tripod created when the stallion stands on its hind legs.

For the second act the group shuffles into a room shimmering in colorful glass vases, decanters, chandeliers, and necklaces, primed for the sales pitch.

The tour guide drops by the tour guide lobby and chats with another guide whose group is now in the furnace room. Meanwhile, his tourists are told about the lifetime replacement promise, which doesn't matter that much because, whack—the salesman hits a cup on the glass table—"you see, it don't break."

Later the tour guide drops by a small window and receives a plain envelope with his card stapled to it. Inside is cash—twenty percent of whatever his group purchased during the visit. (He skips the free glass 'orse.)

My tour company has wrestled with this commission issue. We'd rather forego the commission and offer our tour members discounted prices instead, but the more touristy places refuse to discount groups that don't want the kickback. Rather than lose that money, we used to tell people we'd collect the commission and rebate them accordingly. That worked until one big shopper purchased a $2,000 art vase. He bargained very effectively. Because of the low price, our commission was nowhere near the promised twenty percent. He was angry. We heard from his lawyer after the trip. Thanks to this guy, we no longer rebate commissions. We sink all kickbacks into a Chianti slush fund for the tour. And then, with equal help from shoppers and non-shoppers alike, we drink the kickback.

Dinner with Piero

At sunset I meet Piero at the hotel and we head for his favorite restaurant. Rounding the corner from his empty alley, I tell him, "For the first time I saw a long line just to enter St. Mark's cathedral. Even the back alleys are clogged with people. It's a zoo."

Piero leans toward me. "Yes! Zoo, zoo, zoo! Is a problem. In Venice the people come every day like a wave. There is no high season, no low season. Every morning we are invaded. But at six o'clock the tourists go away."

As if in command of the city, Piero waves a hand across the empty market square grandly saying, "And now Venice lives. Really, Venice is a fine place in the night. Sleep in Venice and you see the quiet Venice. When you see a *menu turistico*, go away. When you see old men speaking Italian in a restaurant . . . this is a good place. I take you now to Bepi's."

We walk quickly past the bruised tomatoes and damaged oranges littering the canalside market square, then we both freeze in our tracks. A three-foot-long rat sits on an empty fruit crate as if waiting just for us.

It wiggles into the canal with a tiny splash and Piero says, "For me the high tide is no problem. Low tide is the problem. It brings out the rats. Never go on the *vaporetto* at low tide—don't write that in your book . . . the gondolier will kill you."

Ahead of us a black gondola with several tired-looking businesspeople is about to push off. At key places along the Grand Canal, where there are no bridges, *traghetti* like this ferry people across. Piero hollers, *"Pop'e!"* (Venetian dialect for "Hey, gondolier!") Rushing through the empty market stalls and scattering a few pigeons, we hop aboard.

Looking warily at the black water slapping at the pier, I ask, "Are there many rats?"

"Yes, Venice is supported by rats. Really, low tide is the problem, not the high tide. We always had the high tide. This is in the medieval text. The high tide is good for Venice. It cleans the streets. It flushes out the canals—they are blue, not green, after the high tide. And it kills the rats."

"How?" I ask.

Putting his hand to his forehead as if to salute, Piero says, "It floods out their homes."

Standing like two Washingtons crossing the Delaware, we glide the width of the Canale Grande. This canal, the biggest and busiest in Venice, actually feels sleepy as twilight gives way to the bare bulbs of outdoor restaurants.

Triumphantly Piero says, "See, no city boats. Only private boats." He's right. The now-floodlit city is drained of its crowds. Locals—no longer selling things—wander like dazed islanders checking for damage after a hurricane.

Earlier in the day, we would have seen five or six *vaporettos*—loaded down with waving tourists and camcorders slam-dancing from dock to dock. Now the Grand Canal is at peace. I count two half-empty *vaporettos* and a dozen or so private runabouts. Dropping 500 lire onto the deck and stepping off on the other side of the canal, Piero promises, "Now we eat like Venetians . . . very, very well."

Greeting old friends as we walk, Piero explains how in Venice, if you open a restaurant you must answer the question, "Do I want to attract tourists or Venetians?"

"To make a tourist restaurant is no problem," Piero explains. "You see the people only one time. Even talking to them is not necessary. One-time visitors, it means bad food."

Piero kisses the cheeks of the waiter when we arrive at Trattoria da Bepi, then continues. "For me, a good restaurant is like home. Mama is cooking. We are maniacs about fish in the North Adriatic."

Sitting down at an outdoor table Piero points out Bepi. He stands as if carved into his *cicchetti* bar, surrounded by toothpick munchies on trays and well-fed neighbors.

Piero introduces me to Bepi's son, Loris. "Loris is a nightmare in fish market. 'This is no good . . . this is okay.' His mama is a Venetian mama, Delfina. I ask her, 'Please. Tell me how you make the fish.' She puts her hand on her heart and says, 'There is no recipe. It is from here.'"

Loris and Piero work up a dinner plan on a scratch pad as if putting together the guest list for a very special evening. They discuss each plate like it's an old friend.

Loris pours a little wine for Piero to test. Piero says, "But I know nothing of wine."

Loris says, "I know."

Soon plates start to arrive. Piero goes immediately for the polenta with cod saying, "In the south they call the people of Venice 'polenta eaters.'"

Piero splashes a hunk of bread into the broth under a pile of empty mussel shells and says, "You can feel the sea here."

The conversation stops as a girl in a short wispy skirt prances by on the arm of a local Romeo. Piero says, "Is incredeeeble. Look at this one, grrrr. This is Venice. I am sorry. I am Italian. I watch the girls."

As a lovely Italian encore struts by, Piero observes, "Giorgione, he is a good artist—yes—but this . . . this is better. Oh, Dio."

"I have a beautiful girlfriend. She is a model. But I cannot be married. It is imposseee—" To playfully show my friend how the default switch in his mind is set on girl-watching, I interrupt Piero by pretending to subtly catch something in my eye over his shoulder.

He stops mid-sentence to see what distracts me. It's nothing—but I make my point.

Loris brings a plate of six crawfish with tails peeled and ready to bite. Piero says "more aliens" as I pick one up and bite off the tail. Noticing how cold and limp it feels I ask, "Is this raw?"

"Yes . . . Italian sushi."

Marveling at the table full of mixed appetizer plates I tell Loris, "I love the antipasto misto. This with pasta is plenty for me. And for me the antipasto misto is more interesting than the chicken and potatoes main course."

Piero, who knows I prefer a meal of tapas-like munchies at the wine bars of Venice to a restaurant meal, says, "You like this because you are a tourist." He slaps the menu. "Be adventurous! Dig deep into the menu."

Loris returns. "Now we have the pasta with crab sauce." He serves Piero and puts the big bowl in front of me.

"Ahhh," Piero says, "For the peasant family, this was the biggest honor . . . to get the original bowl."

Later, watching the heads of five Italian boys turn in unison as another girl walks by, I ask, "Do the Italian girls watch the boys?"

"No, the boys watch the girls. Teenage Venetian boys go to San Marco to make an experience with American girls. Their first words in English are, 'My name eees. . . . You are pretty girl. Where you sleep tonight?'"

Nibbling on an artichoke heart, I say, "For many American girls, Italian boys are nice."

Piero's feet do a gay little tap dance and like a giddy teenager—eyebrows sending happy wrinkles to the top of his bald head—he adds, "Yes, and for Italian boys, American girls are very nice. It is international public relations. I am sorry," admits thirty-two-year old Piero, "I am too old now.

"It is very dangerous because if Venetian girls see the boys on San Marco they are jealous. The girls, they don't look for boys. They are . . ." and he does a couple of quick stuffy sniffs while scratching the underside of his nose with a proud knuckle. "And Venetian girls are not open. They are like a clam. This is typical in the Italian south. Venice is like the south in this way. We say Venice is like the Naples of the north—we sing, we talk with our hands, and our women are like clams."

Antonella, the daughter of Alessandro the barber, trades *ciaos* with Piero as her dog drags her down the lane. We're just finishing up our meal, but I'm concerned that I'm not getting the female side of this story.

Pouring her a glass of Bepi's famous licorice liqueur, I say, "Please, Antonella, help me. We are talking about Italian living, but Piero is giving me only the macho side."

Antonella is no longer the temptress I knew when she was in her twenties. Now she's running a shop. With the reality of business and dealing with Italian men, she is now more savvy than sweet. She's small and tough with a thick head of long black hair. When she talks, her direct eyes and busy hands give an intensity to her words. Stepping over her dog's leash, she grabs a seat and says, "What is macho? There are no macho men in Venice. They are mama's boys. We call this *mammone*."

Piero, as if he's heard the complaint a thousand times cries, "Ahhh, *mammone*."

Pulling an imaginary cord from his belly and petting it rather than cutting it he says, "It is true. I cannot cut the *cordone ombelicale*. I love my mama. And she loves me even more."

Antonella sips her grappa and says, "The Italian boys, ninety-five percent stay at home until they find a wife to be their new mother. Thirty, thirty-five years old they are still with their mothers. Even if they move out, they come home for the cooking and laundry. This is not macho . . . this is ridiculous.

"Aaannn-duh," she continues, lighting a cigarette, "they want a wife exactly like their mother. If they find a woman like me, independent, with some money, perhaps beautiful, this is a problem."

Piero nods like a scolded puppy. "Yes, this is true."

Antonella says, "If I make my hair special and wear strong makeup, they will take me to dinner and take me to bed. But they will not look at me to make a family. They want to be sure their wife won't leave them. A woman like me . . . it is too risky."

We pay and promise Loris we'll be back soon. Antonella unties her dog and we walk through the quiet and romantically lit alleys of Venice.

I tell Antonella, "I could not finish a sentence with Piero. Always looking at the girls."

Piero raises his eyebrows and his hands as if to mount a defense and just sighs.

Antonella says, "I was in England for two years. No boys looked at me. When I come home, in five minutes I was being stared at. I like this. It feels good to be home."

"But why are the Italian boys always thinking about the girls?"

Antonella says, "In Venice, I think it is because the tourist girls come here looking for the boys. Especially the American tourist girls. They like the Italian boys very much."

Climbing over a marble veneered bridge, we pass a gondolier dashing in his straight-brimmed, red-sashed straw hat, obviously well built under his striped shirt and black pants.

As the gondolier hollers a hopeful hello to a cute passing tourist, Piero says, "He hopes to be soo-sess-full."

"Successful," Antonella says to help him.

He tries again, looking at her. "This word, it is difficult, soo . . ."

Antonella interrupts, "No, suc . . ."

"Suc-sex-ful," says Piero.

Antonella corrects him again, punching each syllable, "Success-ful."

As we turn the corner, Piero giggles, "The gondoliers, they get the girls."

With his hands waving melodramatically and his bald head bouncing happily, he plays the gondolier on the prowl, singing, "The moon. Me and you and the lagoon. Oh my, I feel romantic today. I don't know why. My heart is going boing boing. May I offer you a small special ride for free later on? Try something different with me. Here grab my oar." Grabbing Antonella from behind around the waist as if she's about to fall from a gondola, he says, "Be careful, you can fall."

Pushing Piero away, Antonella says, "Gondoliers are the worst.

Here, if a woman marries a gondolier and expects him to be true, we say she has hams over her eyes."

Piero, with suddenly sad eyes, says, "This is true."

Antonella adds, "But I think any Italian woman who trusts her husband has the hams over her eyes. The newspaper said ninety-seven percent of Italian

"The gondoliers, they get the girls."

men cheat. I believe this. It is easy for them because for them sex is for the body and not the mind. When a woman falls in love, she can leave her husband in five minutes. A man can have many affairs and never think about leaving his family. For him, sex is only the body."

We walk to Piazza San Marco, enjoying the Venetian night. The orchestra plays as if refusing to go home. The vast, nearly empty square is claimed by two seniors, waltzing like they did fifty years ago. They twirl gracefully round and round as we pass. The woman smiles with her eyes closed. In Venice, love is a triangle: you, your partner, and the city.

The Stendhal Syndrome

Casanova's defense could have been simply, "It was Venice."

I tell Piero and Antonella about the night I was with a tour group of older American women gazing at the Bridge of Sighs. We were talking about Casanova, the famous Italian author and lover who was sentenced for spying in the Doges Palace. He crossed that saddest of bridges, casting one last look at Venice, before descending into the prison.

My tour group and I were absorbed in Venice. Suddenly, as if stepping out of an old movie, a debonair Italian man walked up, embraced a woman from my group, and gave her a deep and passionate kiss. Her glasses nearly tumbled into the canal. Five other women lined up and took their turn.

The man walked back into his movie and Dave, my assistant guide, took off his shoes, stripped to his boxers, and dove into the canal. Venice is beauty. While the Alps are also beauty, they smell like God. Venice smells like a woman.

For some, the beauty of Venice can be an overdose. The nineteenth-century French novelist and art critic Stendhal became physically ill in Italy, overcome by trying to absorb it all. He gave his name to a syndrome all travelers risk.

Arlene had a classic case of the Stendhal Syndrome. A few years ago, she was on one of our tours a day ahead of one I was leading. Throughout the trip from Amsterdam to the Rhine to the castles of Bavaria she left me notes and messages describing her ecstasy. In the Tirol she left me a postcard—which I still keep on my office wall—of hang gliders soaring through the Alps past King Ludwig's fairy-tale castle of Neuschwanstein. She circled a distant glider and marked it, "This is me!"

My arrival in Venice was initially uneventful. As usual, I marched quickly ahead of my group to the hotel to get room assignments arranged so the road-weary gang could go immediately to their rooms and relax. As I approached the hotel, a chill filled the alley. The boys at the corner gelato stand looked at me as if I were about to be gunned down.

Then, from the dark end of the valley, I saw her. Sprinting at me was a beautiful blonde American, hair flying like a Botticelli maiden, barefoot, shirt half off, greeting me as a drunk bride waiting for her groom. It was Arlene.

I climbed with her up the long stairway to the hotel lobby, humoring her as she babbled about how she loved Venice and she loved me and life was so wonderful. Sergio, my friend who ran the hotel, said simply, "Okay, Rick, now she is yours."

Arlene had flipped out the day before. Her tour guide opted to leave her in Venice and let me handle the problem. Sergio had watched her all day long. Taking me to her room, an exhausted Sergio explained, "She threw her passport and room key from the breakfast room into the Grand Canal. Look at this room." She had been given the tiny room normally reserved for bus drivers. It looked like a wind chime sounds—strewn with dainties and cute knickknacks.

Sergio said if she continued to run half-naked through the streets, she'd be arrested. A doctor on the tour sedated her the best he could. My assistant guide, role-playing the happy groom, took Arlene by ambulance boat to the hospital while I carried on with the tour. Arlene, a sensitive and creative person, had thrown away her regulatory drugs and overdosed on Venice.

Later, while waiting for her husband to call from the States, I packed up her things. Underwear was draped from old-time Venice prints on the wall. Tiny touristy souvenirs—a doll in a dirndl, a tiny glass bear with a red nose, a cow creamer, three shiny Mozart balls, and so on—were lined up on the windowsill and around the top of the dresser.

Arlene's husband flew over and checked her out of the hospital. With the help of her medication, she recovered and went on to love Italy some more. Upon our return, she had flowers waiting for us at the Europe Through the Back Door office.

We understood. It was Venice.

CHAPTER SIX

FLORENCE

*"I hate this Fellini image of a poor Italy . . .
old women dressed in black. I am tired of the
question 'Does your grandmother wear black?'
I say, 'Yes, even her underwear.'"*

After Venice, with its mysterious and feminine charms, my next
stop is the more straightforward Florence. Florence stokes the
humanist in me. It bolsters my confidence and gives me energy. I
can happily lose myself in Venice, Siena, or Rome and just wander.
But the city of Leonardo and Michelangelo is best seen with a careful plan. First on my list of places to visit is the Academy Gallery.

Entering the Academy Gallery is like entering the Church of
David, a temple of humanism. At the high altar stands the perfect man, Michelangelo's colossal statue of David. Like a
Renaissance statue of liberty, *David* represents humankind finally
stepping out of medieval darkness and declaring "I can."

Despite the confidence of our almost post-religious age,
David addresses a more persistent darkness as he turns tourists
into seekers. This hunk of marble offers a light that shines not
on sixteenth-century peasants but on us . . . today.

This 500-year-old slingshot-toting giant-slayer is the symbol of
Florence. The city's other treasures are largely ignored by the hordes
who roam the streets with one statue at the top of their sightseeing
list. Nearby buildings post signs that read: "This is not *David*."

Each morning the line forms as tourists wait patiently to enter the temple. As at any pilgrimage site, the nearby streets are lined with Lourdes-type shops selling *David* icons.

Worshiping at the Church of David

Inside, smartly dressed ushers collect an offering of admission tickets. Dropping mine in the basket, I turn the corner and enter a large nave. Six unfinished statues—brute bodies fighting the rock—line the room leading to *David*. *David's* feet are at a level just above the sea of tourists' heads. Round arches and a dome hover above him like architectural halos. People only whisper. Like sound-bite prayer candles, flash attachments pop. Couples hold each other tighter in his presence, their eyes fixed on the statue.

The scene is black and white under a sky light. I don't miss the color. I wouldn't want color. *David* is beyond color, even beyond gender.

David is fundamentally human. Gathered with people from all nations, I look up to him. Tight-skirted girls who'd cause commotion in the streets go unnoticed as macho men fold their hands. Students commune with Michelangelo on their sketch pads. Kamikaze sightseers pause. Tired souls see the "sure you can" in *David's* eyes.

David is the god of human triumph. Clothed only in confidence, his toes gripping the pedestal, he seems ready to step into the future.

I have only one problem with *David*. The Bible says we're made in God's image. Looking at this statue, I feel it's *David*, not me, who's made in the image of God. I get small as I approach the altar and don't know if I should feel inspired or worthless. Suddenly, what's supposed to be an energizing boost to my self-confidence becomes only a light illuminating my weakness.

Tourists share the pews with Michelangelo's miserable stone prisoners. Also known as "the Slaves," they wade wearily through murky darkness, bending their heads under the hard truth of their mortality.

Michelangelo thought of himself only as God's tool, revealing the beauty that the Creator had put into the marble. Michelangelo's black bust sits sadly in the corner, ignored by his fans. In spite of his success in sculpting *David*, Michelangelo looks at the floor, distraught, wart on his furled brow. His mortality is also exaggerated in the shadow of his towering creation.

I'm with Michelangelo—and the Prisoners. A passing tour guide says, "The prisoners are struggling to come to life." But I see them dying—giving up the struggle, wearily accepting an inevitable defeat. There's a religious message here. Mortality is only a defeat in terms of life on earth. Michelangelo is saying: To overcome ego, set your sights on God.

The Prisoners were intended for the unfinishable tomb of Pope Julius II, a man remembered today mostly for his Vatican-sized ego. Julius is history, the Prisoners bow their heads, and Michelangelo's chisel is lost.

Only *David* stands high, saying in marble eloquence two very different things. As every guide knows, he's the underdog, taking on the neighborhood bully. The message here: "Life is worth the effort." But today I'm getting another message: life on earth—no matter how grand—is transitory . . . just an overrated speed bump in the divine scheme of things.

Michelangelo intended to show the soul imprisoned in the body. While the Prisoners' legs and heads disappear into the rock, their chests heave and their bellies shine. Looking for help, I say to the woman next to me, "Each belly is finished, as if it was Michelangelo's target . . . the handhold of the soul."

Without missing a beat, she replies, "That's the epigastric area. When you die, this stays warm longest. It's where your soul exits your body."

She introduces herself as Carla and her friend as Anne-Marie, both nurses from Idaho. Carla turns from the Prisoners to *David*, raises her opera glasses, and continues, "And *David's* anticupital space is perfectly correct."

"Anti-what?" I say, surprised by this clinical approach to *David.*

"That's the space inside the elbow. Look at those veins. They're perfect. He'd be a great IV start. And the sternocleidomastoid muscle—the big one here," she explains running four slender fingers from her ear to the center of her Florence T-shirt, "is just right."

Carla burrows back into the binoculars for a slow head-to-toe pan and continues to narrate her discoveries. "You can still see the drill holes under his bangs. There's a tiny chip under his eye . . . sharp lips . . . *yeow.*"

Her friend, Anne-Marie, muses, "They should make that pedestal revolve."

Carla, still working her way down *David,* dreams aloud. "Yeah, pop in one hundred lire; get three hundred sixty slow-moving degrees of *David.* He's anatomically correct. Not as moving as the *Pièta,* but really real."

"He feels confident facing Goliath," I say.

Like a bratty sister, Anne-Marie lowers her point-and-shoot, and says, "Well, he's standing there naked so he must be pretty confident."

Turning to Carla, she observes, "The ears are ugly. The pubic hair's not quite right. And his right hand is huge. They always say to check out the fingers if you wonder about the other appendages. So what's the deal?"

"The guidebook says that's supposed to be the hand of God," Carla explains. "You can't measure the rest of *David* by 'the hand of God.'"

Settling back into a more worshipful frame of mind, Anne-Marie ponders aloud, "The Bible says he was like twelve or fourteen."

"This is no fourteen-year-old," says Carla, still lost in her binoculars.

I ask, "What's *David* telling us?"

"He says God made people great," says Anne-Marie.

I say, "No, maybe it's *David* who's made in God's image, and *David* makes it clear that we fall short."

Zipping her opera glass into her daybag, Carla looks into the eyes of *David*. "No," she says. "I think we're each great. And Michelangelo's giving us a sneak preview of heaven. . . ."

Anne-Marie finishes her thought. "Where . . . someday . . . we won't need these binoculars and cameras."

The guards begin to usher people out. I whisper, "I like that." Then, needing a few extra minutes to do my annual slow stroll around *David*, I say *"ciao"* and drift away from the nurses.

David's purity, truth, and beauty are timeless. He was the symbol of a city that led Europe into a new age. And he remains the symbol of a culture in search of inspiration. For 500 years, *David* has stood tall, alone, and just about ready for a haircut, encouraging mortals, turning tourists into seekers and nurses into pilgrims, and shining light on a dark age.

Italian Humanism

At blockbuster European sights—like the Acropolis, the Pantheon, and here at *David*—I try to be the last person ushered out at closing. As the guard nudges me along, I turn and look back to savor the moment when it's just me and a relic of my culture. I find it easiest when I am alone, in the presence of these wonders from the past, to remember, praise, and even worship what we as a culture have accomplished.

Mixing private time with these relics and quality time with European friends is my recipe for good travel. And now it's time for a friend. Late for my appointment, I rush from *David* to the square in front of the Palazzo Vecchio, where I will meet Manfredo.

Manfredo, who runs the hotel I call home in Florence, is calm and classy. Even though he's ten years younger than I am, he seems deeper, more caring and mature. His face is round and serious. With his tightly cropped beard and black hair combed back, he looks like a thin and thirty Pavarotti.

Manfredo is a master at keeping his slice of Italy running smoothly. Once, when I needed a haircut on a Monday—a sacred day off for Italian barbers—Manfredo found a way. On the next trip, he presented me with a fine Italian shirt saying gently, "You

are a successful travel writer. Now you can wear a good shirt."
When my wife and I forgot our stroller on a family tour a few years
later, Manfredo came to the rescue. He motorscootered it to an
autostrada rest stop for a precision pick-up as our tour bus drove
north from Rome past Florence. And now, thoughtfully, he just
happens to be precisely as late as I am. Arriving simultaneously at
the bronze plaque marking the spot where Savaronola was burned,
he greets me with just the correct number of cheek kisses and
shakes my hand with both of his.

Manfredo introduces me to his friend Roberto, a Sienese tour
guide, and proposes that we walk while we talk. Strolling by the
busy tables of an outdoor trattoria, I share my conflicting theories
of the church of *David* and ask, "Did Michelangelo carve *David* to
say Italians are no longer in the Dark Ages or to say that life on
earth is only the appetizer . . . the antipasto?"

"And how would you like your main course, spicy or sweet?"
jokes the pint-sized but cocky Roberto. With his tiny glasses,
scholarly scarf, and a sarcastic intensity, he reminds me of an
Italian Trotsky. Being fond of Manfredo, Trotsky, and Italy, I an-
ticipate a fine time.

Manfredo does his best to be Yankee-direct with me, his time-
is-money American friend. He answers, "*David* is the champion of
humanism. Italy, it is the birthplace of humanism. I try to explain
to the Americans this. That there are ten thousand Italys. In the
Middle Ages we were only in city-states. People lived only inside
city walls. And this forces humanism."

I ask, "What is humanism to you?"

"Humanism is self-confidence in *people*. In the Middle Age
times, people only prayed in church. They felt helpless. Life was
like the weather. You had no control. Then, with the Renaissance,
we gain the confidence."

"Is this anti-Christian?" I ask.

"No. It was scientific, but it was not anti-Christian. For
Michelangelo, the best way to obey God was to use the talent that
God gives him."

Roberto adds, "And humanism is a community working

together. We were divided until 1870. To survive, each state was self-reliant. Every city has its home university. You don't want to depend on other city for nothing . . . water, university, culture, they try always to be the best."

Grabbing my elbow, Manfredo drags me to a point where I can see the towering white and red dome of Florence's cathedral. He says, "Sometimes this competition was ridiculous." He points out a strip of plain brick around the drum of the dome with fine marble work below and above it. At one point, Manfredo explains, even though the city had no money to continue the cathedral project they refused to stop. They couldn't bear to be humiliated by their neighbors for running out of funds. Slowly they marked time, laying the cheap bricks, until they were able to finish in good style.

"But *David* stands alone," I counter, "not part of a community."

Roberto dismisses my observation and continues. "*David* symbolized a community," he says. "The community of Florence. Outside of the walls it is only you, God, and thieves. This is the reason Italy was the most urban part of Europe in the Middle Ages."

Manfredo adds, "And with *David* as its honorary citizen, Florence believed it was the most . . . ahh . . . "

"Cultivated," says Roberto.

"Yes, the most cultivated of Italian cities," Manfredo agrees. "Because of the bandits, we needed the city walls. We wanted the walls."

Roberto swipes a packet of long skinny breadsticks from a streetside table and offers to share them. "Every city had visible limits," he says. "The north gate and south gate. These gates defined the world for that person. For this reason I am Sienese first. After that, I am Italian."

Manfredo—like *David*, taller than the average Italian—seems to grow two inches. Flipping his scarf grandly over his shoulder he says, "And I am number one a Florentine, then Tuscan, then Italian, then European."

Nursing a foot injury, little Roberto limps and scurries at the same time, as if determined not to miss a lick of the conversation and to keep Siena properly represented. Pointing a breadstick at the Palazzo Vecchio, the crenelated symbol of city government, he continues, "The bishops, nobles, and the traders, they were always fighting. The city halls organized this chaos. They were important for the peace. In Florence and in Siena, the tallest tower is on the city hall—not the church. Siena's tower is the tallest in Italy. I feel my roots when I say this. There was a time when Italy was writing the world's history."

Manfredo adds, "What we are doing now is nothing. We only sit on our beautiful past. This is the American age."

Roberto, sounding angry not at America but at Italy, declares, "America is running the fastest, taking the chances, and leaving its mark. America will fill the history books."

Palazzo Vecchio

Enjoying our animated conversation, I walk with my friends back to our starting point, the Piazza Signoria. The tower of Palazzo Vecchio, Florence's city hall, stands high above the square. Blocky, five-story Renaissance-style buildings, sporting every imaginable shade of brown, hold back the crush of the city, creating a vast stony square fronting the rusticated city hall. Cafés landscape their corners of the square with flower boxes and people-filled tables.

Ignoring the tourist crowds and jaunty horse carriages, well-dressed locals spill their welcomes on each other. Pigeons spy a rare piece of open square, spread their tails like fans, and skid to earth. They strut around for a moment and fly off looking for something better.

Next to the city hall, the loggia, a covered courtyard filled with statues, faces the square. It's a kennel of mythical memories: horrified women squirming away from ancient rapes, sage old men sharing philosophy with pigeons, and burly jocks clubbing wild centaurs. A replica *David* marks the spot where the original once stood, guarding the Medici's palace.

The fake *David* seems like a souvenir of those glory days when Florence graduated from being one of Tuscany's big three with arch-rivals Pisa and Siena to the undisputed big kid on the Italian block. But with goony eyes and a pigeon-dropping wig, David seems dumbfounded as tourists picnic at his feet and two police-women clip-clop by on horseback. I scan the *piazza*, its decorated tables positioned for just the right views, and tell Manfredo and Roberto, "This is one of Italy's great squares."

Suddenly defensive, the squirrelly Sienese Roberto asks, "But do you know Siena's Campo?"

"Of course," I assure him. "It's the best city square in Europe." And it really is. Many travelers share sunset memories of Siena's vast brick square. It's a fan-shaped beach without sand or water where the sun and the moon set the tempo. I remembered my last visit. I wandered among lovers strumming guitars and each other's hair. As always, Siena's Campo immersed me in a troubadour's world where bellies become pillows and the community comes to-gether. But not knowing anyone, I felt like an old man in wingtips.

As if attracted by the same ambience, Siena's pigeons gather atop the Campo fountain. They line up and patiently wait their turn. Finally, each gets a chance to skate gingerly down the snout of a marble lion to peck at the water squirting from its mouth.

I tell Roberto, "I love the fountain with the skating pigeons."

Roberto, hopping around Manfredo to walk closer to me, says, "Yes, but this is a new fountain. Before, there stood a statue of Venus."

"What happened to Venus?"

"You know today we joke about how my city is the best," Roberto says, "but before, this was very, very serious. For exam-ple, one time a plague killed most of Siena. Our monks blamed this Venus statue. So we broke it into tiny pieces, put it in bags, and buried it around the walls of Florence. We hoped to share this plague."

Manfredo counters Roberto by walking us past the confused David and into the long arcaded Uffizi museum courtyard. We stop in the center. The permanent line of tourists waits in the shade of the portico to see the Uffizi's best-anywhere collection of Italian paintings. They stand patiently—as if waiting for a ride at Disney-land. Lounging between the columns, artists sketch tourists and display their work. And filling the niches around us are statues of Leonardo, Dante, Lorenzo the Magnificent, and a dozen other Renaissance greats—each life-sized and peeking alertly out at the crowd. Sweeping his hand around the courtyard, as if to acknowledge a triumphant orchestra, Manfredo says simply, "Florentines, every one of them."

I'm enjoying the Siena-Florence tit-for-tat and wonder how Roberto will respond for Siena. Leaving the Uffizi courtyard, we cross a street and belly up to the black stone railing overlooking the river Arno, which cuts through Florence.

Roberto takes off his wire-rimmed glasses for emphasis and says, "Except for Manfredo, I have just one good friend in Florence. His name? Arno."

Manfredo explains, "His *friend* is this river. He talks about the terrible floods. This rivalry gives us centuries of problems. But it was also a good thing. Much of our best art was done only for the pride of our city."

Looking across the river, Manfredo continues. "Real Florentines are rare. In the 1800s this was a small town. Today the last of old Florence is living only across the river. Near Piazza Santa Maria del Carmine the people still talk to each other out the windows."

Emphasizing each point as if holding a conductor's baton, Manfredo says, "Many generations, they share one house. They do everything as a group. The women play bingo together on Sunday afternoon. It is a proud neighborhood."

I break in. "Can you two talk with your arms tied down?"

Roberto strikes back, saying, "Like you Americans at a party without a glass to hold."

"Really," I ask him, "why do you talk with your hands?"

Roberto, placing his hands deliberately into his coat pockets and doing a kind of straitjacket struggle, says, "I think it's because of many invasions. It is in our heritage, trying to communicate with people who speak a different language."

"No," says Manfredo—one hand still at large, "because before we had a thousand city-states, today we have a thousand dialects. Italy is a young nation. To communicate you need hands.

Italians, we are patient . . . we want to understand. But it is not all the time easy."

"This is a problem," says Roberto. "Many Americans don't understand the little meanings of the hand motion. To understand Italian, you must understand the hands."

Quizzing his friend to illustrate, Roberto rubs his thumb and first finger together. Manfredo answers, "Money, expensive."

Screwing his forefinger into his cheek boyishly as a cute girl walks by, Roberto says, "This means something good . . . like a beautiful woman."

Manfredo adds, "Or delicious food."

I drag my fingertips up my chin quickly twice. Roberto translates, "I don't care, it's not interesting for me."

Feigning suspicion all around, the three of us each pull an eyelid down, Italian for "be careful, be on guard."

Manfredo concedes, "It is true, we Italians are lively, especially in giving directions. We wave our arms, even take steps . . ."

Roberto finishes the sentence, ". . . and by the end of the directions you are already there."

The Coffee's Good, but Fellini is Dead

Roberto leads us into a too-crowded café and says, "Two o'clock. This is the after-lunch rush. Everybody is here. But the coffee here is worth the wait."

We crowd into Caffe Fiorenza, pass pizza-sized round tables, and find a place at the bar under a pastel fresco of Renaissance Florence. Cut-glass sconces wash light across polished, knotty hardwood walls. Under whitewashed arched ceilings, the mirrors give the false impression of spaciousness. The happy crowd keeps a crew of trim waiters in white shirts and black vests busy. Three extravagant bouquets of sugar cones decorate the end of the bar closest to the street. And a multicolored see-through plastic bowl of tiny plastic shovels promises countless delights. But all attention is directed at the industrial strength espresso machine directly in front of us.

"In Italy, isn't coffee coffee?" I ask.

"Yes, like wine is wine," responds a sarcastic Roberto.

"Downstairs from my house is a famous bar. The coffee is . . . eeeeeh . . . good for washing the feet."

Manfredo agrees. "I have four bars near my house," he says. "One is very good. If it is closed, number two is okay. If this is closed also, I have no coffee."

Manfredo points to the dark brown stream. "You can see the difference when it comes out of the machine. When the beans are ground correctly, it comes first creamy brown in color, then darker. What do you want?"

Without thinking I say, "Cappuccino."

Roberto rolls his eyes. "Only the tourist drinks cappuccino after lunch. It is incredible. No one in Italy takes cappuccino after eleven in the morning."

Manfredo says "*basso,*" and Roberto asks for his coffee "*alto.*" They wave at me, saying in a tired unison, "cappuccino."

In a two-handed dance the bar man dumps the old grounds, fills new grounds, tamps it down, latches it on, flips on the water, and waits. Every coffee drinker has a style. Your barista knows how you like your coffee.

"I like mine *basso,*" Manfredo illustrates by holding up a tiny coffee spoon. "Half a spoon tall. Espresso *alto* is tall—with more water."

Catching on, I say, "Americans like their coffee very tall."

Looking over his tiny cup between sips, Roberto agrees, "Yes, like *sciacquatura per piatti* . . . the water you use to clean the plates."

"When we were in Florida we saw a wonderful Italian coffee shop," Manfredo says. "Ready for a good coffee, we go in. We get a ridiculous tall cup. If we are so thirsty, we have a Coke."

Wounded, I defend my country. "In the United States, espresso is very popular."

Roberto shakes his head and says, "But in the States you don't push down the grounds enough."

"But if you push down too hard, the water goes around, not through," Manfredo cautions. "Push the beans down just right and the water goes through slowly . . . it stays longer in the grounds and takes more flavor . . . stronger flavor."

Enjoying that flavor, I notice a huge copy of a Botticelli painting on the wall. It's *Primavera*, showing the birth of the goddess Spring.

Botticelli, my favorite Florentine painter, painted a splendid innocence where a maiden can walk barefoot through a garden scattering flower petals from a fold in her dress and call it a good day's work—where three graces can dance naked with no more fanfare than the happy do-si-do of butterflies. To me, the delicate face of Botticelli's Spring is the face of the Renaissance—and an old college girlfriend.

Roberto notices me admiring the painting and whispers, "*Bella.*"

I say, "*Si*, I fell in love with this face many years ago. And I found a girl to match. Her name was Cheryl."

Cheryl was just like this painting. Wispy blond hair, thin nose, thin neck, delicate and innocent. Behind sleepy eyelids, her peaceful blue eyes said, "I'm yours."

"And what happened to Cheryl?" asks Roberto.

I explained how ripping Spring out of that dream and into my arms didn't work. A poster of Spring now hangs in my garage. And I live happily upstairs—not with a classical goddess, but with Anne.

At the next table, a shopping bag rings and an old woman with tinted hair pulls out a phone.

I say, "Botticelli is gone. These days, even Fellini's gone."

Flipping the big steel lid down on the bartop tub of sugar, Roberto says, "Fellini's Italy is dead. It is time to show a real Italy. Movies promote this traditional, quaint *la dolce vita* image. I hate this Fellini image of a poor Italy . . . old women dressed in black. I am tired of this question, 'Does your grandmother wear black?' I say, 'Yes, even her underwear.' Today it is only the tourists who say '*Il dolce far niente*'—the sweetness of doing nothing."

Manfredo cuts in. "My father lived *il dolce far niente*. He said, 'If you feel that you want to work, sit down. Wait. It will pass.' But today, we do not want the 'sweetness of doing nothing,' we want the sweetness of enjoying the good lifestyle . . . no job problems, go home for lunch. But today in Italy, you cannot live without longer hours and more work."

"Fifteen years ago Florence was empty in August," I observe, "Now the long August holiday—the Ferragosto—is gone."

Hunched over his tiny coffee and looking more like Trotsky than ever, Roberto agrees. "Ferragosto is now only little weekends and maybe a week around August 15. Before, even restaurants closed for a month in summer to go to the beaches with their families. *La dolce vita.* Today it is only a TV jingle."

"And with less leisure time, Italians want to buy maximum *dolce,*" says Roberto. "Italians, we lost the sense of having fun without spending money. We buy only the status symbols. Yes. We spend our lives working like slaves to get a second home by the seaside and a mobile phone."

"Look at these young people," Manfredo says, waving at the tables of chic students. "They dress like models. They lose the pleasure of the simple things. They talk money in the restaurants on cell phones. The urban Italians, they are narcissists. If they are not like the magazine image they are nothing."

"Okay . . . this is the money and this is my life," Roberto says, blocking out parts of the table. "It is a battle. Italians are stressed people."

"It sounds like America," I say.

Manfredo agrees. "Yes, we are following your style. The Greek people and the Spanish are not following. The Spanish people, they work like slaves but they have incredible energy for fun. The Greeks, they are just crazy. They don't think what will be tomorrow. It is a southern mentality, like Sicily and Africa: if they normally make one hundred thousand lire in one day and today they make two hundred thousand, tomorrow . . . *il dolce far niente.*"

Roberto says, "The tourists can do the Fellini thing. Take your own rhythm, try just to catch the atmosphere. For the modern Italian, Italy is not a painting or a sculpture. It is consuming."

Downing the last of his coffee, he concludes, "Yes. Fast, good living."

Wasps, Stadium Violence, and Pickpockets

Italian good living may be a pleasurable assault on the senses, but as we step out of the café and back into the streets it is clear that the Italian *vita* is not all *dolce*.

Manfredo hollers above the drone of the motorbikes, "What is yellow and black? It makes a buzz like a mosquito and flies more than eighty kilometers in one day—not too fast but with no problems."

I guess, "A bee . . . a honeybee?"

"No," says Manfredo. "It looks the same but makes no honey. It is a wasp—*vespa* in Italian."

Florentine streets swarm with pesky Vespas—frail-looking motorscooters with small wheels, a flat floorboard big enough to rest your feet side by side, tall windshield, and a black seat long enough for two. As pedestrians slip gingerly by us on single-file sidewalks, the streets teem with motorcycles and Vespas.

As we skirt a construction site that takes up the sidewalk, a fearless Vespa passes a lumbering city bus, sending the three of us up against the scaffolding. A block later, tightroping between too-big buildings and bully traffic, Manfredo points to a line of twelve-foot-tall doors. He says, "Long before the Vespa, Renaissance giants walked these streets."

At a stoplight, he says, "Before we had too much traffic in Florence. We make a new law: no cars in the center. So today, we have traffic even worse . . . no cars, yes. But too many Vespas. In Florence, motorscooters are higher on the head . . ." (Roberto interprets: "per capita") ". . . than any place. Vespa is easy parking, fast in town, easy repair, not expensive. In Italy the typical family dream is two cars and a Vespa. Fifty cc is normal in city—with one-twenty-five you can go to the top of Norway."

Vespas motorized Italy after the war. Like America's Model T, it brought a revolution in mobility to the working class. Anyone could afford one. Anyone could drive one. The signature photo of Italy in the 1950s, symbolizing the birth of a modern and prosperous nation, is a suburban family of four packed onto their Vespa, with a picnic basket going to the beach. Back then, the woman sat sidesaddle wearing a bonnet and never driving.

Surveying the street—a fashion show on wheels—it's clear those days are long gone.

"This is freedom for us," Manfredo says, "No helmet and no license required."

"Italians are narcissists," Roberto adds. "We don't like the helmet."

Like a marine falls on the barbed wire fence to provide his comrades a way to pass, Roberto limps into the street. Sidestepping a couple on their motorbike he beckons for me to cross—waving the palm of his hand down toward his knee as Italians do—saying, "Especially in Florence, the motorbike is independence. It is sexual power. To be modern, you must have a motorbike."

Darting ahead of me, he shoots his head and hands up, saying, "Vespas . . . if I can, I want to kill everyone with a Vespa."

We step down a quiet side street and stop outside a café filled with men crowded around a TV watching soccer—football to the rest of the world. Roberto says, "For Italy in the 1960s opium was the religion of the masses . . . Marx got it backward. But today it is football."

Manfredo agrees. "I read it in the newspaper, a cardinal said, 'Football is the religion of Italy.' Sunday is the only day for the family in Italy. And we spend it around the TV, watching football."

And it's a violent religion. In Italy, the 1970s were a time of political violence—fighting on the streets and at universities. In the 1980s, the political agenda of the '70s was accomplished and this fighting moved to the stadium. Rather than political assassinations, headlines reported football violence: "Roman fan kills Lazio supporter with flare gun."

Stepping into the smoky café, plain and unglamorous compared to Caffe Fiorenza, Roberto whispers, "The press stirs up the violence. You have your sexygate. We have footballgate. We play the game Sunday. Then we talk about it Monday to Saturday. The biggest newspaper in Italy is only for sport, for football."

Manfredo says, "Yes, football is big in Italy. We have no choice. My father said, 'Support Rome, or you get no food in this house.'"

According to Manfredo, in Europe football replaces medieval violence. You cannot stop violence, but you can regulate it. The team captain is the equivalent of a medieval military leader. European fans don't applaud their opponents' good play. They're the enemy. In the United States, sports may be more violent on the field, but not in the seats. In Italy, simply being in the stadium can be dangerous. Manfredo claims the least violent stadium in Italy is Naples—because the streets are violent.

Roberto, whose hometown, Siena, is famous for the brutal horse race called the Palio, says, "There are no rules in the Palio. It is the most violent game in Europe . . . in the most peaceful city in Italy. In Siena, we have no crime, no drugs. Just the Palio. People with anger only wait for the day."

"And peaceful Siena has the most violent stadium in its league," says Manfredo.

Roberto admits, "Inside of every Sienese, there is a piece of our republic. We lost our republic but the medieval anger survives. It is in our blood."

Looking pointedly at Manfredo, Roberto adds, "I like Turin because it is the enemy of Florence."

Back on the street, we round the corner and walk onto the Ponte Vecchio, Florence's famous shop-lined oldest bridge. Sugar cookie–colored walls block views of the river below. But the river to watch is the steady flood of hot, tired tourists. Weaving in and out of the crowd, three children in filthy clothes surround us begging, "Need money. Need money."

Manfredo stamps his foot, like a kid scaring pigeons. They scatter off the bridge, darting almost magically through the traffic.

Manfredo says, "Gypsy children. It is their duty to steal from the tourists. Tourists must be without *pietà*."

Roberto translates, "Pity."

"Police are frustrated," Manfredo continues. "They stop the children today. And tomorrow they are again on the streets. These people are smart, they keep only the money. Money has no name on it."

Across the street, a well-attired businessman shoos the exhaust-stained children away like large pesky flies. Manfredo says, "We have laws to protect people from other countries. These people are political refugees from Yugoslavia . . . Montenegro. This is their way of life. No law can change them. If they go to school and learn a new way, their parents beat them back to the old way. Fathers do nothing—only count the money and drink. They can steal one million a day in Florence."

I estimate out loud, "Six hundred dollars."

"Last year I went to the camping place for the Gypsies looking for my stolen car." Pinching his nose, Manfredo continues, "It is like another world. As you arrive they already know you are not part of them. They ask, 'Why you here?' They live without water, without nothing. At the camp I remember the eyes. Very, very strange eyes. It is dangerous. You see no Fiats, only Mercedes and BMWs . . . these cost seventy or eighty million lire. Why? This is the question for me. Old clothes but new cars. Satellite TV but no shoes on the children. Nothing to eat. Everything to drink. It is a very, very dirty life."

Then, with sudden charity, Roberto concedes, "At least they don't use knives."

"You don't need city walls anymore," I say, "just a moneybelt."

Manfredo adds, "That won't help you at the football stadium."

Roberto gets the last word. "Or under a Vespa."

Edible Patriotism

After a day absorbing Florence, I climb to the roof garden of my hotel for a break. From here, the bell towers and domes stand higher than the TV antennae. Beyond the city walls, it's a misty Leonardo terrarium. The cypress-stubbled hills of Tuscany cradle the city. I wait for the hourly choir of bells to silence the steady buzz of Vespas.

As bells ring, Manfredo joins me on the rooftop. It's one of those fine moments when the timeless beauty of a city overcomes all modern distractions. We savor it. The last bell to ring is the nearest. We watch as the flip-flopping bell coasts, the clapper no longer hits, and the humming bell gradually swings to a standstill. Manfredo, wearing a finely pressed new shirt and more the artistic gentleman than ever, lifts an arm toward the stairs and says, "It's eight o'clock. Come to eat."

Manfredo and Roberto direct me to the big chair at the head of the antique table. Plopping down I say, "*Io sono fame.*"

Manfredo's girlfriend, Ilaria, says, "You say, 'I am a hungry.' If you *are* hungry, perhaps you mean to say, '*Ho fame.*'"

She punctuates the correction by placing a plate of bruschetta in front of me. It's crowded with a dozen crispy slices of toasted bread lying crust to crust. Each slice looks like a little brown ship—a toothpick mast flying a garlic clove—sailing over its oily deck. The four of us hungrily destroy the tidy flotilla. Ripping off a mast and rubbing a sail on the crusty deck, I say, "My family eats bruschetta at home. But for us it is the best only in Italy."

"Good bruschetta needs real Tuscan bread," Roberto says. "This is made with only flour, water, and yeast. Great today. Hard tomorrow."

Manfredo adds, "And even if you could get the right bread, the oil in America—it is not right."

Ilaria, whose dark eyes, hair, and complexion seem to fit this centuries-old hotel, says, "Because bread gets old quickly, in Tuscany there are many dishes made with yesterday's bread."

In unison, all three labor through a short list as if it were long: "*Minestra di pane, ribollita, pappa al pomodoro.*"

Roberto explains, "*Ribollita* is for the poor. You cook and always stir together beans, cabbage, carrots, onions, old bread, and olive oil for at least two hours . . . very filling. It is not good with fresh bread."

Handing me an antipasto plate of smoked salamis and hearty cheeses, Manfredo says, "Salt . . . not necessary in Tuscan bread because here is the salt. I think American pioneers did not know to make a good salami or prosciutto so they could not preserve their meat properly. This is why you have the barbecue sauce. To hide this taste of rotting meat."

"Is there no barbecue sauce in Italy?" I ask.

"No," says Manfredo, "but I like very much to make buffalo wings."

He steps into his kitchen, then returns reading a small bottle. "This is what I like. Could you kindly send me a package of Frank's Original Red Hot Cayenne Pepper Sauce when you return home?"

When Italians sit down together for dinner, a special joy combusts out of their mutual love of good eating. The steam, the memories, the dreams—it's all about fine food.

Passing Ilaria the bowl of freshly grated parmesan cheese, Roberto says, "My wife was born in Florida . . . I know, strange because most people die there. In Florida—and I think everywhere in America—a restaurant is looking not for what is good food. What is good is what sells. Real lasagna is only this thick," he says, sticking his knife through two steamy inches of lasagna on the plate in front of him. "In the United States they make it twice this thick"—flipping another serving on top—"and they fill it with mozzarella."

As he says, "There is no mozzarella in lasagna!" the others cluck in agreement.

"Thick is what Americans want," says Manfredo, trying to sound understanding.

Roberto, talking through a mouthful of too-hot lasagna, continues, "If you go to an American restaurant and say the food is bad, you get a coupon for a free meal. More bad food. If you say the food is bad in a restaurant in Italy, you get kicked out. To get free food here, it is vice versa—you say, 'This is the best beefsteak I ever eat.' Chef will then say, 'You must try the dessert.' You say, 'Oh no.' He says, 'Here. Please. Take it for free.'"

"In a real Italian restaurant when you complain, the chef will tell you, 'I cooked this as a boy the way my grandmother cooked this,'" Manfredo says. "It cannot be wrong. In the United States, what is right is what sells." Roberto jumps in. "And the computer tells you what menu makes good business. In America, you eat first with your eyes and second with your mouth."

Not about to defend America in the battle of cuisines, I ask, "What about French food?"

Manfredo, peppering a puddle of olive oil on a small plate,

responds, "With the French there is two things great: their wine and their art. Since the time of Napoleon, they think only of their wine and their art. In the south they are like the Italians. From Paris and north, they are so proud they are boring."

Roberto says, "But the art in France is like the dust . . . it is everywhere. They don't study the art like the English. It is in their blood. They have good taste. Yes, they are boring—but they have good taste."

Manfredo dips his bread into the oil like a paintbrush. "Here in Italy," he says, "they drink our wine and say, 'Ah, this is good wine. The French wine is better, but this is good.'"

Tearing off a piece of bread and ramrodding it into Manfredo's oil, Ilaria says, "For me the French cheese is the Italian cheese with mold. If we have cheese that nobody buys, it gets moldy. After some days, it becomes perfect French cheese."

Raising my glass of wine I offer a toast to Italian food. "To *la cucina Italiana*."

Manfredo follows that, saying magnanimously, "To bacon and eggs." We all agree that American breakfasts are unbeatable.

"Omelets, hashbrowns," Roberto reminisces. "On my last visit to New York, I gain four kilos in three weeks."

Raising our glasses, we make another toast. "To American breakfasts."

CHAPTER SEVEN

ROME

*"I was born in Rome, and every time I come
to his square I feel the same emotion—like
the past is speaking to me."*

Rome, three hours south of Florence by train, is as far south as I will go on this trip. And it feels southern. Stepping out of Rome's Termini Station, a vast bus-filled square greets me with a blast of noise and traffic. The crowds, cars, and sprawling modern buildings dwarf the tiny crust of an ancient wall. The wall whispers this was the city of Caesar. But the rumble of a subway underneath and noise of the helicopter overhead say loud and clear that now Rome is modern, big city Italy.

A group of American schoolgirls marches by, staying close to their leader. Apparently she warned them about thieves and suggested they wear their rucksacks hanging in front for safety. Parading single file in front of me, they look like a pack of strange, paranoid kangaroo cubs following their mother.

A heavy woman lags behind her husband as they rush toward the station. Dragging her suitcases as if they were reluctant dogs, she yells, "Harold, wait for me!" Her camera hangs from her neck like a ball and chain. Her moneybelt hangs loosely outside her pants, lumpy with coins. Her sweater falls unnoticed from the leash on her suitcase. I grab it and run over to her.

"Rome," she says, sweaty hair pasted to her face. "Never again. I feel like a salt lick."

Her husband is now farther away. She takes the sweater and yells, "Harold!" before rumbling on.

Traditionally, pilgrims came to Rome to climb Biblical stairways on their knees. Today, many Americans tackle Rome with a similar spirit—ready to suffer. But for me, the ability to enjoy Rome is the mark of a good traveler. With charm, color, and cultural vibrancy, Rome ignores the tourist, and thrives.

Trastevere

In Italy "the other side of the tracks" is often found on the other side of the river. When you cross a river you rough up and colorize your experience of a big city. You lose the big museums, but you find the people. After dropping my bag at the hotel, I cross the Tiber.

I tackle Rome's Trastevere as if my high-school poetry teacher sent me here on a cultural scavenger hunt. Laundry and potted gardens fill the scene as if it were sketched by Chagall. Erosion eats at earthy walls while grannies—who brag that they've never crossed the river—grow old with the ivy. Sirens clash with church bells. Lovers ignore thieves. And soccer balls careen past a crusty wallpaper collage of posters and obituary notices.

The people of Trastevere still announce the death of a loved one by posting black and white fliers throughout the area. These obituary notices—once commonplace throughout Italy—are themselves in danger of dying. They're found only in places with a strong sense of community.

The church of Santa Maria in Trastevere is the thumbhole in this urban palette. Adventurous streets, like tiny rivers of paint globbed with Fiats and Vespas, spread out from Piazza Santa Maria into an urban jumble.

Venturing past an amorous young couple gently rocking on their Vespa, I lose sight of the church. More teenagers, riding double on their scooters, slalom around wares displayed on the sidewalk and pony-tailed men restoring furniture.

Very Italian names—Antonio, Massimo, Maria—are hollered

from fifth-floor balconies while baskets filled with gorgonzola, fava beans, and milk bottles are hoisted up and down. Scraps of sun tumble through cracked doors revealing old men who don't get out much anymore. Toddlers try to escape from second-floor balconies while older kids play soccer in the street, rattling World Cup dreams with head shots.

I dodge soccer balls and go deeper into the neighborhood feeling frustrated. Even with my camera hidden in my daybag, I am clearly a tourist. I suspect that to any local I am a stray voyeur at best.

In a tiny deli I break my budget defense rule of always asking the cost before ordering and just let the old lady in a young girl's dress make me a sandwich. But our conversation goes no further than a one-word discussion of the weather—"*caldo*"—and "*grazie*."

After wrapping my sandwich in newspaper and handing it over, she rejoins the card game in progress at the kitchen table across the street.

I sit on a bench to munch my sandwich, noting that this would give locals an easy opportunity to say, "*Buon appetito*." But the only word I hear comes after they walk by—a muffled "*turista*."

So, instead of joining the party, I'm left out. This most Roman of neighborhoods is the least accessible. Tourists are seen as invaders or curiosities rather than as guests or seekers. As if protecting its purity, Trastevere has closed its back door.

I walk back, passing the battery-powered candles of the last nook-and-cranny shrine in Trastevere before meeting the lifeless Tiber, which seeps toward the commanding dome of St. Peter's basilica. Tomorrow morning I'll be there. But now it's time for Rome's ritual stroll, the *passegiata*. I'm going to warm up my Roman wandering with a rendezvous with friends.

Rubbing Shoulders

I hop off the bus at Piazza del Popolo. Its centerpiece, an Egyptian obelisk, stands like an exclamation point marking the start of Via del Corso. This axis of modern Rome stretches from Piazza del

Popolo—appropriately named "Square of the People"—to the Capitoline Hill.

While I sit waiting for my friends, a sea of people, most clad in black, fills this boulevard, which cuts boldly through the heart of Rome. At the far end, capping the Capitoline Hill about a mile away, peeks a tiny bit of the massive Victor Emanuele II monument, that much-loathed glob of marble erected to honor the first king of a united Italy.

Italians hang on each other. Girls walk arm in arm while men adjust themselves. Italy is a land of people-watchers behind sunglasses. Local men have cell phones and cigarettes. Local women have shopping bags. Tourists have guidebooks, maps, and cameras. If you enjoy people-watching, it's hard not to love Italy.

As planned, Stefano and his wife, Paola, the thirty-something Italian couple I met on Mary's Place in Munich, meet me at the obelisk. In Munich I told them how much I enjoyed Europe's street life and how this is what I miss most when I return home. They promised me that the people-in-the-streets scene in Rome beat out the one in Munich.

They greet me as an old friend and Stefano promises, "Now we show you something you never see in Germany."

Each day from late afternoon through early evening the police block off Via del Corso and Rome's main drag becomes a pedestrian zone. We thread our way through a tangle of parked motorbikes, walk between twin churches that straddle the start of Via del Corso, and find ourselves in a meandering river of strolling Italians.

Stefano and Paola, although married just three years and without children, seem very domestic in this crowd. He is short and clean-shaven with a high forehead. She is shorter yet, with a head full of springy black curls. Happily holding hands, each with small, trendy black glasses that look like they were purchased at a two-for-one sale, they seem perfectly matched.

It's a scene of "cruising" but without cars. "In the evening," says Stefano, "people turn Rome's public places into small town squares."

"Most of these people live in the suburbs," Paola adds. "Rome's suburbs are very bad—only big apartment buildings. There is no public space so nice. So, logically, with the fine public spaces in the center of Rome, they come here. These are the *coatto*."

"*Coatto*—the young ones," Stefano explains. "Look at these people. They are all similar. The boys each have short hair, black leather bomber jackets, tight jeans, and maybe a scooter parked nearby."

"At this moment, throughout the Mediterranean, people are strolling," I remark. "In Spain it is the *paseo*. In Italy it is the *passeggiata*."

Stefano corrects me. "Maybe in Sorrento or Verona it is the *passeggiata*. But here with these *coatto*, we call this the *struscio*." He demonstrates by brushing his shoulder along Paola's.

Pushing him away playfully, Paola says, "The principle is looking for the boy or the girl. They walk and brush against each other. This is *struscio* . . . rubbing."

Like a mirage, a mustached grandpa pedals slowly through the crowd with a tiny grandson in sunglasses balanced on his handlebars. Pulling Paola out of the way, I say "*Scusi.*"

"We are friends now," she says, "so you can say *scusa*."

Stefano motions to the sea of black jackets filling the Via del Corso and explains, "This is good and bad. These are not high-class people. They only want to be à la mode. False Nikes, false Levis. This is a small part of the Roman people. But you see them because they are in the squares. This is good because it keeps the city with a human character. I don't think you see this in Atlanta."

Thinking of *passeggiatas* I've enjoyed in other Italian towns, I say, "Let's listen carefully. I like to hear the boys whisper '*bella*' and the girls whisper '*bello*.'"

Paola says, "Again, maybe in Sorrento or Verona. But here, you will hear '*buona*.' This is a cruder sound. '*Bella*' is too kind for this *struscio*."

Stefano says, "*Bella* is something you admire—without touching. *Bona* is something that is good . . . something . . . consumable. Even the girls, they say '*buono*.'"

Every block or two a church sits like a bulldog facing the

struscio, offering a detour. We step out of the crowded street and into a church. Paola gets a coin from Stefano and pops it into a candle box. Considering four ranks of plastic candles, she chooses two switches to flip. Two candles pop on and we enjoy a quiet moment.

Paola says, "Every time I go into a church, I light two candles: one for my mother's mother and one for my mother's father."

Stepping back outside, we cross Via del Corso, drop by a *gelateria* for small cups to go, and wander into a grid of cobbled traffic-free side streets. Stefano explains, "Now the character changes."

A classy woman in a stylish but too-warm coat and confident high heels steps out of a shop. The air is filled, just momentarily, with perfume. Here the people are older. No longer prowling, most walk contentedly with a well-dressed partner. The image, shops, and clientele change: Yves Saint Laurent, Versace, Roccobarocco, Ungaro. . . .

I say, " Do you know the word 'chic'?"

Stefano says, "Yes, this is an international word."

"What is chic?" I ask, scraping the bottom of my gelato cup. "Is smoking a cigarette chic?"

"It depends on how you smoke," Stefano says.

" . . . and what you smoke," adds Paola.

Passing a woman lounging on her scooter with a very thin cigarette, Paola and Stefano look at her and say in unison, "Chic."

"Even her scooter is chic—it's a classic," I note. "How old?"

"It only looks old," says Stefano. "It is classic design, from the '50s, but new."

We pass four men engaged in an animated argument around a parked scooter. They slap their hands, spin away from each other, and shake their heads in disbelief. Stefano says, "In Italy we're all professors—each person knows the correct way."

Paola pulls the tiny blue plastic scoop from her mouth. "We have a strong identity," she says. "If you tell ten Italians to produce this gelato spoon, tomorrow they have ten different variations. In the United States you are good students. You find the best way and then produce it correctly."

Stefano says, "Two French people are a partnership. Three Englishmen make a team. Four Italians are five different political parties. We never agree."

We leave the Via del Corso and wander through the dark and winding lanes of medieval Rome to Campo dei Fiori.

The rough-edged buildings surrounding Campo dei Fiori stand out against the black night sky as if part of an expertly lit stage set. Ivy climbs the walls and, from an abandoned apartment, a tree grows out of a window. Trattoria tables totter as street cats preen. The fountain—a large marble tub spilling water into a coin-filled pool—glimmers floodlit.

And in the center, a statue of Giordano Bruno stands tall marking the spot where this heretic was burned. He challenged the authority of the Church long before Martin Luther made this fashionable—here, a few Hail Marys from the Vatican, no less. I admire Bruno as I admire the priests of Central America who defy angry Vatican pronouncements saying, "Part of our vow of obedience to God is disobedience to the Church." Bruno symbolizes independent thinking and a strong faith.

The swarthy bronze statue towers above the square, a thriving flower market by day and people-filled hangout by night. Floodlights give the monk's body a sheen, but I find myself staring at his head. Buried deep inside his hood, it's mysteriously dark.

Stefano notices a black nose-shaped fountain next to the statue. Brushing a finger down his nose, he says, "We call this the Nasone." He stoops and plugs the spout, forcing water to arc up for an easy but sloppy drink for his wife.

Wiping the water from her cheek, Paola says, "Local boys say, 'Let's go out to the Nasone for a drink. I'll pay.'"

Sitting on a step under Bruno, we savor the square. Paola says, "I was born in Rome and every time I come to this square I feel the same emotion—like the past is speaking to me."

I say, "In America the past doesn't do a lot of talking."

"But in America, you have more respect for your culture," says Stefano.

This statement strikes a chord with Paola, who leans forward.

"Yes, this is true. At the Expo in Sevilla the Italy pavilion had original paintings and work by Leonardo. It was put in the corner with no good lighting. It was not important. But the American pavilion had only this big paper . . . "

Stefano clarifies. "It was your Declaration of Independence. First there was a movie so we could be . . . " —he breathes in and tumbles his hands—"maximum impressed."

Paola continues. "Then the door opens. We see a big, big, big room. In the middle is only this paper. It was fantastically lit. Dramatic. You don't have so much, but you show much more respect. Yes, this is one reason why I like the United States."

Stefano says, "At school in Italy, the teacher don't say, 'You are Italian, be proud.' In the United States you learn this. Or is this only the movie image?"

"No," I say, "it is this way. In the schools every morning children stand, put their hands on their heart and promise—in unison—to be loyal to our flag and country."

Stefano shakes his head and says, "Each morning they do this? Each morning the only thing we do in unison is drink cappuccino."

Leaving Bruno brooding over his square, we walk to a place Stefano says will be perfect for my guidebook. Two blocks off Campo dei Fiori, we turn a corner and come to a classic, crumpled little *piazza* filled with scooters. A grand but tiny neoclassical white church is crammed into the corner. And, on the far side, a single business is lit and open. The sign above the door says "Filetti di Baccala."

"Stefano, this is perfect," I say, walking ahead of my friends through the lonely rabble of motorbikes to the restaurant. A long line of tables covered with white paper tablecloths stretches to a neon-lit kitchen. The place is packed with locals. In the back, two grease-splattered cooks are busy cranking out *filetti di baccala* . . . fish sticks.

There's one table open, near the back past an old man in a black suit playing the violin. We limbo by the violinist and grab it. Above our table an old sign reads "Specialita Filetti di Baccala 60 lire." They're 5,000 lire now. The waiter drops a menu on our

table. Several appetizers and salads
but only one main course: *filetti di
baccala*. The harried waiter asks,
"*Da bere?*" ("To drink?")

With a tall bottle of white
wine, breaded and fried zucchini,
and a salad of greens I've never before encountered, we enjoy our
filet of cod. Far better than fish
sticks, it's about what you'd expect
at a top-notch London fish and
chips joint.

I don't tell my friends this is   *"A sweet caressing Roman wind"*
nothing new. But buried deep in
Rome, in a tarnished and varnished eatery, without a tourist in
sight—my fish sticks are a delight.

The violinist plays Sinatra's "My Way" to an appreciative
crowd. Eventually he makes his way to our table, standing just beyond Paola's plain but radiant face. It's a classic Roman moment.
Her dark brown eyes, framed by those little black glasses, are
locked on Stefano's. Tiny rings of pearls set in gold swing from her
ears. A gold necklace is a perfect complement to her smooth olive
complexion.

Like a hungry camera, my eyes compose the scene: carafe of
golden white wine shimmering in foreground, Paola's face looking
lovingly at her husband in the middle, and the violinist—jaw tight
on his instrument but still smiling—in the back. The happy chatter of people eating finishes off the scene.

As if for Paola, the musician plays a Roman anthem to the
night. Paola whispers to me, "This is *ponentino* . . . a special wind,
a sweet . . . ," brushing her hand gently along her cheek in search
of the word, "caressing Roman wind."

Then she and Stefano face the music and, with the entire
room, sing the song:

Rome don't be foolish tonight.
Give me the sweet wind to let her say yes.

Turn on all the stars that you have . . . the brightest ones.
Give me a small flash of the moon, only for us.
Let her feel that springtime is arriving.
Give me your very best crickets to sing to her.
Give me the ponentino.
Be a partner with me.

Paola explains the rest of the song to me. In verse two, the woman answers: "*Rome, give me a helping hand to tell him no,*" and so on. But in the final verse, the wind blows them together.

With the room still singing, the elegant older couple at the next table looks around. Seeming pleased that three younger people are enjoying this traditional moment, the woman says, "*Bella.*"

Looking at Paola, I say, "Roma. It's *bella*, not *buona.*"

Pilgrim Tourist, Tourist Priest

The next morning I catch a bus to the Vatican. I'd like to start a conversation with the good-looking priest sitting next to me, but all I can think of to say is, "You look like the kind of priest who would have trouble with the women in your parish."

As the bus lurches to a halt, a frail old woman hurtles past us, artfully keeping her balance as if this were a daily routine. "Ooooh, Maria," she exclaims.

The priest, assuming I'm an English-speaking tourist, says, "Many would finish that with, 'Oh Maria, mother of God, pray for me.'"

"But how many who say this actually go to Mass?" I ask.

"Even though fewer people are going to Mass these days, the Italian people have religion in their blood," the priest replies. "You can see it. Even the young Italian tourists—they do the sign of the cross when leaving a church. And if you speak Italian, you can hear the religion. It's on the tip of every tongue."

I introduce myself and he says, "My name is Renato. I am a tourist, too. I come from Torino."

"I guess if a tourist can become a pilgrim," I say, "then a priest can become a tourist."

Together we leave the bus. I stick close to Renato as he darts between speeding cabs. Pausing a moment between four chaotic lanes of traffic with the immense dome of St. Peter's and its vast circular *piazza* just out of reach, he says, "If we get hit here, we are dead in the right place."

Surviving that dash, we hike through the massive Piazza San Pietro and climb the long steps to the church.

St. Peter's is a cocktail of religion and art, culture and history, tourists and pilgrims, yesterday and today. A gaggle of tourists in tank tops and cut-offs—figuring wrongly that the modest dress code would not be enforced—grumble at the gate.

With the masses funneling through the one open door it feels like rush hour at the base of a huge skyscraper. The vast lobby, or portico, inside the outer doors is just a big room. But stepping from here into the actual church is one of Europe's great thrills. As if about to jump into a swimming pool without checking the temperature, we climb the three big steps of the threshold. Then we leap into St. Peter's.

The best payoff of my work is seeing my tour members wowed by a slice of Europe that has always wowed me. Stepping around the corner from the Métro stop at Trocadero to see the Eiffel Tower standing bowlegged beyond the Seine, or rounding a corner to pop St. Basil's onion-domed cathedral on first-time visitors to Moscow is one of my greatest thrills. My Turkish tour guide friend Mehlika actually stalls to arrive in a village after dark so the group wakes up to a never-before-seen view. When guiding a group through St. Peter's I orient them briefly in the portico. Then I step through the door first in order to see the interior of the greatest church on earth suck their breath away.

Then I gather my groups just inside the church on a six-foot-wide purple slab of porphyry. This huge royal dot marks the spot where Charlemagne was crowned by the pope in A.D. 800—back when neither papacy nor royalty wanted each other but both realized they needed each other. Together, papacy and royalty lifted each other to the top of medieval Europe's feudal order. Once there, the pope made it clear, kings would kneel at the throne of St. Peter.

Charlemagne's stone, in the back of the church, is the kickoff

point for the promenade
up to that throne and the
tomb of St. Peter, marked
by the largest dome on
earth. The bronze bal-
dachin stands seven stories
tall—like a giant four-
poster canopy bed. As if
seventeenth-century scav-
engers were trying to drive
home the point, the bronze

*St. Peter's: A cocktail of
religion and art*

of the baldachin is from melted-down panels that once adorned the
Pantheon, ancient Rome's temple to the pre-Christian gods.

The best way to visit St. Peter's basilica is not with a guidebook but with a friendly priest. Father Renato and I wander
through the greatest church in Christendom. Surrounded by busts
of popes carried heavenward by six-foot babies, we stare at a statue
of St. Peter stiffly giving the peace sign as patient pilgrims slowly
kiss away his foot.

"The statues and art in a great church can speak the theological
wisdom of a library," Renato says. Watching pilgrims kissing the toe
of a statue that is actually of a Roman senator, whose head was replaced with one designed to look like Peter's, I try to see "theological
wisdom." It must have something to do with unquestioning faith.

High above us a mosaic banner declares *"Tu es Petrus"* ("You
are Peter" and upon this rock I will build my church).

In spite of the Lutheranism woven into my genetic makeup, I
have a respect for and fascination with Catholic intellectualism. For
years I went into this grandest of Catholic churches as a
Reformation soldier. Like some Japanese fighter who stumbled out
of the bush forty years after V-J Day, I refused to believe the war was
over. My determination to hold a grudge made me blind to the
beauty. Since I learned to check my cultural baggage at the door,
St. Peter's has become a friend instead of an enemy.

As I walk under the dome, head back, mouth wide open,
Renato politely reminds me about the birds. The size of St. Peter's

is hard to comprehend. Birds live inside St. Peter's and hardly know they're caged.

Europe's tallest dome makes me feel small and less sure of my-self. A huge beam shines through the window accompanied by star-bursts of alabaster. Choral streams of praise, wafting through Europe's ultimate religious and architectural space, seem to rise like heat off the candles and mingle like the sweet smell of incense.

We walk among gilded and marble memories of the struggles of the faithful; the organ trills and old men in red robes fling in-cense. We come to one of many side chapels. On its altar, like a finely carved pearl under the towering roof, sits Michelangelo's *Pietà*. Looking at Mary holding the dead body of a crucified Jesus, I marvel, "How could a mortal carve such a divine work?"

Renato says, "We can be thankful that creation can cooperate with the Creator."

After a thoughtful silence, he repeats, "The theological wis-dom of a library."

I tell Renato I don't understand the importance of Mary to Catholics. Realizing I am a Lutheran trying to be open-minded, Renato explains the theology of the *Pietà*.

"Mary and the apostle John were with Jesus at the cross. As he died Jesus said, 'Mary, here is your son. John, here is your mother.' John symbolizes the faithful here on earth. In the *Pietà*, Jesus is gone. Mary holds only his body. And she looks not at him. She looks at us. Mary is prepared to care for John and that means all of us . . . the body of Christ on earth."

I tell Renato I hope Mary will care for me as I begin my walk across Rome to the Colosseum. He walks me to the door.

From the top of the threshold, the blinding Roman daylight pours past the columns and arches of the outer wall. Placing the back of his hand flat against his nose he says, "Cover the sun and look up."

I do and the black ceiling of the portico suddenly becomes vis-ible, revealing a huge mosaic of Jesus calming the stormy sea for the frightened boatload of disciples. He says, "Today, maybe Jesus is better than Mary for you."

I say, "*Grazie*, Renato," step across the portico, pass the grumbling gang in cut-offs at the main door, and stride down the broad steps back into Rome.

I squint down the Mussolini-built boulevard that leads grandly up to Piazza San Pietro. It also leads grandly away. I walk past the soulless fascist columns and along the parallel elevated and fortified escape route leading from the Vatican to the pope's fortress, the former Tomb of Hadrian. From there I cross the Tiber, thread the tangle of streets marking the heart of medieval Rome, and find the grand monuments of ancient Rome.

Atop the Capitoline Hill, I find a peaceful perch overlooking the Roman Forum. This perch is symbolic of my coming of age as a traveler. In 1973, midway through our summer-long high-school graduation trip, my travel buddy Gene Openshaw and I dangled our feet from this same Forum viewpoint and played tour trivia. We reviewed the magic moments of our first month on the road. While our three-dollar-a-day budget focused our priorities on simply getting enough to eat, we were completely satisfied with our trip just the same. To prove to ourselves that travel is good living, we recalled each of the meals we had bought, begged, or stolen since leaving home.

Twenty-five years have passed and, while I've changed plenty, the Forum has changed little. But 200 years ago, the Forum was known as the cow field. Old prints show a few columns sticking out like the fingers of a man buried prematurely. Back then, Romans knew their cows were grazing on the ruins of greatness, but they needed milk more than history. The rubble of the Forum was interesting only for its value as a quarry, a handy source of precut building blocks.

Today the cows are replaced by tourists wandering through the sweltering rubble enjoying "*Et tu, Brute?*" fantasies and struggling to piece together the puzzle of Rome.

Walking down the Capitoline Hill towards the Arch of Septimus Severus, I stumble onto a gang of note-taking tourists following a scholarly-looking young Italian guide. I hang out within earshot to pick up some information.

Most tour groups are territorial about their guide's services. Self-appointed vigilantes sheriff the back row making freeloaders feel cheap and unwanted. This particular guide has a fine spiel: "Back when Rome had more thieves and wolves than decent people, the great palaces of the Foro Romano were only used as quarries. It was a crude time . . . not a good time to be pope. In the tenth century alone, nine of twenty-four popes were murdered. . . ."

Suddenly I'm being leaned on by a large woman who whispers harshly, "Private tour, private tour."

Leaning back I whisper, "Public attraction, public attraction."

Surveying the Forum, in every corner I see tour guides teaching and entertaining their tired but fascinated groups with "tour guide history." I like to think that what I've learned over twenty years of taking and leading tours is all correct. But much of what is accepted as "history" by tourists is only clever storytelling. As Napoleon said, "What is history but a fable agreed upon?"

When touring with a guide who seems reputable, I like to confirm points I want to believe but have doubts about. I remember following one wonderful old man through some B.C. rubble and soaking up piles of great ideas. Scampering ahead with him as he led the group to the next stop on his tour, I'd confirm and check things with him.

"I've heard that columns from the three classical orders follow a canon of proportions," I began. "Doric, the simplest, is eight times as tall as its base width. Ionic columns are ten times as tall. And the Corinthian are eleven times as tall as their base width. Have you heard this?"

The guide admitted that this was news to him.

Later on that same tour, standing before a lone Corinthian column, he turned to the group and said with authority, "Columns from the various orders can be identified by their height. There is actually what we call a canon of proportions. A Doric column is eight times as tall as its base width. . . ."

So now when I say that Stonehenge is at the junction of Britain's two strongest leylines, Mozart kissed more queens than any pre-teen in history, or Michelangelo secretly dissected corpses

illegally and at great personal risk in order to understand what was
under the skin, I have a nagging fear that "tour guide" history is
closer to entertainment than the truth. The least reliable form of
a tour guide fact is one that starts with, "It's been said . . . ".

I walk the giant black cobbles from the Forum to the
Colosseum. A woman recognizes me from my TV show. After
chatting for a minute she says, "My purse was stolen on the bus."

I ask, "And your moneybelt?"

"It was in my purse," she confesses.

"Bus #64?" I ask.

"How did you know?"

Bus #64 is notorious. It laces together the most-visited sights
and is filled with rich and vulnerable tourists—probably the
most crowded bus line in Rome. I ride it, pockets empty, for the
entertainment: to watch pickpockets at work. While tourists are
on guard against street urchin–type thieves, they don't suspect
prosperous-looking businessmen. The thieves on bus #64 are dis-
tinguished gentlemen, well dressed, with suit jackets folded over
their arms for distraction.

I wrote my anti-theft tips into the script of our Rome TV
show. While we were filming this bit right here in front of the
towering Colosseum, I said, "In Europe thieves target American
tourists, not because they're mean but because they're smart. Be
on guard. Thieves will target you when you are distracted."

As I continued with "A mother changing a diaper is an obvious target . . . ," a thief made off with our camera bag, complete
with a wide-angle lens, battery, and film. To this day, I wonder
where our $400 lens is doing time as an ashtray.

Now, especially when in Rome, I'm on guard. I don't sit at the
corner table of an outdoor café. Unobserved, a thief can sneak up
and grab a wallet or bag.

And I have a great respect for Gypsies pleading on the
streets. Since my first trip, they've approached me with newspapers and babies in shawls to distract. I recently met a tourist who
was the victim of a new trick. A Gypsy mother tossed her baby
into his arms, then grabbed his wallet. Making a commotion

as if the tourist were taking her child, she grabbed her baby and fled.

I ride bus #64 back to my hotel ready for a spectacle. But my second day in Rome ends with only my hands in my pockets.

The next morning I awake ready for the Riviera. I check out and walk to the train station. Along the way, I pass both good and seedy budget hotels. They are often stacked four or five tall in vast soulless blocks. Recommending cheap hotels in Rome can be dangerous, because what may be a good budget find one year can be overrun by prostitution the next.

Walking down Via Principe Amedeo, I pass #76. The Frommer guidebook to Italy once recommended several cheap pensions here. Doing my research rounds a few years ago, I poked into this building. A broad set of stairs wound around a dark old elevator shaft up seven or eight stories. Climbing the stairs, I passed a stressed-out older American couple. With Frommer tucked under their arms— their bulging suitcases on tiny one-inch wheels careening down the stairs—they were fleeing. Wondering why, I looked up the shaft. The place was swinging with prostitutes.

Nursing a latté from a café across the street, I studied the scene. A steady flow of single men, walking quickly with eyes down, came and went. Then a young tourist came running out of the building like a kid escaping an angry parent.

Crossing the street, he stopped just beyond my table to catch his breath. I asked, "Why the rush?"

Plopping into a chair, he told me that he was lured into the building by a big party girl. Three flights up she put her butt up against his crotch, grabbed his arms, and pulled him around her. To his surprise she began an incredibly dirty dance and eventually put his hand in her wet and most private of corners.

He stretched out that same hand to introduce himself. Waving it away, I said, "I'm Rick. Nice to meet you."

"I'm Kent, from Wisconsin," he said. "This is my first time in Rome. Wild city, huh?"

Kent, a red light voyeur, continued his story. He couldn't believe that the woman enjoyed this sleazy encounter. Enjoyed it, it seemed, even more than he did. It went on and on until suddenly a man opened a door. The party girl freaked out and pushed Kent away. She screamed, "Run, run away!" and he fled down the stairs two at a time and back into the brightness of the street.

Wringing his hands as he finished his story, he suddenly grabbed his empty ring finger. The horror on his face said it all. In an instant the entire puzzle came together. With all that lubrication and gyration, the party girl had managed to remove his wedding ring while it was in that most inappropriate corner. Now Kent sat in this café, suddenly stunned, wondering how he'd get it back. After a silent moment, he muttered, "Be careful what you wish for."

Now, several years later, I pause at #76 to see if there's any interesting action. It's all new hotels with a security door flanked by a new beauty salon and a twenty-four-hour Laundromat. The café is still there but there's not a "party girl" in sight.

Around the corner I see the big, bold Roman train station. I walk briskly by the rough street crowd and the tired mothers lounging with their pickpocket children, then step into the station. Scanning the schedule board, I am happy to have survived Rome unscathed. It's a great city, one of Europe's greatest. I don't feel like a salt lick. But after a few days here, I'm ready for a small town. The longer you keep your guard up, the heavier it gets.

Catching a train, I share a compartment with two boys from Denver. They pore over their guidebooks. With a picnic spread atop their Eurail map, they munch bread and prosciutto and pass a huge plastic bottle of Coke back and forth. Give them longer hair, put an external frame on their internal frame backpacks, replace the ham with jam, and switch the Coke for Fanta, and it could have been me and my buddy twenty-five years ago. In a few hours I'll be in a tiny Italian Riviera harbor town. I pass the time remembering my best trip ever.

Europe Through the Gutter, 1973

My childhood horizon had been steadily broadening, pried wider by first a bike, then a car, and then by two European trips with my parents. Now, nearing graduation, with a passport, plane ticket, and a few traveler's checks, I was ready for the Europe beyond piano factories and Norwegian relatives . . . beyond parents.

As I'll be when my kids are ready to travel, my parents were nervous. They decided I could go only if I had a travel buddy. Confidently, I put my "help send a poor student to Europe" coin jar on the mantelpiece. I talked up my dream of a graduation trip at school. I even advertised "feel the fjords and caress the castles" in the classified section of my high-school newspaper. But no one had the necessary combination of will, money, and parental permission.

My friend Gene wanted to go, but his mom and particularly his dad were against it. Seeing Gene as my only hope, I talked his parents into giving me thirty minutes to sell the idea. They gave me the time slot between the local news and Lawrence Welk. Mixing the skills of a lawyer, school counselor, and travel agent, I made my case.

After I finished my presentation, I looked hopefully at Gene's dad. He looked insulted that a schoolkid had just wasted his time—an entire episode of *Lucy*. There was silence. He sat, fixed to the sofa. Slowly he turned to Gene's mom, then to Gene. Finally he looked at me and said, "Where do I sign?"

Now I had a partner. To earn my parents' blessing, I had to make two promises: I wouldn't go to Turkey (and risk being sold into the white slave trade) and I'd write home every other day. My dad figured that if the postcards stopped coming, at least he'd know where to begin looking.

We graduated. On the next day, Gene and I flew.

In 1973 flying was a ritual. People dressed up. Travelers gathered with next-of-kin around flight insurance boxes. With a solemn ceremony, they'd fill out the form and, like gamblers at a wake, drop in their purchase. On board, passengers yawned and chomped on gum trying but failing to avoid the pain of popping ears. And people applauded captains for a safe landing.

Back then, "affinity club" charter flights were cheapest. We were flying from Seattle with a German club. Jean-clad and uninsured, we walked under "Auf Wiedersehen" banners and past oompah bands as if they were for us. Gene was short with a pixie haircut. I was tall with longer, red hair. We were both scrawny—looking like Simon and Garfunkel before their first hit—and a bit afraid. Our nervous parents slipped us some extra postage cash. Promising postcards from Europe, we did our Nixon wave, boarded the plane, and began our seventy-day adventure.

Within hours of landing in Frankfurt, the reality of surviving on three dollars a day sank in. On that budget, gutters had gravity.

Shell-shocked by the prices, we spent our first evening sharing bread with German-speaking riffraff in the streets of Heidelberg.

We couldn't afford a double room. Instead, Gene rented a single from a surly woman. Through clenched German teeth, she made it clear that "*Ein einzel ist nur für ein*"—"a single is only for one."

I fell asleep on the floor next to Gene's sliver single bed with a map over me. If discovered, I was ready to claim that I dozed off while planning our next day and had no intention of spending the night. Night one and we were off to a clumsy start. But within days we were on track, tackling each day like a big new candy bar.

There were glorious times. I remember hitchhiking across western Ireland. We'd stick our thumbs out in whichever direction the sparse traffic was rolling. When asked where we were going we'd say "Ireland" and hop in. Immersing ourselves in wide-ranging conversations we were wide-eyed students of the road. On one ride, a truck-driving poet would discuss the notion that in Europe a hundred miles is a long way and in the United States a hundred years is a long time. On the next, a beer-bellied philosopher explained why the Irish have as many words for "drunk" as the Eskimos have for "ice." And tonight he planned to get pissed, wellied, sloshed, bevvied, paralytic, and ratted all at the same time.

There were scary times. Arriving in Naples we were greeted by doctors in white robes who said they needed blood for a dying baby. Without hesitation, we jumped back on the train and headed for Greece.

And there were simple delights. With the wonder of newborns, we caught fireflies in Bulgaria, discovered Gummibear jellybeans, and got creative with the choco-nut spread Nutella. And with Europe as our class-room, we relived the second rise of Napoleon while following a city walking tour from *Turn Right at the Fountain*, a guidebook that inspired us to later write our museum tours book.

Europe on $3 a day

We spent nights resting our chins on train windows as thunderbolts lit up La Mancha and a murky midnight twilight glowed over endless Swedish birch forests.

One night, as we picnicked on a bench in front of a floodlit Chartres cathedral, a bum noticed we had no wine to go with our baguette. He offered us his plastic bottle of red wine. Looking past a week's worth of bristles, I saw the happy and caring face of a man who had almost nothing in common with me. Sharing that same tiny bit of floodlit Europe—if not the wine—made the world more real . . . less mine, more ours.

Stumbling upon magnificent pipe organ concerts made me miss my dad. Setting up the perfect Dutch dike campsite made me miss my mom. Nothing made me miss my sisters.

With our budget, we couldn't expect clean rooms. Our goal was simply sleepable rooms. When checking out a dive, we learned to rush into a room before the hotel clerk, flip on the light, and check for bugs before they could scurry for cover.

Flies were a problem. We learned that if you waited until they rubbed their front legs together they were easy to swat. The institutional yellow walls of Europe's worst hotels were speckled with smudged bugs.

Hotels in our price range came with bare bulbs dangling from water-damaged ceilings and sagging "ship-shape" beds. Mattresses were made of a sweaty beige foam and sheets didn't fit. A hot, muggy Barcelona night in the clammy bilge of a one-star hotel bed was just another part of "Europe on the cheap."

Plumbing was also primitive. For us, a trickle of tepid water drooling from a broken nozzle down the wall of a rusty shower stall was a triumph. As wispy Roquefort-fringed shower curtains clung to our bodies, we'd press up against the wall to rinse. With bare feet straddling spooky drains, we never picked up the fungus my mom predicted.

While air conditioning was out of the question and fans cost extra, we took our sheets into the shower for temporary relief from hot Mediterranean nights.

We made mistakes. We spent one evening wandering through Salerno in search of our youth hostel . . . until we realized it was actually in Sorrento, a three-hour bus ride away. Our backpacks—complete with tube tents, Boy Scout mess kits, "patrol boots," and, for the last half of the trip, a huge bronze chess set—were a lesson in bad packing. And, uncertain how to order in units less than a kilo (two pounds), we'd eat our produce in bulk quantities. One day would feature carrots, the next tomatoes, and the next we'd walk around with a kilo bag of plums.

But seventy days in Europe gave us a year of living. For this first summer of our adult lives we were like pipe cleaners happily blackening ourselves in Europe's offbeat nooks and remote crannies.

Other than freedom, the only thing we had in abundance was rail travel. Our $150 Eurailpass gave us two months of unlimited second-class travel. From Lapland to Gibraltar to Sicily, it was recess and Europe was our playground.

To travelers of our means, a railpass provided accommodations as well as transportation. And on more than one early morning we were jolted out of sleep by a train station loudspeaker blaring the name of our destination. We'd leap off the train, trailing sleeping bags like groggy butterflies unable to rid themselves of busted cocoons. As the train sped away, we'd do a nervous inventory of our belongings, make certain we were in the right city, and begin a new day.

To maximize nights on trains, we structured our trip by artfully connecting the dots with eight-hour train rides. On occasion, to enjoy more time in a town and the budgetary boost of another free night of sleep, we'd ride a train for four hours out, cross the track, and catch a train for four hours back.

Although trains had rentable berths, the extra cost was beyond our budget. Besides, the cheap seats pulled out to make a bed for free. All we needed to do was to make our compartment undesirable enough to persuade others to sit elsewhere.

While some travelers did this by putting a hand down their pants and a smile on their face, we developed the Hare Krishna approach: sitting cross-legged on the seats, staring deep into each other's spacey face, and chanting. People would slide open the door, shake their heads, and shut the door quickly, preferring a seat in the aisle rather than a night with us.

One Belgrade night was particularly fitful. We arrived late. Rather than pay for a hotel, Gene and I spread out our tube tent as a ground cloth in a park near the station. As the night wore on, the park got busier and busier. Lying there, two frightened virgins under a tree, we realized this was a rendezvous spot for gays.

A medley of Yugoslavian faces poked into our dim little corner, smiling approvingly at the four wide, teenage eyes shining out of two cute little sleeping bags.

Realizing this was no way to get any sleep, we returned to the station ready to spend the night on a bench. Then I saw the perfect answer: a lonely single train car sitting on a grassy train track as if it would be there, uncoupled, forever. We'd have the entire car to ourselves until daybreak. Within minutes we pulled out all six seats in a compartment. We sprawled across a wall-to-wall bed, cozy in our bags . . . smug dreams and deep asleep.

Then, with a humping jolt, we lurched into motion. Barreling through the darkness, heads out the window, only one thing was clear: we were leaving Belgrade. Not knowing when or where the train might stop next, we bundled our belongings and made the dumbest move of our trip. As the train slowed down at a suburban station, we tossed our rucksacks off the train, and—like stunt actors—leapt after them, sprawling across the concrete platform.

Shaken by the thought that we could have easily jumped into a pillar, we counted our limbs and gathered our bags. The station guard, a lonely figure swinging a lantern, walked toward us as if we were a still-hot meteorite. He wondered why we dropped into his off-the-beaten-path domain at three in the morning. Without knowing a word of Serbo-Croatian, we managed to communicate and spent the rest of the night on the floor of his locked waiting room, happy to be warm, safe, and uncomfortable.

Early in the morning, before the decent workaday crowds arrive at the station, vagabonds are cleared out—often with brooms, sometimes with hoses. Our guard woke us with bread, tiny apples, and coffee.

This was the summer I learned to like coffee. Throughout the trip, friendly locals bought us coffees and Cokes. Since Gene was Mormon and anti-caffeine, I routinely ended up with double servings.

Hunger was our incentive to budget carefully. Each week we'd do a frightening financial check. Stacking our kroner, francs, marks, dollars, and traveler's checks neatly on the bed, we'd see how we were doing and determine what we could spend next week. I kept a journal obsessively detailing each of our expenses. Many times we went forty-eight hours without spending a pfennig.

Our budget guard was always up. We knew which bottles were returnable for deposits in which countries and which small coins from one country worked as big coins in vending machines across the border.

Like exhaust-stained orphans with an appetite for art, we slipped into museums and historic buildings through back doors and freeloaded on guided tours. For all but the most essential cultural and historic treasures, an admission fee meant the same as a locked door. To afford a Vienna Boys' Choir concert, we shared one ticket, taking turns sitting in the balcony and snoozing in the courtyard.

While we had a healthy appetite for high culture, we fed our bodies before our souls. My most vivid memories of that trip were edible.

Canned ravoli is actually cheaper than dog food. That's a fact worth knowing and sharing. There's a camaraderie on the road and vagabonds happily compare notes. We weren't as desperate as the travelers who hung out in Greece harvesting their hair and blood to support their souvlaki, retsina, and suntan oil existence. But we were inspired by the girls on the cruise ship to Helsinki who feasted on unfinished salads and picked "untouched" doughnuts out of "clean" garbage cans.

To eat well and free on long train rides we'd bring on leftover picnic scraps and sit next to a group of Europeans with bulging picnic baskets. Our offer to share a hunk of our bread would kick off festive potlucks.

Midway through an all-day bus ride across the mountains just north of Albania, the driver stopped for lunch at a rustic mountain lodge. Having just arrived from Greece and without an opportunity to change money, Gene and I were penniless. We walked, sad and hungry, past long tables, surrounded by boisterous Yugoslavians feasting. My glasses steamed up with the happiness of other stomachs being filled. Yugoslavians were poor and we were rich. But at this moment, the meat and potatoes were on their plates. The only thing separating us from food in our belly was pride. With the help of hunger, we overcame that, and begged. Asking for just a piece of bread and a hunk of meat, we got full plates and a rustic table of friends.

Now, a generation later, when I collect the remains of tour group picnics into three or four paper plate meals and find some hungry teenage backpackers to feed, I remember how that Yugoslavian charity lunch fueled another day of good travels.

Gene and I encountered a similar situation when we were in a desperately poor oasis village in Morocco's Sahara. Children walked around with lifeless babies hanging from their necks— tiny faces crusted with dirt and buzzing with flies. The village's one eatery was busy with locals munching a gruel-like soup that, hungry as we were, we couldn't imagine eating. Everything was dry and filthy, like an ugly growth on a pristine desert. Balancing the last of our bread on a lens cap and taking turns shooing away the flies, we pondered this ironic scene. A dozen thin but satisfied Moroccans were sucking down this nutritious gruel while two grossed-out Americans—who had more money in their moneybelts than the entire village combined—went hungry.

A dusty little girl, escorted by a scrap-seeking dog, brought us a big, hot bottle of Fanta. Parched and eager, I attacked the cap with my Swiss Army knife. The glass top crunched off with the cap. After a short pause to consider the consequences of drinking broken glass, we sucked the pop through clenched teeth.

While good Boy Scouts back home, our lack of funds turned us into petty thieves in Europe. We knew which of Scandinavia's famous smorgasbords came with protein that traveled well. Hard-boiled eggs and wrapped cheeses were ideal. We'd pay for a breakfast and walk out with bulging day bags. I remember nearly free meals—eating fresh Italian bread in Milan with eggs and cheese from Copenhagen. But this trick had its risks. One time I swiped six hard-boiled eggs that weren't, and the bottom of my daybag became an over-easy punishment.

When picnic shopping, I had rationalized a moral compromise: I'd pay for all the food but shoplift the dessert. At the end of a picnic, I'd pull the cookies from my coat pocket with a triumphant grin. Gene would look at me with disgust and refuse to eat the stolen sweets. But after watching me savoring my treats for a few minutes, he'd grudgingly say, "Okay, I'll have one."

Gene packed a zip-lock baggie of Tang. I left home with a hiker's squeeze tube filled with peanut butter and grape jam. Regrettably, my clever mix curdled. With the sadness of a pet burial, we dropped the squeeze tube into a garbage can. Before long, our Tang ran out too.

One day in Garmisch, our spirits went from a record high to an almost fly-home-early low. Romping down the aisles of the U.S. military commissary store we sorted through our edible hometown favorites like a pirate alone with his treasure chest. It was wonderfully American—with a vast selection and impossibly cheap prices. We filled our shopping basket with peanut butter, Tang, graham crackers, beef jerky, even Triskets. Then, at the check-out line, the cashier—who had no idea how important this was to us—said flatly, "Without a military ID card, you cannot buy this."

The military personnel we asked to help us out reacted as if they'd be court-martialed for buying us Tang. Reshelving each delight one by one, we battled back a strong wave of homesickness.

Halfway through our trip Gene and I planned a week with my relatives in Norway. This was a chance to wash our stinking rucksacks, take a break from our economic fight for survival, and be part of a family. By the time we reached Oslo, we had shrunk our stomachs. Two sandwiches a day kept hunger at bay . . . until Norway.

It seemed Norwegians measure hospitality in calories. Meals came in two assaults: first a lavish table of smoked salmon, creamy fishballs, vegetables, and delicate open-face sandwiches. Then, after waddling to the overstuffed furniture of the living room, a parade of cakes and cookies with pop or coffee followed. Between meals we would visit other relatives who'd show their love by feeding us again.

Caca is one thing in Spain. But in Norway, *kaka* is cake: *Kransekaka, Napoleonkaka, Julekaka,* and—my favorite— *Krumkaka.* Every time I moaned "I'm full," uncles would laugh, explain that "full" is the Norwegian word for "drunk" and put another fancyfrostedkaka on my plate. I remember fjordside jogs with Gene actually stressed out about our inability to face another festive table piled with food.

We left Norway with bulging bags of goat cheese sandwiches and fancy pastries. But when the last *lefse* was eaten, we were on our own again—stomachs stretched out and more demanding than ever.

We spent the last half of our trip on a crude diet of Fanta and crusty bread with a thin icing of strawberry jam. We suffered from painful cases of baguette mouth. About once a week we'd need bread-free days to give the perpetually roughed-up roofs of our mouths a chance to heal.

As departure day neared, we made up words to the tune of Paul Simon's "Kodachrome": *"When I think back on all the crap I ate in Europe, it's a wonder I am here at all. Although my lack of good nutrition never hurt me none, I got maggots on my stomach wall. Mama don't take my jam and bread, mama don't take my jam and bread, mama don't take my jam and bread away-ay-hey-ah-hey. . . ."*

I didn't know that I would return home to a kind of mental

breakdown. The doctor called it "chronic fatigue." Exhausted and undernourished from this trip, I was mentally AWOL for my first month of college. I couldn't teach piano. I couldn't keep score in ping pong. And I had a terrifying ability to make bad things happen just by thinking about them. Before turning the key in my car's ignition, I'd be afraid nothing would happen. Then I'd turn the key . . . and get silence.

I couldn't cope with the world. It scared me back to Mom and Dad. I spent a week reclining in a big chair, throwing magnetic checkers at metal things in my parent's living room.

I was back on track by my second quarter at college. And, astonishing my mother, I took a class on nutrition. Since then I've never touched a Fanta or a jam sandwich. In fact, I'm passionate about drinking one-hundred-percent pure orange juice.

But while in Europe, exhaustion and fatigue were not options. With impressive teamwork, Gene and I never let up. If one of us was down—jaded, homesick, or vomiting—the other was up enough for two. We were vagabonds with a mission: to experience Europe.

Managing on our budget required more than skimping on food. Gene and I learned from other vagabonds that you could buy a ticket from Brindisi in Italy to the island of Corfu, "miss" your stop in Corfu, and sail free all the way to Patras, Greece. As the boat pulled away from the shrinking Corfu harbor, we screamed as if we left our loved ones on the dock and raked in undeserving sympathy from the crew.

We put a similar trick to use in Eastern Europe, which our Eurailpasses didn't cover. We bought a train ticket to Sofia in order to go somewhere farther . . . like Plovdiv. When the conductor checked our tickets after Sofia, we said simply, "We go to Sofia." He motioned that Sofia was already past. We acted as if we didn't understand, convinced that Sofia lay ahead. When we finally got it, we were mad that we missed our stop. The conductor, thinking we were stupid rather than dishonest, kicked us off the train . . . in Plovdiv.

Our tight budget didn't prevent us from buying quirky souvenirs.

In a small Spanish town, we hung out behind the bullring and watched the post-fight skinning of the bulls. As if the matador were the underdog, the butcher and his crew celebrated the death of these animals with bravado. They hoisted the bulls tail first, leaving them swinging like traitors from a bloody gallows. Between long swigs of red wine, they peeled and processed the losers. For a couple of dollars, the butcher sawed off the horns and we each had a trophy.

The butcher explained that we should carefully hollow out the horns. Thinking "rubbish," we said, "*Sí, sí, sí*" and took the horns back to our hotel. Shampooing the cute tufts of hair still upholstering the fringes and marveling at how bangles from the matador's coat were lodged under tiny horn splinters, we dreamed of having this evocative bit of Spain on our bookshelves at home.

Rather than clean the horns, we left them on the rooftop outside our hotel window to air out for a few days before heading north. The horns began to smell. In fact they smelled so much, we no longer needed the Hare Krishna trick to keep our train compartments empty. But—far from Spain—when a persistent and thriving colony of bugs infested our pointed prizes, we gave up and abandoned the horns.

Our best souvenirs were memories of the people who carbonated our experience. Like a bubble-wand makes more bubbles when you wave it, a traveler meets more people while on the move. I meet more fascinating people in a week of European travel than I do in a year at home.

Coconut, the Israeli flower child who left her country rather than take up arms, took the chill out of Paris. In Morocco, we palled around with a professional photographer who taught us to relax your local subjects by acting so crazy they write you off as a fool. Visiting Linz, Hitler's hometown, we were adopted by a grandmotherly friend of a friend. Referring to me and Gene as "*meine kinder*" ("my children"), she told us stories of the Führer's youth.

Vagabonding drives you into the youth hostels where shoestring travelers from around the world rely on conversation for entertainment. Youth hostel doors are locked by ten o'clock and the lights are out by eleven, but bunkbed conversation rages long after curfew. We found ourselves propped on our elbows staring intensely into each other's darkness, passing around travel tales like a bucket of popcorn.

Finishing off our 1973 trip with one last cheap stunt, Gene and I rode the train from Frankfurt to its airport on an expired Eurailpass. Nothing gets by German conductors. Our only hope was that we'd reach the airport before they finished their sweep through the train. Starting at opposite ends of the train, they methodically worked their way to the middle. Watching them approach like collapsing walls of knives, we nervously clicked off suburban stations as the airport neared. With a conductor within six rows on either side of us, the train lumbered to a halt at the airport. Gene and I squirted out . . . ready (and needing) to fly home.

We flew home with two dollars and fifty cents between us, clutching overstuffed journals, ready to resume our decent and properly funded lives. On this first "Europe Through the Gutter" trip, I learned that spending money had little to do with the richness of our travel experience. We had rooms with a Jungfrau view—even if on hay in a barn. We danced into the wee hours— at a neighborhood inauguration of a new public toilet in Geneva. We hobnobbed with the jet-set at the roulette tables of Monte Carlo—until kicked out. And we shopped for unique—and fragrant—souvenirs.

Gene and I did our final expense tally on the plane. In seventy nights we spent fifty-two dollars each for beds. The twenty nights we splurged in hotels or pensions cost three dollars and eighty cents per double. The eighteen nights in youth hostels ran us eighty-three cents per bed. About half our nights were free. We each spent $111 for seventy days of food, $243 for our round-trip airfare, $150 for the two-month train pass, and $202 for sightseeing admissions and everything else. Total cost: $758 each. Today a two-month youth railpass alone costs more than that.

Flying home, I finished my journal with, "My future is precarious but I feel a strange, almost cocky, optimism . . . a feeling that I'm climbing a ladder with plenty of rungs to go."

On the nine-hour flight, Gene and I double-teamed a trip

1973: The best trip ever

fresco, each of us drawing alternate frames. By the time we were over the Rockies we had two identical souvenirs of our trip. I didn't know it then, but this was the first of twenty-five summers in a row that I would spend in Europe. And, twenty-five years later, it's clear, this trip was the best.

CHAPTER EIGHT

VERNAZZA

"Only two Vernazza families still fish
for a living. Before we harvest the sea.
Now we harvest the tourists."

E Pericoloso Sporgersi . . . The sign on the train window warns
in four languages: "It is dangerous to lean out." But the five-
hour ride from Rome to the Riviera is just about over and I'm
hurtling through a tunnel, window down, face in the wind and
eyes wide open.

From out of the darkness each break in the tunnel brings an
explosion of Mediterranean brightness. Each scene is grander than
the last: azure blue tinseled in sunbeams, carbonated waves hitting desolate rocks, and the occasional topless human camped out
like a lone limpet.

This is the Cinque Terre, the most dream-worthy stretch of
the Italian Riviera. And the danger here is not leaning out but
actually getting out. Nowhere else does the lure of the
Mediterranean, Italy, and village life combine so potently to ship-
wreck speedy itineraries.

The Cinque Terre, which means "five lands," comprises five
towns tucked along the rugged coast. Each is a variation on the
same theme: a well-whittled pastel jumble of homes filling its gully
like crusty sea creatures in a tide pool. These days the castles, which

used to protect the towns from marauding pirates, protect only glorious views.

Trains tie the villages of the Cinque Terre to each other and to the outside world. Screeching along the tracks as if they don't quite fit, these trains are a common target for tourists' insults. But the first train cutting through this tough, mountainous coastline was an engineering marvel for its day and an important early wave of the new Italian flag.

The Cinque Terre train line laced together the regions of Piedmont and Tuscany shortly after Italy's unification in 1861. With just one line, local trains stuttered from town to town, venturing out only when no big city expresses were near. With the addition of the second line, built to celebrate the 100th anniversary of Italy's unification, things went from miserable to just bad.

The train lumbers to a halt at Vernazza and I hop off. As I stand on the platform that stretches like scaffolding over the town's only street, I hear a ding-a-ling warning—sounding like a cartoon alarm clock—announcing the arrival of a train on the other track.

Cold wind pours out of the tunnel and a screaming intercity express barrels through. The doppler-created two-note melody of its tooting horn reminds villagers of the harsh, fast-paced world beyond. Conversations pause as hair, dresses, and newspapers slap and flap. Then, suddenly, once again, the air is thick, warm, and quiet, and voices travel. My slower commuter train struggles away. As it disappears into the mountain it leaves me alone, suspended in car-free, roosters-on-the-loose, pastel-village Italy.

I'm alone only momentarily. Like most arriving tourists, I'm accosted by the room-pirate widows. They ambush new arrivals—bound for pre-reserved rooms—and try to talk them into renting a room from them. Ignoring them, I head directly for the beach.

Italy, with 65 million people and as many Fiats pressing firmly against its coastline, is not a great place for idyllic beaches. My first memory of an Italian coastline—in 1969 with my family—left a strong impression. From a noisy freeway car park we walked down to a polluted beach and met a family enjoying a barbecue in squalor. The gravelly beach was papier-mâchéed with sunburnt seaweed and dried Kleenex toilet paper. Ever since, I've had a fascination with hellish Italian beaches. Try Rome's.

I like Vernazza's tiny port-town beach. It's a humble little working beach—a pebbled cove littered with the jumble of a community that lives off the sea . . . and travelers who love the views. Well-worn locals fill the benches while tourists sunbathe on rocks. Yellow webs of fishing nets, umbrellaed tables, kids with plastic shovels, and a flotilla of tough little boats provide splashes of color.

Vernazza is my favorite Cinque Terre town. At the top end of town a cruel little road hits a post. No cars enter this village of 600 people. Like the breakwater keeps out the waves at the bottom of the town, the post keeps out the modern storm at the top.

In England, people go to port towns to gaze out to sea. In a good Italian port town, people go to the end of the breakwater and gaze inland. Artists from northern Europe perfume their landscapes with an Italian mist. Italian artists stay at home. Their world is Mona Lisa's backyard.

Vernazza's ruined castle no longer says, "Stay away." And its breakwater—a broad inviting sidewalk edged with seaside boulders—sticks into the sea like a finger beckoning to distant excursion boats. Grabbing a comfortable hollow in a boulder on the tip, I study the arrangement man and nature have carved out here over the last fifteen centuries. Crumpled hills come with topographical lines: a terraced, green bouquet of cactus, grapevines, and olive trees.

The hills are rugged, but the fifth-century author of the first-ever account of the Cinque Terre may have overstated his case when he wrote the hills were "so steep that even the birds strain to fly over them."

With a closer look, the hills silently seethe with activity: locals tending their vines and hikers working up a thirst for the fresh white wine these hills produce. The single silver rail of the tiny grape pickers' train—the *trenino*—scales the hillside like a rock climber's rope. In autumn the *trenino* is busy ferrying grapes down into town from the high terraces.

Like a gangly clump of oysters, the houses seem to grow on each other. Locals are the barnacles. Trains spurt from the hillsides bringing in tourists. And accompanying the scene is the sound-track of a dream . . . a white noise of children, dogs, and waves.

Below my rocky perch, a fisherman cleans his nets after a long night at sea. The cool mist, which follows each crashing wave, reminds me how easily this breakwater is conquered dur-ing winter storms.

High above the breakwater, at the base of the castle, is a restau-rant called Il Castello. This pricey place was my private little splurge back when I stretched lire by choosing popsicles over gelato.

Vernazza feels populated by descendants of the pirates who plundered this coast. Lorenzo, who ran Il Castello, was a rare Vernazzan who didn't take advantage of tourists held hostage by his town's beauty. He'd sit me down under an umbrella with the most commanding view in town. And with the love of a small-town priest, he'd put a cookie next to my glass of cool sweet *sciacchetrà* wine, and say, "Rest here. The view is nice."

Cancer took Lorenzo quickly one winter. Now he's king of the Vernazza mountain. He's resting and enjoying the best view of all from a hotel booked out by locals for years, the hilltop cemetery.

Leaving the harborfront, I climb the long, crooked staircase up to Il Castello. Monica, Lorenzo's twenty-five-year-old daughter, greets me warmly. With her Barbra Streisand lips, bony nose, and black hair backlit by the sun, she seems to have an aura. Her pene-trating eyes find me with each visit. In her caring face I see Lorenzo as if he were still standing there with the bottle of *sciachetra*, saying, "Rest."

I tell Monica that I've been thinking about her father and she suggests we visit the cemetery. Hiking through narrow back alleys that smell of damp cats, we find the road that leads uphill to the cemetery. After a funeral Mass, the entire village spills out of the church and parades darkly up this same route.

At the top of the lane, a black iron gate is open. Inside, the cemetery is fragrant with fresh flowers. Quiet lanes separate marble walls of niches, stacked five high. Walking down a lane closest to the sea, Monica explains that coffins are not put into the ground but slid into a *loculo*. Squinting at a wall of niches, reflecting bright white in the late afternoon sun, I review names and dates carved into the marble. Each niche is wired with a tiny light and comes with a built-in vase. And next to each vase is an inset oval window filled with a black and white portrait.

Stepping around a rolling ladder—left out for loved ones with flowers for those resting on the top row—Monica arrives at her father's *loculo*. She leaves me long enough to cross herself. Then, turning toward the sea, Monica sits on a flat rock just big enough for two. Patting the other half of her perch, she invites me to sit down.

We ignore the red tiles, flapping laundry, and tourists lounging on the breakwater below. From here, the world is a peaceful green and reassuring blue that blends the sea and sky. To the left and right, I pick out each of the Cinque Terre towns along the coast. Each is alone in the world—seemingly oblivious to the march of time. I wonder what could possibly improve this setting. Then the church bells ring.

Doing Laps in Vernazza

Monica and I hike back into town as the sun is setting and Vernazza's main street begins to fill with people.

"Every evening the town does its *vasca*," Monica says. "We walk up and down the street. "*Vasca*" means laps, like when you go swimming."

At the train station, we see Vittorio, the town playboy, camped out—fishing for tourists. He works at a competing restaurant, Il Capitano, directly below Monica's Il Castello on the harbor.

"*Ciao*, Vittorio. *Come va?*" I ask.

The roar of a passing express train interrupts us. All conversations stop until it's gone, then resume as if nothing happened.

"*Ammazzare il tempo.* I'm killing time," he says, knowing I like slang. "Where have you been?" he asks in Italian.

Monica answers coolly, "*Cimitero*." In a town this small, they must have been schoolmates.

Seeing my notepad filled with notes, Vittorio switches mainly to English. "Hotel *completo*. Too many bodies. Now when you die you have to take a place in the new *cimitero*. No views."

As if to earn a place in our walk, Vittorio kicks in another thought. "Cremation is not acceptable in Italy. Because of the Church." Watching me jot something in my notepad, Vittorio assumes he is welcome to walk with us.

I like Vittorio. But he's a hustler: hustling girls and, when I'm in town, hustling me for a good recommendation in my guidebook. His sweatshirt shows he supports the Genoa soccer club. He wears it like he could be on the team. Above his thin black beard, his dark sleepy eyes have a playful sincerity about them. They seem to say, "Trust me. Any trouble we get into will be good trouble. Really. I promise."

With the help of gravity, the three of us sift through Vernazza toward the breakwater. I miss my alone time with Lorenzo's daughter. But the competition Vittorio infuses into our walk might shine a different light on Vernazza.

On our *vasca*, Monica and Vittorio nod hellos to various friends and comment on others. Pointing to a one-armed man walking up the street between two rotund women, Vittorio says, "He could use another arm."

Not finding that funny, Monica explains, "As a boy Maurizio fell from the *mulino*, the water mill. In Vernazza everyone knows every step you take. If you are together before you marry. . . ."

Shaking her finger, Monica mimics the old women's scolding. "'Look at that girl. Why does she go with him?' they say. And they build a big story. In Vernazza people are living very close. If you open your window every morning at nine and then one morning you do this at ten, everybody asks what's going on. When a boy is with a girl the old ladies ask, 'When will you marry?' When you do marry, the village has a big festival."

"As big as the funeral," Vittorio adds.

I ask them about Vernazza funerals.

"When someone dies, the body is dressed up and lies in bed for two days as everyone in the village comes by," Monica says.

"The house must be open all night. The law requires this for twenty-four hours. Forty-eight in the case of a heart problem to be sure the person is really dead."

Vittorio jokes, "When someone is about to die, the family calls the ambulance so the person can go to the hospital and die there. This way you don't have the village in your house."

"Trust me. Any trouble we get into will be good trouble."

Monica nearly agrees. "It can be a hardship on the family. Such a sad time. But it is a time when a community is strong together. In the big cities, it is different. My professor died in the hospital—we were sent away at eight o'clock at night. He was behind glass."

"You better be where you want to be buried when you die," Vittorio advises. "It is complicated to move a corpse."

"Recently a strong communist who was dying asked for a civil funeral," Monica continues, ignoring Vittorio. "No priests. This is rare and courageous in front of death. It may be okay to have a civil wedding, but death . . . it is the finish."

"My uncle . . . ," Vittorio starts to say, then spies an attractive young woman with a big backpack. With a "See you later!" he heads off in hot pursuit.

Because so much of good travel involves the locals, any time I can plug my readers into an interesting character, I feel like I'm doing each a favor. Three editions ago I wrote, "And the English-speaking waiter Vittorio likes the girls" at the end of my description of Il Capitano. Vittorio told me, "This has changed my life."

When Vittorio's off duty, he's on duty. He knows when every cute tourist arrives and when she plans to leave. The basil on his *trenette* is a hit. Vittorio is always looking to score.

If Europe is a body, Germany could be the head, France might be the heart, and the peninsula of Italy must be its penis. A fact of travel is that the most interesting male characters in Italy are also the horniest. Several American women have told me that if they leave Italy without getting a single whistle, pinch, or stare, they feel that they haven't experienced the real Italy.

How am I to handle a situation such as Angelino from Bagnoregio? Angelino, aging but ever-young, loves wine, women, pasta, and singing with Americans in his wine cellar cantina. He has delighted hundreds of my readers, yet too many solo women have had terrible experiences—being kissed, touched, or grabbed. One angry woman reported that midway through a cantina chorus of Volare, Angelino exposed himself down where the kegs are empty. I sent that letter with an Italian translation to his family in hopes they would rein him in. And in my guidebook, I added a clear "no holds barred" warning to women.

Vittorio catches up with us, saying, "She had reservations." I wonder if he means hotel or in general. Unless I hear otherwise, I'll assume Vittorio is as innocent as the look in his puppy eyes. And I'll continue to keep his off-duty life as interesting as my readers' Riviera experiences.

We venture up a spindly lane from Vernazza's only real street. Stairs and the stony hillside mingle. Ramshackle drains lead to tin cisterns and water pipes hang like afterthoughts on walls. The aroma of frying onions and garlic seeps from a few doors and windows. Like a neighborhood gang adding to its treehouse, tight spiral staircases lead to sun decks that struggle for the best Mediterranean view. Oblivious to views, a woman hoists laundry along the wall away from her window. We pass a father patiently teaching his daughter to count by climbing stairs, with him, hand in hand.

Brick-laden tractors the size of a child's sled climb the back lanes to a small, messy construction site. An old man covered in plaster runs a screeching saw. When it stops, nothing could be quieter.

Vittorio, the silence catching him by surprise, yells, "When I was a boy porks lived in this room."

"You mean 'pigs,'" says Monica, turning to me. "Carlo is making an apartment for tourists. Because he is retired from the train work, he can ride the train for no money. He even goes to La Spezia to get tourists. Like fishing."

Vittorio continues. "Italians don't like the private jobs. They like the state jobs. You know, where four guys watch one person. In America if you work like that, they kick you out."

Wearily, Carlo looks up from his work. Monica greets him and introduces me. He snarls something in Italian. Monica translates, "He says to take his sister out of your guidebook."

"He is nervous because of the tax man," Vittorio explains.

In Italy, tax evasion is—if not a patriotic duty as it is in France—at least a respected sport. Across Europe, people who run bed-and-breakfasts are tempted not to declare their income. The temptation to hide B&B income goes up with the tax rate. It's highest in Scandinavia. Because a guidebook listing raises your profile and makes it difficult to convince the government you don't make a lot of B&B money, many prefer not to be listed at all.

Carlo's sister rents rooms with prime harborview balconies. It's my challenge to collect small-time operators like this who are bold enough to risk the publicity a guidebook offers.

Carlo nods goodbye even though we haven't left yet. Hoisting the saw, he flips it back on and attacks a board. The sound of the screaming saw follows us down the stairs as we head to the main street.

Enrico, hanging out at a coffee bar, seems to be waiting for us. Like the town George Burns, he's easy-going, with the stub of an unlit cigar locked between his fingers and plenty of time to talk. Waving his cigar, he launches into the same conversation we have every year.

"Eh, Rick," he says, "you been here two days. Why don't you come by? And why don't you do me better in your guidebook? You know my bungalow has a nice garden and a big view."

I used to hope that in Enrico I'd find a contact that could help me understand the social puzzle of this almost incestuous little community. Enrico spent time in the United States, and I'd hoped he'd be able to give me some perspective. But, while he understands Vernazza, he can't understand what I need to know about it. He may have worked in New York, but he never really left home.

Unlike Carlo, Enrico has no fear of the Italian tax man. Like Carlo, he supplements his retirement by meeting trains to snare tourists in need of a room. He joins us in our walk, saying, "Come visit, Rick."

Every year I give him the same answer: "I'll try to come by."

Someday I'll just level with him. A place renting only one room causes more frustration than joy for my readers. The garden's okay, but the view is peek-a-boo at best and the term "bungalow" is too generous for his hut. It's more like a treehouse without the tree.

I tell Enrico of Carlo's demand that I remove his sister's listing from my guidebook. He says, "It don't surprise me. Did you hear about the police raid last September?"

"The police raid?"

"It was like World War II all over again," Enrico says. "Last September. It was half-past six one morning. Sixty police invade Vernazza. They had a list of places renting rooms with no tax registration. I don't know. Maybe they read your book."

"What happened?"

"They knocked on all the doors. Woke up all the tourists. It was very, very fast. And then they know who is renting rooms and tax cheating."

"Did people go to jail?" I ask, crossing my wrists.

"Oh, no. You got to kill someone to go to jail in Italy. They just make them pay the taxes."

Monica points out a building that appears to be closed down. "This is the clubhouse for the boys who went into the hills to fight Hitler."

"The resistance?" I ask.

"Yes," she says. "Most are dead now, but to close it down would be bad politics."

Trying to pull a few memories past his cigar, I ask Enrico to tell us about World War II in the Cinque Terre.

He slows his pace as if to divert his energy to thinking. "In

1943 Hitler said all Italian men over fifteen must go to Germany to work in the fields. They even took strong boys as young as twelve. We weren't stupid. 'The fields' was really the front. Another Hitler lie. Boys escaped into the mountains. The resistance fighters were escapees first. To stay free, they became partisans. They had no choice."

Biting down on his cigar, he says, "To call them heroes and give them a clubhouse . . . I don't know."

Monica whispers, "Some towns supported Mussolini. Monterosso has no club for the resistance fighters. Vernazza was more communist. Anti-fascist. My oldest uncle is a communist. Since the end of the Berlin Wall, the communists are quieter now."

I ask one of the most common questions in European tourism: "Did any bombs hit here?"

Pointing his soggy cigar to the mountain that stands between Vernazza and a big navy town, Enrico says, "La Spezia had the navy. It was destroyed by bombers—American bombers. Vernazza was hit once. We ran into the train tunnel for shelter. But twenty-five people died.

"Riomaggiore had a big cannon. We called it Raccia, 'the ugly girl.' It was for shooting down airplanes, but after 1944 the Nazis used it to bomb the villages. Two days before liberation, Raccia shot off the tower of the Corniglia church."

Pausing at the steps leading up to his bungalow, Enrico shakes a nicotine-stained finger at me. "You come up and see me, right?"

At the sidewalk tables on main street, a few stray tourists study menus, sip coffee, and watch us discreetly watching them. The bakery wafts a fragrant invitation. The grocer signals the closing of his store by pulling tarps over the fruit and vegetables. Wearing his white, blood-smudged apron like an advertisement, the butcher fills the doorway of his shop, waiting for a last customer.

Passing a bench of widows, each wearing the wrinkles of a long weather-beaten life, Monica says, "Women outlive the men here."

Taking his turn, Vittorio continues. "You can see them at the five o'clock Mass. It is only the old women. The men are in the billiards hall. Women and men are apart. The young people, they are together. But the old ones, they are apart. This is some kind of a social sickness."

"Japan is this way," I say. "Salarymen work and play together. And the wives stay at home."

"In Burma, the women walk ahead, a tradition left over from the days when World War II mines were a risk," says Monica.

Vittorio interrupts, saying, "Ladies first." Monica rolls her eyes.

We stop for gelato at the town's only *gelateria* and, eyeing the long line of tempting bins, I ask about the quality.

Monica explains that the metal tins show that the gelato is homemade. "I don't eat the gelato from the plastic boxes," she says.

"To test the quality you must eat the *crema*, vanilla, or chocolate," says Vittorio. "Never the fruit flavors. What do you like?"

We walk to the little harbor square, no longer talking—just licking our cones and nodding our approval.

The tower bells of the church jerk into motion. We stand, licking and listening—facing the bell tower as if pledging allegiance to the past—until they stop clanging.

"The bells wake me in the morning," I say, "but I like it. Six rings and they stop. I think, 'Great! More sleep.'"

"Church bells remind us of the old days," Monica says. "The fishermen five kilometers out at sea could hear them. The men in the vineyards high on the mountain could hear them, too. In one village the hotels tried to stop the bells for the tourists who couldn't sleep. But the people of the village, they nearly had a revolution. The bells ring about thirty times at half-past seven, reminding everyone to start their day with the Ave Maria—to pray to Mary."

I ask Monica, "Are you Christian?"

"Catholic," she says. "In Italy, we are Catholic."

Vittorio crinkles his nose, rubs his beard, and confesses, "I don't go to the church, but, yes, I am. We have a strange relationship with God. Everybody says they don't believe. But every big festival, it's always Catholic. We have Catholicism in our blood.

"My father is a fisherman," he continues. "On his arm he has a tattoo of Jesus on the cross. When he catches many fish he kisses it. When he catches nothing, he spits on it. Maybe we are opportunistic with God." He looks off as if pondering what he said. Surprised by his depth, I follow his gaze—as if tracking his thought— to a group of backpack-toting American women

Monica and her fiancé

. . . Vittorio's specialty. The train must have just arrived.

"A moment, please," Vittorio says, and leaves us. The women are following my guidebook as if on a school assignment, trying to match words with buildings. As Vittorio reels them toward his restaurant, I realize that I've caught them first. The impact of my guidebook is making Vernazza touristy—filled with Americans looking for the "untouristy Riviera."

While sending travelers to a place because it's "undiscovered" is contradictory, it's the essence of my travel writing. I'm like the whaler who screams, "Quick, harpoon it before it's extinct!" But, sooner or later, the modern world—with or without tourism—will drown the charm of Vernazza. My mission is clear: to help my readers find and experience this slice of Italy. Maybe I'm their hired gun. But finishing the last cool crunch of gelato and cone, I see a world very happily mixing old and new, locals and tourists.

Monica and I linger in the little harbor square. The people looking out of the windows of the faded pastel buildings are a gallery of portraits hanging on ancient walls. It's said Americans watch six hours of TV a day. Here in Vernazza the generation that didn't grow up with television must spend that much time just posted at their windows, watching over a world as predictable as the Mediterranean tide.

In my office in Edmonds, Washington, I have a photograph of an old woman framed by her blistered windowsill reading the newspaper. After seeing this, a customer brought me a *National Geographic* article with a photo showing the same person reading a newspaper in the same window . . . ten years earlier.

Years ago Vernazza had almost no outside exposure and little money. Now, even with each train dumping out wads of wide-eyed, lire-laden tourists, it seems little—other than the source of the local economy—has changed.

Vittorio rejoins us with a cheerful "*Ciao*" and we walk out to the breakwater. I ask Vittorio and Monica about the rising tide of tourism.

"Before tourism," says Vittorio, "in the 1960s, having land to farm was most important. People now prefer to rent rooms to tourists or work in an office. Time is too valuable to work the land."

"We still fish," Monica says. "And we still grow the grapes, olives, and lemons. But now it is mostly a hobby."

Vittorio looks at Monica and says, "I own a piece of land."

With a "doesn't everyone?" tone, Monica says, "Me also."

"It is a one-hour walk," Vittorio says. "There are olives, lemon trees, and the best view of Vernazza. I could make postcards."

"Do you go there?" I ask.

"I visited it one time fifteen years ago with my grandmother," Vittorio pauses, then confesses, "and one time again with a girl from Brazil."

We reach the end of the breakwater, boats nudging the sidewalk pier. "Come tonight to my restaurant," Vittorio says to me, taking my arm. "I will tell you more about fishing, about seafood, anchovies, wine. . . ."

"Okay, okay," I say, and Vittorio flashes a victory grin at Monica. The hustler has scored again. Trapped, I flop willingly into his net.

Anchovies, Hold the Pizza

I join Vittorio for dinner, images of his father kissing his crucifix in my head. But tonight, Vittorio is the one who has the catch of the day: the American travel writer. To score with me means a pumped-up listing in my next guidebook. Just a little phrase can have a huge impact.

My annual visit can cause restaurateurs and hoteliers to stutter. For people in the tourist business, a guidebook listing is extremely important. It's important to me, too. Mistakes last an entire year. I hate discovering I've promoted an unworthy place as much as I enjoy praising a deserving place.

Adjusting the dishes at my table and taking an English menu from my hands, Vittorio says, "No menu. Tonight I give you an education in seafood."

He starts me off with small plates of seafood. "The red on the shrimp is phosphorous. It's good for your brain. And *tegame Vernazza*—this is anchovies Vernazza style."

Noticing my reluctance, he explains, "I know. In the United States anchovies are the most hated. People say, 'Pizza, no anchovies.' But here we cook them fresh with potatoes, tomatoes, white wine, and oil." His graceful hand yanks in each word as if pulling in a net. Then, as if sprinkling some imaginary seasoning, he says, "*Prezzemolo*. Parsley. *Exacto*. And to drink?"

"Mineral water," I answer, anticipating a long night at my laptop.

Disappointed, Vittorio says, "The fish will swim in your stomach. You must have wine. Angelo!" he hollers to another waiter, "*un bottiglia di vino bianco. Per il mio amico!*"

Vittorio serves a fine meal. Beaming at my very clean tiramisu plate, Vittorio plots to meet me before breakfast tomorrow to talk fish. He says, "At seven o'clock, Vernazza is not a tourist town. It is a fishing village. At this hour you can buy anchovies, but no suntan oil."

I promise to meet him first thing in the morning and offer to pay for my meal. He pushes my lire away. I could insist, but it doesn't seem polite to turn down his gift. We help each other in our work.

Stomach full, with just enough wine in my belly to make threading the beached dinghies fun, I step down to the harborfront and zip up my jacket.

As predictable as the mountain tunnel slurps up the local

trains, Antonio Sorriso stands tall in a bright white T-shirt and swimsuit on the harbor square. Antonio is a huge man. Ever since he retired years ago from cooking at Vernazza's only pension, I've seen him only here, supervising the lethargy on the harbor square.

"*Ciao*, Antonio. Aren't you cold?" I ask.

"No, I'm drinking the wine," he says.

The sun has settled and a cold wind sends the temperature diving. I shiver. "*Freddo.*"

He looks up past the cemetery at a wisp of cloud heading out to sea. "The wind from the north. This will bring clear weather, but cold. Very clear. Tomorrow you will see Corsica."

The people of the Cinque Terre have many words for wind. Tramontana means "from the mountain." The mistral brings good weather. And the sirocco is a warm wind from the southeast. Three days ago, in Rome, a friend took me to his rooftop and kicked through a sprinkling of white sand saying, "This is from Egypt . . . the sirocco."

Returning his glass to the bar, Antonio turns back to say, "If you know the winds here in the Cinque Terre, you know the weather better than CNN."

I climb to my tiny room and hang out of the window—surveying the huge view, chasing away the horrible thought of headline news. I pull the shutter shut over a wad of Kleenex to keep it from clattering as the wind builds. After my laptop chores, I climb into a bed lumpy with Cinque Terre ambience.

While Tourists Sleep

The morning sun touches the tip of Vernazza's bell tower and greets a peaceful world. This time when the bells chime six, I know it's time to get up. The wind is gone. There's a refreshing damp cool in the air and a rare Italian silence. Head down and lost in thought, I wander downhill, passing under the tracks. Then, out of nowhere, a train rips like a tablesaw through town. In the wake of the train, distant roosters angrily crow "kee-kee-ree-kee" (as they say in Italian) at the modern world.

The harbor square is quiet—littered with calloused little

boats, still beached for the winter. After the town wakes up, the townspeople will hang out here—where painting and puttering is a spectator sport. Next week, umbrellaed restaurant tables will push the boats into the water, marking the opening day of the tourist season.

Throughout Europe—on medieval ramparts, in churches, produce markets, Alpine farmsteads, and Riviera villages—the local culture thrives while the tourists sleep. In the early morning shade, Vernazza's working boats are busy helping power the slow grind of the town's traditional economy. A few mobile market stalls await locals and restaurateurs preparing for another round of cooking.

Vittorio, still in his red Genoa sweatshirt, greets me enthusiastically. Together, we wander through the tiny open-air market. An old lady in boots and gloves plops down her fish-filled wheelbarrow.

"Her husband is retired now but he still cleans the nets," Vittorio says. "The son does the fishing. Fishing is a family business. If the man tried to sell the fish he would take home everything he caught. The woman is smart with the fish cart."

Sorting through the wheelbarrow like a sale bin at the mall, Vittorio introduces me to the *frutti di mare*: a tiny red snapper, electric eel, big octopus, and *pesche azzuro*, or "blue fish," the term for miscellaneous fish—anything from anchovies to tuna.

Picking up a shiny six-inch anchovy and threatening me with it as if it were a rattlesnake, Vittorio says, "This was swimming this morning at three o'clock. He will be dinner tonight. To preserve it, soak in salt for two months. But fresh, this is very tasty."

Then, screwing a forefinger into his cheek, he says, "Fresh anchovies stuffed with bread, eggs, parmesan, and a little parsley . . . it is the best funeral for them. Don't you think so?" he asks the fisherwoman, repeating the recipe in Italian.

She sweeps her fingernails up her chin, indicating, "I don't care."

It's obvious she doesn't like Vittorio. I can imagine what she thinks of the town's playboy showing an uncalloused tourist the market as if it were a museum display of endangered livelihoods.

I say quietly, "It's a tough life."

"Yes, but good money," Vittorio says, pointing to the brightly painted house atop the town. "Anchovies built her house."

"I will tell you how we catch the anchovies," he says. We walk the few steps to the harbor, and sit down on a colorfully painted dinghy with our backs to the still sleeping town.

Pointing past the jumble of beached dinghies out to sea, he says, "Sail out in the evening for an hour and set out a net with lamps shining. When darkness comes in, the fish stay with the light. After midnight the fisherman returns to ambush these fish."

On my first visits years ago, Vernazza's inky nighttime horizon was a milky way. I'd count the anchovy boats, their lights slowly blinking between the waves.

Tapping on my wedding band, Vittorio asks, "What is this word? Ah, 'ring.' A rope pulls a big ring around the float to make the net a bag. They take in the fish and when the sun comes up, they are here in the cart."

"We saw only a single wheelbarrow of anchovies," I say, "but there are so many restaurants."

"Now we get most of our anchovies from Monterosso and La Spezia," Vittorio admits.

"You said that Vernazza is a fishing village at seven in the morning. I see just two boats."

"Only two Vernazza families still fish for a living," Vittorio says, shrugging. "Before we harvest the sea. Now we harvest the tourists."

"Want a cappuccino?" he asks.

"Rick Steves Make Me a Very Rich Man"

On my first visit to Vernazza I slept at the only pension in town, Pension Sorriso. *Sorriso* is "smile" in Italian. For the next ten years, as my business grew, so did Sorriso's. Paolo Sorriso was my main man here, the lead listing in my guidebooks and the beach home of all my tours.

He never tried to impress me. I was charmed by his barnacle tongue approach to business. Slowly, as the flood of tourists rose, so did his prices. And like a sand castle at high tide, his concerns about good service crumbled. As demand exceeded his building's room supply, he gradually annexed nearby apartment flats. He began requiring that guests take dinner at his restaurant and charged more than the prices he had me list in my guidebook. I woke up only when he started bragging to my mistreated readers, "Rick Steves make me a very rich man."

I remember my first visit here. Sorriso, his brother, and his sister were a family of huge people. They filled their kitchen like giant gears, slowly turning out a menu that hadn't changed in fifteen years: breaded herring, green tomatoes, and spaghetti . . . bolognese or with clams. Breakfast was last night's bread and a hasty cappuccino.

Sorriso resisted change. His elevator ran on 10-lire coins long after these ridiculously worthless coins—they actually float—were out of circulation. For a decade I assumed his family name was Sorriso and called him by that. He never bothered to tell me his name was Paolo Fenelli. I still call him Sorriso.

For years Paolo was surrounded by the town's children playing crude, noisy video games. They still play but the volume is way down. And children still dig through Paolo's popsicle cooler. *Fruttidoro*, my favorite back when it cost 50 lire, is still there . . . at 1,200 lire.

But change comes even to Vernazza. Paolo's sister grew too big to help in the kitchen. For years she sat, like a record-breaking pumpkin, filling the doorway across from the pension. Now, I'm told, she stays inside. Paolo's brother, Antonio, retired to watch the varnish blister on the harbor boats and track the wind. And the old footprint toilet in Sorriso's bar has been replaced by one you can sit on.

"Ees beeg problem" was the heavy, tired, slow-motion response to any need our tour groups had. We had a tradition of toga parties with our groups. Gathering for dinner wearing our bedsheets and strategically placed leaves, sporting names like Magnus Rhododendron and Coitus Interruptus, we'd entertain each other. But modesty is a virtue in this town and, understandably this time, Sorriso pulled me aside and explained, "Ees beeg problem."

When Sorriso met Graziella, a sophisticated woman from Milano, he retired and bought a fine house in the big city. His nephew, Giovanni, a young man with the size and energy level of Paolo, took the reins. He carried on the "Ees beeg problem" ambience of the place.

Vernazza: My cover-girl village

Stopping by to see Giovanni, I'm surprised to find Paolo. "Where's Gio?" I ask.

"The young generation, they don't like the responsibility," explains Paolo, with less weariness than ever in his smile. "So I come back, now with Graziella." Pouring me a *sciacchetrà*, the graying but thin and lively Paolo says, "Graziella makes me young."

And I made him rich. He makes more money from my Italy guidebook than I do. But in a way, Sorriso made me a rich man, too. Vernazza has been my cover-girl village as I've earned my niche in the travel writing world as the guy who finds the undiscovered gems. Vernazza is the quintessential "back door." The best way for me to get people to take my books or articles seriously is to tack on a photo of Vernazza.

Riviera on the Rocks

I'm unable to travel in Europe anymore without doing a little research. Hoping to round out my coverage of Vernazza, I have a list of reader-recommended B&Bs to check out. First on the list is Ivo. Ivo, who runs the best bar in town, spent his college years in San Francisco. Now, with his three-year-old diploma and a postcard of the Golden Gate Bridge sharing a thumbtack on the wall behind the espresso machine, he is reportedly a kind of Vernazza welcoming committee for Americans in need of a private room, good gelato, or advice on hikes. Through Ivo, I hope to learn more about how this town works.

At the bar, I'm told that Ivo is at home. I head down the street in the direction the man in the bar waved. Two men approach me. Both wear dusty too-tight sweaters. They seem to be brothers and know who I am. Feeling curiously threatened, I ask, "*Dov'è la casa di Ivo?*"

The brother with the thin face and stringy hair gives me a rooms-for-rent business card, printed crooked with the faded blue ink of a tired rubber stamp. He stutters, "When you write the book, speak very well from us."

Assuring him I'd visit later, I repeat my question. He looks up and says in a soft, matter-of-fact voice, "Ivo."

Ivo, wearing a red cape and halfway through a haircut, pops his head out the window. I introduce myself and, like the gate-keeper of the Emerald City, he welcomes me upstairs.

Upstairs, Ivo greets me like an old friend from the Bay Area. He says, "So, finally I meet Rick Steves, the man who sends America to the Cinque Terre. Everybody with your book seems to know you."

Returning to his stool, repositioning his Soviet flag cape, he introduces me to his friend Simone. Surrounded by a floor furry with black hair, a newly trimmed Simone digs his hard-working scissors back into Ivo's hair. This trading of haircuts is a four-times-a-year ritual excuse for a lazy afternoon together.

On a stool in the corner, bent over his guitar, is Graham, from Arizona. When I plop into a chair near him, his head rises like an upbeat on a conductor's baton as if to say hello and then drops like a downbeat back into his own musical world.

Ivo's flat is evidence of how the Cinque Terre destroys a traveler's momentum. Not moving his head, but motioning with his eyes, Ivo directs me to a small pile of postcards from American friends. They litter the top of a bookcase under a poster of Jim Morrison—testimonies of tourists who became travelers in the Cinque Terre.

As I read through cards, Ivo and Simone reminisce happily as if the sight of each card brings their friends back to Vernazza.

"Oh, that's Chef John from Austin. He come here, he goes

away. He come here, he goes away. He come here again, he goes away."

"Yes, Catherine and Colleen. They're from Portland, stayed for eight days."

After a few minutes, Graham steps out of his music as if stepping out of a car. Impressed by the song, I ask, "You wrote that?"

Graham says, "It's called 'More Than You Know.' Lying on a rock, looking up at the sun, guitar on my belly, it came to me. I've been writing a lot here. New environment, people, the sea. And the rocks."

"The rocks?" I ask.

"Yes, there's something about the rocks. I was in Figueres, where Dalí lived and painted. Near Barcelona. It was the same. One look and I thought, 'No wonder.' I love Dalí's art. It's the rocks."

Abandoning Ivo momentarily, Simone pours me a cup of spumante. Setting it in the unfinished zone of a jigsaw puzzle of a nude woman, he returns to his scissors.

Graham explains, "'More Than You Know' has no words yet. It's about how important a girl I met at the hostel is to me right now. The words will come. I hum and strum. First some false words, and before you know it, the right words find their way into the melody."

I ask him to play more, and he does.

Simone stows the scissors and a trimmed Ivo puts on a leather jacket, tucks a football helmet under his arm, and strikes a James Dean pose. Simone snaps a photo as Ivo explains, "For my sister in San Francisco."

My conversation with Ivo wanders from cheap beds and good pesto to linguine and linguistics.

"From Genoa to Levanto it is one dialect," he says. "Then each of the Cinque Terre towns has a distinct dialect."

"Each village has its own slang," Simone claims. "You speak five words and I know where you live. 'All of us' in Vernazza is 'see-ah moo tutti nooee.' In Monterosso—only six kilometers away—you'll hear 'say moh tutti deh nooahtre.' If you say 'see-ah moo tutti nooee' in Monterosso, that means 'we are all naked.'"

Plopping onto his couch, Ivo adds, "Everywhere in Italy this is a sofa. But here it is 'ottomana.' Maybe because of the pirates. They came from the Ottoman Empire. Here, everybody loves a legend."

Head buried in his guitar, dancing alone atop his flexible stool, Graham sings, "*Crossing a bridge I passed in a dream, ain't it funny life always shows you which way to go. It's a leap of faith.*"

As I leave, Graham gives me a farewell downbeat with his head and Ivo warns me about the brothers in the sweaters. "All this year they make a plan to get into your book."

The wind is back. Knowing that waves crashing over the breakwater bring out the town, I head for the foam. Antonio Sorriso, supervisor of the peeling paint, hollers "mistral" as if heralding good news. Vittorio, posted outside his restaurant, waves a quick hello. I know Monica is up at Il Castello earnestly serving satisfied customers. Here at the harbor, old men pace the rough concrete breakwater, kids bop a soccer ball, and tongues of tourists chase gelato drips down sugar cones. As for me, I've got an appointment with a train for Switzerland. But I can't get Graham's tune out of my head. I love this scene "more than you know."

In the spray of a wave that sends the crowd dashing up main street, a young couple hails me: "Mr. Steves!" They're from Edmonton on their honeymoon. "Just like you say in your book, Mr. Steves, the children in Riomaggiore helped us peel a cactus fruit. And we found the old man in Corniglia. He invited us into his cellar. We drank wine from his keg with a straw. Thank you so much!"

Despite the B&B godfathers, tourist excursion boats, ATMs, and English menus, the Cinque Terre still casts a powerful spell. No matter who the pirates are these days, we all end up sharing the riches.

CHAPTER NINE

GIMMELWALD

*"Half a day is spent on steep rocks harvesting
what a machine can cut in half a minute on a flat field.
It's tradition. It's like breathing."*

Aiming for the heart of the Alps, I leave my train in the belle
epoche resort town of Interlaken. From Interlaken, a long, lush valley leads south to the snowy tips of the Eiger, Mönch, and Jungfrau.
Climbing onto another train—almost a toy in comparison to the
one that took me here from Italy—I head into the mountains.
Once in my seat, I slide open the big panoramic window. The lush
air, perfumed with the sweet, sweaty smell of freshly cut hay, fills
my car. Grassy banks speckled with alpine flowers remind me of my
first ride on this train. While my girlfriend and I eagerly hung out
the window at a slow corner, overwhelmed by the views, a railroad
worker surprised her with a bouquet of alpenroses offered through
the window.

Below me a swollen stream charges noisily down the center
of the valley, chattering excitedly about the wild ride it just survived. I crane my neck so I can see what all the excitement is
about. Slowly we glide higher and higher into Lauterbrunnen
Valley, a glacier-edged garden of traditional Swiss lifestyles. This
scenic rut has kept me from exploring the rest of Switzerland.
From the Alps, I need nothing better.

The track ends at the town of Lauterbrunnen. The air is brisk, the colors vivid. I feel healthy and happy to be small. Brutal cities like Los Angeles, Moscow, or Mexico City make me feel sadly insignificant. But here in the Alps I celebrate my smallness. It's a place where locals go about their work nonchalantly, and tourists are easily identified as the ones with heads locked back, marveling at the Alps.

Avalanches are a part of life here. Upon hearing them rumble across the valley, travelers train their eyes on the edges of the distant glaciers. I remember bringing a tour group into Lauterbrunnen. My tour group had seven days of Italy ground into their clothes. Not only had I been lifting spirits all day with promises of a self-serve laundry, I promised that our assistant guide would wash clothes for the entire group. Spirits were soaring as we approached the corner where I would reveal Lauterbrunnen's Laundromat. Then we saw it—or at least its freshly crumpled remains. Our Laundromat had been crushed under an avalanche.

Looking past the bare patch of land where the Laundromat once stood and down the valley, I follow the cliff past several waterfalls to the end of the valley. The village of Gimmelwald and the chalet I'll call home tonight sits, ram-tough, just beyond the bluff.

It's early and the sunshine energizes me. Rather than catch the funicular up and the train over, I decide to get to Gimmelwald by hiking along the river to see the waterfalls then riding the gondola at the end of the valley up into town.

Staubach Falls marks the end of Lauterbrunnen town. For years, I've marveled at it from a distance. Today, as I hike out of town, I climb for a close-up look. Scrambling up a pile of glacial gravel—as if struggling up a sand dune—I eventually work my way to the roaring base of the waterfall. Through the noisy storm, a black rock face soars 600 feet straight up. What was a river bursts over the cliff into a galaxy of excited drops. The sun glints through the mist as wet and fleeting prisms of color break into liquid fireworks.

I feel alone, engulfed in the roar. Then I notice a gray silhouette—a man—on the far side of the rainstorm. Suddenly, he grabs his head and falls to the ground. Racing to help him, I realize that

Staubach Falls hurls rocks (and that the small mountain of rocks he and I had climbed didn't get here by dump truck). I feel under attack.

As I help the injured man climb down the glacial gravel, we pass a sign that causes us both to pause. It says, in very clear German: "Vorsicht: Steinschlag." Looking up past the hand holding his wounded head, he translates it for me: "Beware, flying rocks." In Lauterbrunnen Valley, tourists learn to respect the power of nature.

In early trips I visited only touristy Interlaken. I shrugged and wondered, "What's the big deal?" I didn't understand that Interlaken was only a springboard into a land of raging natural waters crashing into deep and persistent cultural pools. The name Lauterbrunnen means "clear spring." From Interlaken you take three steps and leap into this Alpine world where man and nature share the same crib. But nature rules.

Just up the valley from Staubach Falls, Trummelbach Falls—a waterfall inside a mountain—makes its point differently, but with equal power. I climb a series of wet switchbacks to a tunnel that leads deep into the mountain, to an elevator. I buy a ticket, enter, and it zooms me up.

The elevator doors open into a misty cavern. The river roars, busy at work, cutting—like God's thundering bandsaw—through the mountain. Sheltering my camera from the angry mist, I try to capture this spectacle on film. A guard in an orange raincoat cautions me to watch my step. Last year, he tells me, a Japanese man, camera at his face, backed into Trummelbach Falls. He was found six months later in a log jam. His skin looked like wood.

Hiking down the switchbacks to the valley floor, I look back and notice a Swiss flag. While many flags signal conquest, this tiny red-and-white Swiss flag flying from the top of Trummelbach signals surrender. Nature flexes its muscles as if determined to teach us that the best way to control her is to obey her.

A big gondola station marks the end of the valley. The Schilthornbahn is the all-powerful lift that connects the valley floor with the mountain communities of Gimmelwald and Murren on its way to the 10,000-foot Schilthorn summit. This artificial vein pumps life's essentials—mail, bread, skiers, schoolkids, coffins, parasailors, and tourists—to and from each community. Last year the gondola was given a new function, and 2,700 people enjoyed the world's highest bungee jump.

Making Hay in Gimmelwald

Leaving the gondola station at the edge of the cliff high above Lauterbrunnen Valley, I step into the hamlet of Gimmelwald. Everything's out . . . flowers, kids, cows, and sun. I sigh the slogan I picked up from some graffiti at the youth hostel here on my first visit: "If heaven isn't what it's cracked up to be, send me back to Gimmelwald." My goal is Gimmelwald's Hotel Mittaghorn, but I'm in no hurry.

With every visit I look up at the next town, the built-up resort of Murren, and remember how cleverly Gimmelwald escaped development. At the dawn of Switzerland's age of big-time tourism, the farmers inhabiting the tumble of rough-hewn log farmhouses called Gimmelwald voted "no" to development. Led by the town's visionary schoolteacher, Emil von Allmen, they had their land classified "avalanche zone" so no building permits would be allowed. While other cliff-hanging villages became soulless resorts, Gimmelwald survives as a home for its farmers and their families.

Gimmelwald is a community in the rough. Its two 700-year-old streets, a zig and a zag, are decorated by drying laundry, hand-me-down tricycles, and hollowed stumps bursting proudly with geraniums. Little-boy cars are parked next to the tiny tank-tread cement mixers and mini-tractors necessary for taming this Alpine environment. White-bearded elves smoke ornate pipes. Cow troughs outnumber mailboxes. Stones called "*schindels*" sit like heavy checkers on old rooftops, awaiting nature's next move. While they protect the slate from the violent winter winds, today it's so quiet you can hear the cows ripping tufts of grass.

Gimmelwald has three dominant families: von Allmen, Brunner, and Feuz. With nearly all the 130 townsfolk sharing three surnames, there are probably ten Hans von Allmens and a wagonload of Maria Feuzes. To keep prescriptions and medical records

straight, the doctor in nearby Lauterbrunnen goes by
birthdate first, then the patient's name.

But townsfolk are more
creative. Fritz, the first man
with a tractor in the village,
is called "Motor Fritz." The
first time he fired up the
engine, the noise fright-
ened him. He ran away,

Traditions are stubborn in Gimmelwald.

and the story became part of Gimmelwald's folklore. Motor Fritz
has a friend known as "Hee Hee Ernst" for his funny laugh.

Buebi means "little boy." There is a von Allmen called Buebi.
His son, who works on the gondola, is Beubi's Buebi. And his little grandson is called Buebi's Buebi's Buebi.

Hans von Allmen was the first guy in town to have fiberglass
skis. Neighbors asked what the hell they were made of. Hans said
"fee bee glass." Hans became "Feebee Hans." And Hee Hee Ernst
laughed.

The Gimmelwald Hostel, Petrafied

Petra, the new owner of the hostel, sees me trudging up the hill
from the lift. "Hey Rick," she calls from the hostel's balcony.
"Come up for a drink."

I head up to the hostel. For years this was Switzerland's most
rustic youth hostel. It was managed by a sweet old lady named Lena
von Allmen. Lena sounded like a goat when she spoke English. Her
commitment to hosteling was admirable, but she grew too old and
frail to do anything but come by once a day to collect her three-
dollar fee and feed the goats who inhabited one wing of the place.

Because this was an official youth hostel, Lena had to send a
cut of each overnight fee to headquarters. When she realized she
was getting virtually all of her business through my guidebook, she
quit the hostel association. The youth hostel got a new name—
the Mountain Hostel—and Lena got all the money.

The hostel survived only because of the caring spirit of the travelers who visited. To shape their attitudes and expectations, I wrote it up very carefully: "This relaxed hostel survives with the help of its guests. Please read the signs, respect its rules, and leave it cleaner than you found it. The place is one of those rare spots where a family atmosphere spontaneously combusts, and spaghetti becomes communal as it softens."

I remember enjoying nights in the family room passing travel tales like a pipe. It was—and is—a high altitude, benevolent Loreley luring travelers with good company and natural beauty. The togetherness, warmed by itineraries tossed into the fire, made even the party-hearty student crowd philosophical. Conversations were meaningful. Cultural cross-dressing was accepted as the norm.

One night, beer-buzzed, I climbed upstairs to the dorm. It was dark. I didn't want to disturb my sleeping roommates. As I settled in the hammock-like top bunk and pulled the blanket up around my neck, the German in the next bed whispered in a perfect Rat Patrol accent, "You're climbing into the germs of centuries."

In later visits, when I had minibus tour groups in tow, Lena took good care of me. I'd get the coveted "teacher's room"—the only single in the house. And in her goat scrawl, Lena thumb-tacked notes on two other rooms: "For the girls of Rick Steve" and "For the boys of Rick Steve."

My tour groups aged even faster than I did, and soon we migrated up the hill to Hotel Mittaghorn in search of more comfort, more privacy, and younger germs. But I'd still make an annual visit to the hostel to chat with Lena, who every year leaned harder on her cane.

I feared that aging Lena would turn the hostel over to Eric Balmer, the entrepreneurial tornado of Interlaken whose hostel—"Balmer's Herberge"—ranks among the top four or five endless frat party zones in Europe. Eric is a great guy, but it's generally agreed by connoisseurs of small-town paradises that another Balmer's would fit Gimmelwald like a Pizza Hut.

Lena sold the Mountain Hostel to Petra, the best thing that

could have happened to the future of Gimmelwald-bound vagabonds. Lena could have sold to Eric for more, but Petra lived in
Gimmelwald.

Petra meets me at the door. It's the middle of the day and the
hostel is nearly empty. While a few lazy hostelers are reading on the
balcony, most are off hiking. Petra invites me for a drink outside.

I tell Petra she's the most driven person I've ever met in
Gimmelwald. She tells me she's always had a passion for hosteling.

"I grew up in Interlaken, next to the Böningen hostel," she
explains. "It's a big place right on the lake. I saw travelers coming
and going throughout my school years. Working at the hostel, I
fell in love a hundred times with travelers. I dreamed of marrying
an American and being called 'honey.'"

As her hard-working husband, filthy as a muddy boot, plops
himself down at our picnic table, she finishes. "Then I met a farm
boy named Wally. Love took me to Gimmelwald."

With an entrepreneurial vision unknown in Gimmelwald,
Petra took out a loan and, with her husband's help, renovated the
crude little hostel. Wally's father—with his small-town outlook—
worried that the loan would ruin the family. Petra laments that
her father-in-law has never visited the hostel. Translating for
Wally, she says, "Wally says if he had cows, his dad would celebrate. But Wally left farming and his father will not forgive him."

Petra's hostel is a home away from home for new alpaholics.
Nostalgically touring the renovated place, I poke into its little
graffiti room, upstairs under the eaves. The graffiti is gone and on
the mattress, the hostel blanket heaves up and down. Not wanting
to interrupt a lifelong travel memory, I close the door quietly.

Downstairs in the much-used family room, Petra hands me
her guest book like a new mother shares her baby album. It's filled
with reports from people intoxicated by Gimmelwald.

Mark from San Francisco writes:

I've lost track of time and date
Here between the meadows of yellow and the skies so mellow.
If the clouds are kind, nature will show a sign.
And she's telling me to never let it cease.

Oh, how wonderful is this peace.

Petra and Wally invite me for a walk through town. With Petra translating for her husband, the conversation is slow. But the hostel is set for the day and they seem to be in no hurry.

Petra and Wally: Their hostel is a home away from home for Alpaholics.

I see only women and children about. Petra says the men are out making hay. Wally explains that Gimmelwald is so consumed by its making of hay that the fire brigade—breaking all local traditions—allowed women to join. This way, if a fire hits when the men are far off in the fields, there'll be people to toss the buckets. The people of Gimmelwald have always been farmers first. And many—like Wally's father—can be farmers only.

Passing the big new farm of Esther and Johann, Petra says, "They have two small boys. One will be the farmer. These things, they don't change." The numbers 1995 are carved above the door of their new barn. We walk around the corner to the old barn—in the same style, but dated 1656.

"Here in Gimmelwald," says Petra, "the people's farming work is their life. When they don't work they talk about work. Farming is in their blood."

Farmers systematically harvest the steep hillside above Gimmelwald. They cut and gather every inch of hay like children of the Depression polish their dinner plates with the last crust of bread. After harvesting what the scythe can reach, they pull hay from nooks and crannies by hand.

Petra says, "Half a day is spent on steep rocks harvesting what a machine can cut in half a minute on a flat field. It's tradition. It's like breathing. And there's one right way to do it."

Petra explains how excitement mounts in the village as the late June day approaches when the cows leave the barns to go to the high Alps. The choice of the right morning to take the animals to the high country is a delicate decision. It's a mix of tradition and superstition, founded on what worked in the past.

I tell her that early one morning last year, I was awakened by the lazy rhythm of an Alpine bell choir. From my hotel balcony I saw a happy but ghostly procession cutting through the pre-dawn darkness. Folk-loric fathers gazed past my hotel toward the high meadows. Sons wielded their grandfathers' crooks and staffs. Lanterns swung with the bells, softly lighting the cows—decked out with their finest bells—as they evacuated the town.

"Yes, this is a big day," says Petra. "Children take a day off from school."

Centuries of trial and error are folded into the folk farming culture. More milk is the bottom line. Wally says that not every scheme works. One man heard that if goats hear music they'll give more milk. He wired up speakers. A goat ate the wires and was electrocuted. No milk at all.

Modern Swiss farmers know that chemicals would improve production. But the Swiss government subsidizes Gimmelwald's less productive, natural approach.

"Even without the government's help, these farmers take good care of nature," Petra says. "Wally's family uses no soap on dishes because the water goes on the fields. In Gimmelwald the only fertilizer you find comes directly from the cows."

Suddenly a bright modern gondola swooshes by with thirty tourists gawking out the windows. "Imagine Gimmelwald without the gondola," I say.

"In Gimmelwald the twentieth century started in 1965 when we got the cable car," Petra tells me. "Before that, mothers ready to give birth had to hike an hour downhill to the valley floor for a ride into Interlaken. Many mothers didn't make it all the way to the hospital. Outside Interlaken, a curve in the road is named for a Gimmelwald baby who was born right there."

Not that an easier route to the hospital made any difference, but these days Gimmelwald has lots of babies. There are twenty kids in the village school. Murren, the resort on the next ridge, has four times the population but no more children. Gimmelwald is a stronger community.

I ask Petra about the new "Magic Mountain" slogan painted on the side of the gondola.

She confers with Wally and says, "We copied this name from Disneyland." She explains that the Swiss government is starting to tighten up on farming subsidies and Gimmelwald is changing its ideas about the tourist dollar.

Murren, up the hill, feels like a resort because it was built that way. Gimmelwald is different. Gimmelwald, with its farmers manning the T-bars in the ski season, feels quaintly antiquated. But today, tourism slumps in overbuilt Murren. Its tourism director is seen as a fool. But Gimmelwald's modest economy is robust.

While Murren has the huge elegant chalets, Gimmelwald houses its guests more simply. Walking through "downtown," I count a hotel, a pension, a youth hostel, and the schoolteacher's B&B.

Wally points to a sturdy well-cared-for barn and Petra says, "And now we also have 'Schlaf im Stroh.'"

The sign at the barn is trilingual: "Schlaf im Stroh, Aventure sur la Paille, Sleep in Straw." A clever solution to the need for budget lodgings, this barn, one of 200 such barns in Switzerland, artfully shuffles cows and people. In summer cows go to the high Alps, leaving the barn empty as tourists stampede into town looking for cheap beds. The place is hosed down, the straw is changed, and the barn is opened to humans. Tourists lay their rucksacks on the feeding troughs and bed down in cow stalls filled with fresh, sweet-smelling straw.

Inside the barn, Petra reads the sign aloud: "Welcome here. Please enter the barn free and easy. Install yourself anywhere in the straw. If the weather is nice we are out making hay. We will come and see you the latest in the evening. Strictly no smoking."

The switch from heifers to hikers depends on the snow level. If there's too much snow, the cows stay, because the grass in the high meadows will be inaccessible. This week the cows are grazing in the high Alps but tonight one cow is sick. She'll share her barn with the tourists.

Petra has more vision than your average villager. Closing the Sleep in Straw barn door, she explains her proposal to creatively merge farming and tourism by letting travelers help with hay work. "For tourists, it is perfect. They can make hay, eat mountain cheese and fresh bread, and actually see our traditional Alpine lifestyle. And they would help the farmers at the same time."

Petra is enthusiastic about her plan, which would be free and helpful at the same time—a high altitude win-win arrangement. "But old people stopped my idea," she says. "They said, 'A tourist helping to cut hay would need a helicopter in five minutes.' 'Need a helicopter' is the village phrase for needing an emergency evacuation."

We're nearing the top of the village and my hotel. Our walk has taken us on the entire Gimmelwald zigzag. Christian von Allmen putt-putts by in an empty two-cylinder hay wagon. I know Christian from years of after-dinner accordion performances for my groups at Walter's Hotel Mittaghorn. He wears a tattered gray felt hat and a huge red beard, and gnaws a droopy old pipe. He doesn't say much. But his bright eyes, gentle smile, and the way he answers most questions with "yeeeahhh, yah, yeeeahhh" make me think he understands a lot. He's heading up past Walter's, so the three of us hitch a ride on the back of his wagon.

Petra jokes, "It's good Wally is with us. Otherwise, after our walk and this ride, villagers would talk." A girl can't be on the first cable car up in the morning without setting the village abuzz with talk of an affair. Courting in a village is more complicated than courting in a town. Romances are everybody's business.

So are funerals. In Gimmelwald they are attended by at least one person from each home. There is no cemetery in the village. Men carry the coffin as the whole community rides the cable car down to Lauterbrunnen Valley.

At a traditional funeral dinner, the village sits together, eating as a family. The meal of coffee, bread, cheese, and mustard is simple so that no grieving family will experience financial hardship in providing it.

We hop off the truck at Hotel Mittaghorn, perched at the top end of Gimmelwald. From the porch, we survey the town.

"Something is missing," says Petra. " Gimmelwald has no church. They say if the biggest building in a Swiss village is a church, its people are Catholic. If it's a school, they're Protestant."

She points to the biggest building in town. "Gimmelwald has a school . . . we are Protestant."

"How do people go to church then?" I ask.

"Once a month the valley pastor visits. The church service is in the schoolhouse. Elizabeth von Allmen teaches a weekly Sunday school class to the village kids. Locals who go to church for more than their marriage, baptism, and burial hike to Murren on Sunday mornings."

Petra warns me that Walter's bar is filled with youth hostelers who've come up to see me. As she and Wally skip down the stairs—a shortcut back to the hostel—I step into my hotel.

A Friendly but Hostel Crowd

The graffiti wall at the Mountain Hostel used to be my sounding board. Since most of the hostel's guests were my readers and the remainder were generally vagabonds who refused to follow any guidebook, an entertaining mix of comments filled the wall. My fans referred to themselves as "Stevesians" and called their picnics "Ricknicks."

Because of my work, people consistently describe me in two peculiar ways: "bigger than you are on TV" and as a guru. A guru is a teacher whose students honor his advice nearly without question. If I say airport X-rays won't hurt your film, it's believed. If I say do Dordogne but bag Bordeaux, my will be done. But it's also common that people thank me for great experiences they have on Malta or Mallorca—places I've never been, much less written about. With that kind of following, my research seems worth the trouble and doing a careful job remains paramount. And as TV screens get bigger and bigger, so will I.

You can't have fans without foes. Some people are downright resentful. This hostel graffiti board was where they got even. Each year I'd lie back on a musty old bed and read the wall from top to bottom—enjoying the accolades of fans and marveling at how people who'd never met me could decree: "Kill Rick Steves."

Petra painted over the graffiti wall. Now I get my feedback in person up the hill at Walter's bar in Hotel Mittaghorn. Word travels quickly in Gimmelwald. When I'm in town with a tour group, the hostelers hike up and gather in Walter's bar after dinner. While I enjoy my tour guiding and the people in our groups, my heart is with the independent travelers. Each evening, after stoking a polka with my tour gang in the residents-only dining room, I'd slip into the smoke- and farmer-filled bar to find a gang of hostelers.

It's about six o'clock and a gang of hostelers have gathered in the bar for a pre-dinner beer. Cheeks radiant with Alpine sun and high altitude memories, they are high in the Alps and loving it.

I join them, clustering around a table crowded with beer glasses. Mike, a Canadian, wears a ponytail and his first beard. James and Jan, a sunburnt guy and girl from California, share a chair and a beer. Val, who says she loves me, is a young school-teacher from Maine. Kate, an Australian free spirit, has never heard of me but is pleased to meet a travel writer. She buys me a beer. After that, introductions peter out and I just greet the rest of the gang en masse.

James broaches the delicate subject of how I, his inspiration—who must have noble and well-thought-out intentions—can justify abandoning my backpacker roots for soft, wealthy, older travelers. Nearly indignant, he asks, "How can you be a tour guide?"

The others chime in, "Yeah, Rick."

"My tours are for people who have more money than time. They hire us to be sure that things go smoothly," I explain. "You guys can just fly to Europe, make all the mistakes without even noticing, and still have a blast."

"But people on tours don't have any time to explore," says Jan, the sunburnt Californian. "Today we found the meadow locals call the Dancing Floor. And we danced on it."

"And a lot more," James says, chuckling as she blushes and the gang smiles.

Mike, who keeps pulling on his beard as if to make it grow, says, "Just like you say in your books, I picnic, sleep on trains, and never make any reservations. But do you still travel like that?"

"With all my tours and research, I don't really blow with the wind like I used to," I admit. "I still sleep on trains and picnic as much as I ever have, maybe even more. But the problem with travel for me these days is that I've always got more work than time."

Several hostelers look disturbed at the thought of combining work and travel.

Feeling suddenly older, I continue, "I do anything to get more use of my time in order to do more research and writing. To save time, I take a taxi or even a plane. I pay a hotel to do my laundry."

The gang looks stunned, almost shaken.

Fortunately Christian von Allmen joins us before I confess I've used porters in Turkey. Christian drops by without his accordion for a change. Today he's here just for a drink. I order him a coffee schnapps. Clinking glasses, I thank him for keeping our groups dancing. With a twinkle in his eye that says we're on the same team, he gives me a long, friendly mountain man's "Yaaaa."

I introduce Christian to the hostel gang, but they aren't done with me yet. The schoolteacher, Val, asks, "Do you have any new discoveries?"

After downing some beer, I answer, "Just this year I learned you can reload a small travel-size tube of toothpaste by docking it tightly against a big tube and squeezing slowly."

Raising my glass, I offer a toast: "To travel's magic moments."

"Like making love on the Dancing Floor," says James, raising his glass triumphantly.

"Or picnicking under the Sprutz waterfall," says his embarrassed girlfriend, trying to change the subject.

Val, helping her out, says, "Cheap travel really is best."

Mike pulls out a bag of peanuts, tears off the corner, and sends it around the table.

"Good travel is making friends," I say, "like this."

Val pulls a camera out of her bag and James and Jan bring out my guidebook. Enduring the ridicule of a few back-bench onlookers, my new friends ask me for autographs and pose with me for photos.

They share obscure bits of my books. James says, "You wrote that you put those huge kilometer markings on the Rhine to make your book easier to follow. There's no way!"

"Yeah, you're right," I say. "Sometimes I get bored and lonely writing. So I pop in something to tease my readers. Some people actually believe I put those signs up."

Jan offers, "In Morocco, we used your trick for checking out a cheap room. Open the door, flip on the lights, and count the bugs."

The hostelers repond with a resounding chorus of "Yuck!"

"If you weren't doing your travel work, what would you like to do?" Val asks.

I answer, "Teach piano," and she compliments herself on what interesting answers that question always gets.

Mike says, "Why don't you write about the nightlife in Europe? I love the nightlife."

"Then what are you doing in Gimmelwald?" Kate asks. The gang laughs.

"My readers spend their days sightseeing and their nights sleeping," I say. "I use my evenings for writing."

And although there is no sign that this discussion is winding down, that provides me with a handy excuse to say goodbye and relax before Walter's dinner.

Climbing the stairs to my comfortable room at Walter's while they stay for another beer, I feel gratified but sad. I feel more like their father than their friend.

But, stretching out on one of Walter's lumpy old beds, I'm reassured and thankful that experiences I had a generation ago still contribute to the dream trips of travelers born after I took my graduation trip.

Walter and Hotel Mittaghorn

Hotel Mittaghorn sits at the top end of Gimmelwald. The black-stained chalet has eight balconies, a couple of picnic benches out front, and a few umbrellaed tables on its tiny terrace. Everything comes with huge views. As if anchored by pitons into the steep grassy hillside, the hotel is disturbed only by the nearly silent twice-hourly whoosh of the cable car and the two-cycle clatter of passing tractors.

Walter Mittler, the owner, is Hotel Mittaghorn. In the mid-1970s he got sick of the rat race, turned in his Swiss Air chef's apron, and made Gimmelwald his "Green Acres." He had an aunt with emphysema who needed the fresh environment. For several years—the last years of her life—Walter's hotel rattled with her struggling wheezes.

Walter never married. I doubt if it ever occurred to him. Hair thinning and belly bigger, he seems to live in his dirty white apron. Shuffling around and breathing heavier each year, Walter is slowing down.

Old-fashioned sleds hang under the chalet's eaves. One time Walter stowed his apron and showed a little youthful craziness. During my only Swiss ski visit, Walter invited me—with a playful wink—to Murren for an after-dinner drink. Carrying Walter's sleds, we rode the gondola up to Murren. After a schnapps, we strapped flashlights to our heads, miner-style, and zoomed through the night down the trail back toward Gimmelwald.

Suddenly, halfway down, Walter pulled over. The snow-covered world was perfectly quiet. Nothing moved. Walter turned off his headlamp. As he reached for mine I expected to be engulfed in darkness. But as Walter switched off my lamp, he switched on a moonlit dreamscape. Everything was silver on black. The moonlight reflected off the trees, the trail below us, and the icefields across the valley. After a silent moment, Walter asked, "How many tourists see this?"

Back in the hotel, Walter dusted the snow off his pants, tied his apron back on, and once again became the grumpy but lovable old innkeeper. I never saw him out of Hotel Mittaghorn again.

Never quite accepted by the "peasants," as he calls the towns-folk, he's still the village city slicker. Even so, they fill his pub with their smoke and drink his beer.

When the village council allowed one farmer to build a small silo directly in front of his hotel marring the view, Walter hit back by deducting an "inconvenience fee" from each visitor's bill and sending that money—without paying taxes on it—to his pet charity in Ecuador.

While his logic is clear only to him, Walter is making a difference. In the last five years more than a quarter million dollars of his money has built roads and clinics in a town halfway around the world that Walter will never see. The hotel's creaky stairway is lined with photos of his Ecuador project and formal but unintelligible letters he's written to explain his grounds for compassionate, measured, and entirely fair—as far as he's concerned—tax evasion.

With the help of my promotion, Walter runs a thriving hotel. When the mercenary Paolo Sorriso, who runs a hotel I recommend on the Italian Riviera, boasted, "Rick Steves make me a very rich man," I was perturbed. But it feels great to provide Walter with a booming business.

Our alliance started years ago. Noticing that the steady stream of tourists in town were nearly all Americans toting my guidebook, Walter sent me a letter inviting me to check out his hotel. It was a couple of years before I made the trek to the top end of the village to visit Walter. When I finally did, I was bitten by Walter's feisty little dog, Luchsi. I was also bitten by the possibility of staying here in relative comfort with my tour groups.

Now all that remains of Luchsi is a big photo in the dining room. My groups are more comfortable, and Walter even arranges for a "peasant" to meet us at the gondola station with a tractor wagon to haul our groups' luggage. Invariably there's one particularly frail senior in the group who is placed carefully on the top of the pile of suitcases for a free lift up. As she waves like a 1930s Rose Parade queen, cameras click and people cheer.

Walter's hotel is a creaky treasure chest of memories. It's hard to forget the time one of our Belgian tour bus drivers invited his wife, Nina, to join him at Walter's. The driver forgot that in an old Alpine chalet voices travel several floors. In the wee hours, our entire group was stirred from their sleep by rhythmic grunting:

"Nee-nuh, Nee-nuh, Nee-nuh." Nina is the only bus driver's wife whose name I remember.

The stepped lane that leads from the gondola to Walter's makes me think of Glen. Able-bodied tour members sometimes complain about the steep ten-minute uphill hike, but not Glen. He suffered from cerebral palsy and was unable to walk. On the way to Walter's, he refused help, throwing his body up the hill one step at a time until he landed on Walter's doorstep—sweaty, dirty, and smiling, like some unstoppably happy punch-me toy.

Glen's disease steeled his determination to live life with an everything's-a-blessing gusto. While he had a friend on the bus who always offered to carry him, Glen was determined to manage this climb on his own. To some, the climb to Walter's "pitted them out." To Glen it was "conquering the Alps."

Life is simple and good here at Hotel Mittaghorn. And, in hopes of maintaining Walter's sanity, each year he and I have a state of the alliance meeting. I encourage him to hire help and he complains, "The peasants are impossible." And each year we end up lightening his load by whittling back on the services my guidebook promises he provides.

Walter's menu is extremely simple: a board printed on two sides. One day he serves chicken and spaghetti. The next, he flips the board and it's veal stew and rice.

A tour guide friend asked me, "How long are you staying at Walter's?"

I responded, "Till the food gets old."

My friend, who knows the drill, replied, "Two days."

Tonight, it's the veal. Walter may keep his menu simple, but he uses only the best ingredients. His salad is one hour out of the garden. I eat it with my fingers one leaf at a time.

Walter sets down a basket of bread and apologizes. "Murren's baker is sick. His bakery is closed. This bread is terrible. I get it from Interlaken. Now, for the first time, I have leftover bread. People taste the difference and eat less."

Emerging from the kitchen with a platter of meat dishes, Walter mutters about how tainted British cows have scandalized kitchens all over Europe. As he sets down my veal he promises he uses only New Zealand beef grown with no hormones. "No one eats British meat, "he grumbles "and Swiss meat is a scandal, too." Apparently, Swiss hospitals gather all the post-operation scraps—including placentas and human body parts—into a mix that is fed to the cows.

"You can put a Swiss flag on it and I still won't eat it," Walter declares. "Animal hospitals do this, too. They put the cats and dogs to sleep, put them in a barrel, and we have it on the table in six months."

I ask Walter if he remembers that a few years ago the restaurant near the lift station advertised a "Rick Steves burger."

Walking some dirty dishes back into his kitchen, he wonders out loud, "I wonder what they put in *that* meat."

Walter and I joke about how tourist industries create traditions to make a buck. One year we tested our culture-bending power by creating our own new "traditional" drink. While a coffee *fertig* (coffee with peppermint schnapps) is a well-established local favorite, we created the "Heidi Cocoa": Swiss hot chocolate with schnapps. Today our Heidi Cocoa is considered as "traditional" as a coffee *fertig* in Gimmelwald. And it's the best-selling hot alcoholic drink in town.

Nothing makes Walter laugh more than the poetic justice of the greedy overdeveloped and overpriced hotels in nearby Murren struggling while his humble little Hotel Mittaghorn thrives. Yet to Walter, money has lost meaning. The leader of any group that stops by is tossed the change bag and given the job of collecting the beer, wine, and schnapps money.

Walter could retire. But this is his only life. He has no relatives. He rarely leaves his hotel. Hikers need his beds and the village in Ecuador needs his continued support. As long as he's able, he'll keep shuffling and providing for both.

Teachers with Nail Shoes

With plenty of daylight left on this long June evening, I skip Walter's dessert and slip out unnoticed by the hostelers still in the bar. I hike down the shortcut stairs through the village to the home of Gimmelwald's schoolteachers, Olle and Maria.

Looking from the trim and tidy rough-hewn homes of Gimmelwald up to the towering hotels of Murren, I marvel at the vision of Emil von Allmen. Gimmelwald's retired schoolteacher foresaw the struggle between maintaining traditional life and developing tourism and pulled his village out of the coming rat race. A wise and visionary community leader, he became part of Gimmelwald's folklore.

When Emil retired, the town decided that the next teacher needed to be an outsider—above village squabbling— who "wore nail shoes." Nail shoes are used for hay making. Someone who wears them respects and understands the farming culture.

The new teacher is actually a couple who split Gimmelwald's one teaching position. To some, Olle and Maria are known not by their surname (Eggimann) but as Olle and Maria Nail-shoes. Olle and Maria, while here for fourteen years now, are still learning about the power of village tradition.

Olle and Maria are on their back porch, which sits above the cliff. Not a nail shoe in sight, Maria sorts through a basket of berries and Olle studies the far side of the valley with his telescope.

There's nothing but air between their deck furniture and the rock face of the Jungfrau a mile or two across. Kick a soccer ball wrong and it ends up a mile below on the Lauterbrunnen Valley floor.

Olle knows the view from his back porch like those with a sea view know the shipping lanes. With strains of Mozart tumbling through the sliding-glass door and onto the deck, Olle spots an ibex with his telescope. Ibex, the size of a big deer with four-foot-wide ram-like horns, majestically roam that zone between people and glaciers. Panning to the next rock face, Olle shows me the spot where the rock ruptures and an underground river spurts out mightily—like a gargoyle in a rainstorm. Just another cascade in the clear springs.

Olle and Maria seem to welcome my visits as a refreshing break.

I'm curious about the life that modern, cosmopolitan teachers lead in this confined social world. Conversation flows easily.

As teachers, honoring both traditional and modern ways is as challenging as teaching evolution in a Catholic school. They are paid to teach the 3 Rs—not to change the culture.

"Here in Gimmelwald," says Olle, "when you plant, you do it on certain days. You harvest on certain days. People are close to nature. They don't need some modern city-taught teacher messing with their ways. Their relationship with nature is almost mystical."

Olle and Maria have designed the ideal life. They have a fine house and a good income (together they make double what an American schoolteacher would make). Their minds are freed by a modern university outlook but not chained to a big-city pace of life. And their two kids are growing up in a traffic-free village wonderland.

While my father treats his father's wood-working tools with a reverence for old-time quality, he never uses them. That lifestyle is dead and buried in the stress we call American success. Here, in Switzerland, that same reverence honors old-time skills and tools by using them.

Olle unwraps a brick of mountain cheese and slices it with his grandfather's plane. "This is Hobelkase. The word *hobel* . . . is a woodplane . . . and *kase* . . . is cheese," he explains, carving a tasty curl for each phrase. "You cut it like wood. Must be at least two years old. This is the very best. Like a woman, it gets flavor with age."

Olle says, "Rick, the proof that you really are the travelers' god is that even when you are wrong, they won't believe me." Olle and Maria rent rooms to travelers. Olle gently corrects some of my book's advice on local hikes: "A trail you recommended became an ugly service road. The flowers are gone. If I walk there I weep. But your readers refuse to accept my correction."

Maria remarks on the restlessness of American tourists. "We have this impression that it must be some sort of illness—to arrive on one night and leave the next morning. When they finally get rested they are on their way."

Popping an elegant sliver of Hobelkase into my mouth, I bring up my concern that Switzerland is becoming too expensive for the average traveler.

"In Switzerland there is no place where you have to be afraid," Olle responds. "There are no slums. The minimum wage of eighteen Swiss francs is nearly triple the minimum wage in the United States. There is no homelessness."

"All this is not cheap," Maria admits. "But what is it worth? We choose to pay for it. Is there not enough money in America to overcome hunger and homelessness?"

I try to explain. "In America caring people take a drunk to dinner for Thanksgiving. But a favorite Bible quote is 'We'll always have the poor.'"

"In Switzerland we also have a national day of prayer," says Olle. "But in Gimmelwald we don't pray. We only eat plum cake."

"But we feed our hungry and all the people of Switzerland have a place to sleep," adds Maria.

"And this is a safe country," Olle says. "We don't lock our doors. It's hard to get some of the tourists to relax about this—but we don't lock anything."

"Is there no crime?" I ask.

"We had one robber in Murren. Wasn't that two years ago?" he asks Maria.

"Yes," she says. "He robbed a hotel. Since the valley has only one way out, the road was closed at midnight. At three in the morning he was captured trying to escape the valley."

I joke to Maria that Olle would make a good politician, but Olle breaks in. "That's one job I do not want—politics. But in a village so small, my day will come. The town meets once a year. Everybody goes to this meeting to be sure they won't be chosen to a political position. Whether local or national, we Swiss are afraid about too much power in any one person. In Bern (the national capital), we have seven people who are the governmental inner circle. The president is chosen from these seven. He only organizes the work. The office rotates. We have a new president each year."

Maria says, "Many Swiss don't even know who the current president is. We have government by three parties sharing power, so in Switzerland politics is the art of compromise. In our country we like our political change watered down."

Olle explains that because of the strong regional differences throughout Switzerland, no one wants a strong national government. He and Maria show how Swiss cultural diversity is caricatured in popular regional jokes.

Appenzellers are short and traditional: Why do Appenzellers laugh when they play football? The grass tickles their armpits as they run.

Folks from Friburg are dirty: Why did the Friburger pour hot water into the garbage? Quick lunch. Why do birds fly in circles over Friburg? That happens when you hold your nose with one wing. Where do Friburgers hide their money? Under the soap.

Olle follows the jokes by saying, "One thing is true of every region: Here in Switzerland we love our country and we love our way of life."

"For example, today at the village co-op local eggs cost double what Dutch eggs cost," Maria say. "But, like many people here, I buy Swiss eggs."

Olle agrees, adding, "And when the Swiss franc is overvalued and tourism is down, the Swiss vacation here in Switzerland to help out."

Tempering their enthusiasm for the local culture, Maria says, "But getting to know us Swiss can be slow. Here in Gimmelwald, we are still considered outsiders."

Maria pauses as a hay wagon jumbles by, then continues. "The people here are very conservative. Women couldn't vote until the 1970s."

"And some regions gave women the vote only in the 1990s," says Olle. Noticing the shock on my face, Olle then jokes, "German women had the vote much earlier and look what happened there."

When I push them for some explanation, Maria explains that, traditionally, it was practical for each family to have one vote. This way, if the woman needed to stay on the farm with the children, the man could go to the square on voting day and raise the family sword. But in places like Walter's bar, men would brag about how they voted independently of their family decisions. Women, feeling betrayed, wanted their own vote. Slowly, the vote was changed from one vote per family to one vote per adult.

Europeans have a habit of carrying on an evening conversation through the coming darkness without turning on a light. With a pause in the conversation, long after darkness surrounds the candles on our table, we realize how much time has passed. Sharing the last slivers of Hobelkase, I invite Olle to join me on a hike in the morning at eight. He jumps at the opportunity and suggests we start at seven.

I climb the stairs through the sleeping moonlit village back to Walter's hotel. At the top of town, I stop. Except for distant loud waters, it's silent. On distant snowfields, beyond the Dancing Floor, I see just a little of that silver-on-black world.

In Search of Edelweiss

It's a glorious Alps morning. As planned, I meet Olle at the gondola station. After a fifteen-minute gondola ride, we walk to a small lake. Opening his rucksack on a rock, he asks me to take off my shoes and socks. Muttering that he can't believe how tourists tackle these mountains without good hiking boots, Olle fits some moleskin around my tender toes.

As Olle works, I lie back on the rugged tufts of grass growing through the pebbly shale. Completely alone, we're surrounded by a harsh and unforgiving Alpine world. Anything alive is here only by the grace of nature. A black ballet of rocks is accompanied by cow bells and a distant river. Wisps of clouds are exclamation points.

The Alps put you close to God. A day like today has Lutherans raising their hands and holy rollers doing cartwheels. I remember what someone wrote in the hostel guest book: "I'm not religious. But while I walk on a ridge, I have to raise my hands to the sky."

On a solitary ridge we meet Elizabeth von Allmen, who's in her seventies. Elizabeth, Gimmelwald's Sunday school teacher, climbs a towering ridge all alone with her walking stick and binoculars. Sharing a delight in the day she says, "*So schön . . . fantastisch . . . ay yai yai.*"

We follow a faint path along the ridge. I stop every few steps to enjoy vast views of the Schilthorn on our left and the Jungfrau on our right. Olle takes on a teacher's voice. "We respect nature more than the tourists do. When there's an avalanche warning we take the gondola down. Tourists continue sledding. There are many accidents. In Lauterbrunnen, maps show red flags for places of mountain injuries and black ones for deaths."

Pointing to the towering rock cliff of the mountain over the valley directly ahead of us, he says, "The Eiger is solid black."

As I squint up at a wasp-like helicopter, Olle answers my question before I ask it. "These are mostly sightseeing trips. But even sightseeing trips are related to mountain rescue. As they show a tourist around, they are practicing for emergency rescues."

"Are there really dead climbers hanging from ropes on the Eiger?" I ask.

"Yes," says Olle. "It's sad when bodies are finally recovered. Sometimes it's twenty years later—they look like they did when we saw them last, except with a very light beard. The family has to identify them."

The weather can turn at any time. Just last month, a storm hit fast. Within a few minutes five people died: three mountaineers on the Eiger, one on the Mönch, and one in the air—a parasailor.

I tell Olle of a harrowing experience I had back in my youth hostel days. We'd hike up the Schilthorn from the hostel with a plastic bag, sit on the bag, and slide down the glacier—breathtaking fun. As a reckless young tour guide, I'd lead my groups down the mountain in the same way.

One day, late in the season, with an icy but smaller-than-usual sliding field, I got going out of control. Hurtling directly toward the rocky edge, everything but my mind went into slow motion. After almost too much time to consider my options, I dug my hands like brakes into the rocky ice. Going through several degrees of burn in a matter of seconds, I ground to a halt with blackened, blistered, and bleeding hands—and a bloody butt.

My group heralded me as a hero. But in the Murren doctor's office I was scolded as a fool, the whipping boy for all the stupid tourists who toy with the power of the mountain. The doctor didn't even bother to clean my hands. He lectured me, sprayed something on my wounds, and bandaged me. I left knowing that the little bits of Schilthorn embedded in my palms would come out only in the pus of a later infection.

Olle nods, as if in support of the doctor, and says, "This happens many times."

Olle tells me that even cows become victims of the mountains, occasionally wandering off cliffs. Alpine farmers expect to lose some of their cows in "hiking accidents." These days cows are double the weight of cows a hundred years ago and no less stupid. If one wanders off a cliff in search of greener grass, the others follow. One time at the high Alp above Gimmelwald, forty cows performed this stunt . . . and died like lemmings. The meat must be drained of blood immediately or it's wasted. Helicopters fly them out, but it's only meat for the dogs.

With a local friend leading the way, the Alps become a lively world of tumbling cows, joyriding helicopters, and Sunday school–teaching grannies straddling ridges. The scene is trimmed by a pastel carpet of flowers: gold clover, milk kraut, bell flowers, daisies.

"This is a good mix for the cow's milk," notes the schoolteacher of the farm kids, suddenly all but abandoning me for the flowers. "For me, it's like meeting old friends when the flowers come out again in the spring."

Rummaging through his rucksack, Olle pulls out a big handbook describing the local flora: "My bible."

Olle announces, "Okay, Rick, you will now risk your life for a flower." He leaves the trail and creeps over an edge and out of sight to find an edelweiss. Loose rocks, huge drop, no helicopter in sight . . . I don't really care about an edelweiss.

Then I hear Olle holler, "Yes, I found some! Come around."

"This spot must not go in your guidebook."

Feeling fat and clumsy, I leave the trail. Pulling gingerly at weed handholds, I work my way around a huge rock and across a field of loose shale. The suddenly younger Olle comes into view. "There are three edelweiss here. But this is a secret for only you and me. This spot must not go in your guidebook." At this point I am concerned only with my survival. Olle grabs my hand with hands that even as a teacher have grown strong and tough after fourteen years of village life.

He whispers, "For me, it would not be a hike without a little danger."

I whisper, "That's why your school's so small."

"*Edelweiss.* It means 'noble white.' In the valley, it's noble gray. Only at high elevations do they get this white. UV rays give all flowers brighter colors at this altitude."

Creeping with me to the ledge he gently bends three precious edelweiss toward the sun. Pinching off a petal he assures me, "This will not affect reproduction."

Petting the petal I note that it feels like felt.

"Yes, like felt," Olle agrees. "This protects the plants from dehydration. I collect and press flowers but have never pressed an edelweiss. Edelweiss is a promotional flower. It has been picked nearly to extinction."

As we struggle back to the trail, Olle talks on. "Here in Switzerland we are getting serious about our environment. Twenty years ago our rivers and lakes were very polluted. Today you can nearly drink out of Lake Thun. Now we understand. You don't pee in your living room, do you?"

Finally reaching the trail, I assure him I don't.

We are walking quickly now, with ease, along the trail.

"Tourists often ask, 'Do farmers mind if we walk through their property?'" Olle says. "That is for me perverse." Olle's environmental passion crescendos with his voice. "This is a human right—to walk through the land. When I was in Boston, I asked, 'How can I get to the lake?' They told me, 'You can't, it is private.' This is unthinkable here in Switzerland. We are guests of this earth."

Feeling like welcome guests, Olle and I make it to our target, a peak that stands dramatically high above Gimmelwald. After a steep descent, we step out of the forest at the top end of Gimmelwald. We're cheered by a fragrant finale . . . a field vibrant with flowers, grasshoppers, bees, crickets, moths, and butterflies.

Olle says, "This year farmers obeyed tradition and not their eyes. They waited too long and had to take cows directly to the high Alps. They skipped this lower field. For these flowers, it is a fine year—no hungry cows."

The bench that sits at the high end of Gimmelwald is one of my "savor Europe" depots. When we get there I thank Olle for the hike and sit down. Watching him hike slowly into the village and home, it hits me: I'll be on the train tonight and in Paris for breakfast.

Switzerland feels storybookish. It embraces its traditions with such gusto that locals like Olle fear visitors think it's an underdeveloped nation. And the greatest news since the birth of the Eurailpass: the traditional Alpine culture survives most heartily—like an edelweiss—in the most scenic corners.

Subcultures thrive, remote from each other, in Switzerland's wild geography. Even today, small-town Swiss routinely spend entire lives never traveling beyond the nearest big city—an hour away by train. Walter, after twenty years in Gimmelwald, has visited the popular resort of Grindelwald—just ten miles away—only once. Grandparents marvel at the exotic adventures of Gimmelwald's schoolchildren as they ride the train with Olle for three hours to France.

A great dimension of travel is finding the right spot and just sitting still. Crickets rattle their happy castanets, a river blurts out of a glacier, and Murren crowns a bluff above me keeping all the fancy tourists where they belong. An Alpine farm that has intrigued me for years still sits high above the tree line, forever alone amid distant flecks of brown and white, cows and goats. And beyond that is another place I've never been: the Dancing Floor.

A gang of college kids—tourists still wet from their jump under the waterfall—bumble by. Below me the village schoolyard tumbles with children. Christian, the accordion player, who went up to the fields early this morning, rumbles by on his mini-truck towing a wagon wobbling with towers of hay. His two pre-schoolers bounce like cartoons on top.

Enjoying this alone is fine. But share this bench with a new friend, the sun of a daylong hike stored in your smiling faces, and you too will sing, "If heaven isn't what it's cracked up to be, send me back to Gimmelwald."

CHAPTER TEN

PARIS

"You see there is the boulangerie *problem: the man is either a good bread man or a good pastry man. The man at that* boulangerie, *his heart is in his pastry. The bread suffers."*

Lying in bed on a lazy Paris morning, I wake to a comforting buzz and "phoop." It's a Chirac, spotting and sucking up a poodle turd on its search and destroy mission down rue Cler.

An activist mayor of Paris in the 1980s, Jacques Chirac created a small army of mobile pooper-scoopers. Known as "Chiracs," these motorcycle vacuum cleaners doggedly patrol the streets of Paris. In this wealthy neighborhood with more than its share of poodles, Chiracs are commonplace.

Stepping to the fourth-floor window of my room at the Hotel Leveque, I see hungry seniors lining up for their still-warm baguettes and merchants setting out boxes of fragrant, ripe red strawberries.

Then I see him, the soldier in green, methodically making his way down the street. He parks his motorcycle next to a dropping, covers it with the vacuum nozzle, and *phoop!*, the poop is gone. After an appendage soaps and rinses the spot, the Chirac—proud of a job well done—motors on in search of the next road hazard.

From my window, I see the tip of the Eiffel Tower peeking over the grand city of Baron Haussmann. He was the nineteenth-

Phoop... the poop is gone.

century architect who helped turn Paris into the elegant city it is today. Only the churches and the Eiffel Tower exceed the city center's six-story building code.

Paris is packed with buildings, each topped with Lego-like chimneys and Kandinsky-esque antennae. Stately black grill work, frosted with big city dust, treats humble windows like royal balconies. Top stories squeeze maids, students, and winded backpackers under slanted ceilings with peek-a-spire views out dormer windows.

Paris is Europe's greatest city, its grand capital. And Parisian culture is resilient. Tourists bounce off it like bugs off a window. With so much of Europe dolled-up for tourism, a city that nearly ignores its tourists is refreshing. Paris offers an American the traveler's equivalent of finishing school.

Below my window is village Paris and the market street I call home, rue Cler. This cobbled pedestrian street is lined with all the necessary shops—wine, cheese, chocolate, bread—as well as a bank and post office. And the shops of this community are run by people who've found their niche: boys who grew up on quiche, girls who know a good wine. Connoisseurs of good living keep rue Cler in business. If you want to learn the fine art of living, Parisian-style, rue Cler provides an excellent classroom.

In the street below, Mimi—the receptionist and my friend for ten years of visits—pops out of the hotel with a tourist. As she points him in her idea of the right direction, her laughter echoes in the street. She is endlessly entertained by her inability to understand her English-speaking guests at the hotel.

Proudly sporting its one star, this hotel—the "Grand Hotel Leveque"—pries apart a café and a cheese stall just wide enough to plant its front door on rue Cler. Hotel Leveque calls itself "grand" in the sense of grand old days.

As the singing maid's thin soprano wafts up from the no-view courtyard, I get ready to take my morning shower. For those of us who come from a country that starts and ends with squeaky hair, Europe has made great strides in plumbing. There was a time when slumber mills proudly advertised their sinks as having "hot and cold water in every room." I remember entire hotels that had no showers anywhere.

For a decade of visits, Hotel Leveque was classic one star: a sink in the room—plastic cup, tiny soap, and maybe shampoo in an unrippable packet—and the shower down the hall. The shower was equipped with a frail piece of rubber shower hose; water spun from its base and sputtered out its hand-held nozzle. Never able to count on hot water, I'd start hot and scrub quickly, waiting for warm to become room temperature and then worse. Today my Leveque shower is in my room, not down the hall, and the water bursts out stresslessly hot from a modern no-leak nozzle.

Pondering the water babbling in the walls long after my shower is done, I think of my Bulgarian friend, Svetoslav, who used the sound of running water to mask intimate conversations in his dining room.

Svetoslav was a Francophile who had never set foot in France. In the 1980s, Bulgarians were forbidden to travel west. But globe-trotting via books, stories, and dreams, Svetoslav was a frequent flier. He knew Paris as if he had lived there.

As we sat in his Plovdiv dining room with the faucet running, I'd bring my friend to Paris, spinning tales of the Latin Quarter, the rue de Rivoli, the Louvre, and Notre Dame. In the 1990s, Sveti finally turned the faucet off and went to Paris.

Spiraling down the hotel staircase to breakfast, I know exactly what to expect. Breakfast is half a baguette, a flaky croissant, a basket of jellies, and two hot pitchers—one of milk and one of coffee. The coffee will be strong; it needs the milk. The wet pitchers will stick to the paper tablecloth; they invariably dribble during the pour. One French breakfast in a hotel costs about what two people would pay for eggs, toast, hashbrowns, and endless coffee in the United States. It's better not to compare.

To supplement the breakfast, I make my ritual trip outside to the white-bonneted cheese man.

"*Cinquante grams emmental, s'il vous plaît,*" I say.

Like any good merchant, he slices not fifty grams, but eighty.

"*C'est bon?*" he asks.

"*Oui, c'est bon.*"

When I step into the breakfast room with my discreet packet of cheese, Mimi kidnaps me into the kitchen. Whispering in French and gesturing as if her throat were being slit, she makes it clear that the new owner is firing her. She's in her sixties but energetic. Thinner and in better shape than she was last year, she wears a bright scarf and a sporty haircut. Still, in two weeks she'll be gone.

At breakfast, a young woman introduces herself as Ariane and sits at my table. She's the daughter of the new owner of Hotel Leveque and a photographer here in Paris. She wears her hair cut short and died a black-cherry red—the same color as her lipstick. Except for lipstick, she wears no makeup. She's confident and, though half my age, connects as an equal. She wants to talk about my TV series.

Our conversation is interrupted by travelers with my book apologetically asking for itinerary advice. Ariane says, "Your series must be very popular." Mimi, whose cackle fills the breakfast room, was featured in my last series. Sounding like Cinderella's stepsister, Ariane continues, "Mimi is like a star around here."

"It is too bad your father is firing her," I say.

"She speaks no English," says Ariane, ripping a flaky croissant in half. "He had no other choice. Tell me how you produce your shows. I have some time this afternoon. What about meeting me here after lunch?"

For the same reason I used to risk taking a stranger for a dorm roommate back in college, I agree.

Rue Cler: Can a Street Be a Sight?

As I leave my hotel I pass the cheese shop. A man, thrilled he's found his favorite goat cheese, tells me, "Vieux Corse, it can only be found on rue Cler."

Rue Cler is very French. It makes me feel like I must have been a poodle in a previous life. You could live well and never leave here. Flower shops add fragrance to the breeze and every shop (except the health food store) is jammed. The crêpe man makes crêpes like he just invented them. A man with working-class hands cradles a bouquet and a baguette in his arms. Aproned fruit-stall attendants coax doll-like girls into trying their cherries. Even bums drink a better wine on rue Cler.

Stepping past huge tables balanced high with colorful fruits and leafy vegetables, I spot my friend Marie-Alice. She runs my favorite local restaurant. Each morning, she picks up the ingredients for the day's menu here on rue Cler.

"Oh, Rick," she says, noisily kissing the air an inch in front of each of my earlobes, "the strawberries are beautiful today." She buries her nose, then mine, in a basket of the lush fruit.

Ready to give a polite "Wow," I actually give an honest "Wow," having never quite enjoyed the smell of a strawberry so vividly.

"You must shop with your nose," she says. "These Gariguette are French. A beautiful smell. Better than the Spanish strawberries."

Reaching back for a less expensive Spanish strawberry, she holds the stem to my nose and I smell nothing.

"Oh, and this basil," she says, moving on "It will be great on a salad."

Marie-Alice is short, barely reaching my shoulders. But she's a force in the market. With a dark dress, brightly-colored sash, and beautiful long black hair, she power-dresses to shop. Her lipstick is as fresh as the basil and bright as the berries.

"May I join you?" I ask.

"Yes, please, Rick," she answers. She knows I'm a TV-dinner kind of guy; I suspect she welcomes this opportunity to give me a little cuisine culture.

Pawing through bundles of tarragon as if the brown herbs were a bouquet, she says, pouting, "No smell. If I want to make a chicken tarragon, I cannot do it today. It seems that the herb delivery has not arrived. Ah, these asparagus are also not good. I must take them off the menu tonight."

I flip at the tough leaves of an artichoke saying, "These are good with butter."

"Artichoke. We say it is the vegetable of the poor people. It takes a long time and much work to eat."

Waving a gnarled white ball at me, she says, "You know this?"

"It looks like a brain."

"No, Rick, this is the root of the celery. Stronger taste. We grate it for a salad. Delicious.

"It is not the season for melon. *Ooo la la,* look at that price," she says, pointing to the sign with price, name, and country of origin chalked onto it. "What is that, about six dollars per kilo. You see, it came from Guadeloupe. There is an obligation to say where it comes from. Many people will buy only the French products. I try."

French women, thick and crusty after a lifetime of baguette munching, debate the merits of the street's rival *boulangeries*. A young girl, who looks chic in just-out-of-bed hair, walks quickly out the door of the bakery eating a *pain au chocolat*.

"Rue Cler has two *boulangeries*. Is one better?" I ask.

"Oh, yes. This one is good. That one," she points down the way and shudders, "it is horrible."

"Can you taste the difference?" I ask as we step in.

"*Ouff!* Absolutely. You see there is the *boulangerie* problem: the man is either a good bread man or a good pastry man. The man down there, his heart is in his pastry. The bread suffers."

Pointing to a fancy cake, Marie-Alice says, "The baker here is a good bread man but he has a special pastry man. A bread man could never do work like this. When you do good bread, you have no time to do good pastry."

A friend passes Marie-Alice. Greedily hurrying home with his tart, he giggles, "*Poire et chocolat*."

"Jean Pierre loves his pear and chocolate tart," she says. Then she walks me to the most tempting storefront on rue Cler.

Tarte Julie's windows are filled with various pies. The shop's classy old storefront is a work of art that survives from the previous occupant. The inset stones and glass advertise horse meat. The sign still says "Boucherie Chevaline." The decorated front, from the 1930s and signed by the artist, would fit in a museum. But it belongs right here. And everyone knows this is a place for a fine tart, not horse meat.

A long, narrow, canopied cheese table brings the *fromagerie* into the street. Marie-Alice bounces her finger over a long line of cheeses: wedges, cylinders, balls, and mini hockey pucks, all powdered white, gray, and burnt marshmallow—it's a festival of mold.

Sounding blessed as can be, she says, "So many different cheeses. This is goat, and goat, and goat, and goat. All different kinds of goat cheese. *Ooo la la la la.*"

Picking up a glob of cheese misty with mold, she holds it close to her nose, takes an orgasmic breath, and exhales. "Yes, it smells like zee feet of angels."

Just inside the door she points a happy pinky at a crumpled wad of cheese the size of a pocket watch. "Ah, Rocamadour. To make this tiny piece, you need half a liter of milk."

The owner of the shop, seeing me peek past the heavy plastic curtain into the cold, tiled back room, proudly pulls back the drapes and invites me to see "*la meule.*" These are the huge rounds of cheese from which the "hard" cheeses are cut. Bending down to the second shelf on a big wooden rack, he hefts out a wheel the size of a truck tire. He declares, "Eighty kilos, made with one thousand liters of milk [250 gallons]."

Marie-Alice translates his warning: "Don't eat the skin of these big ones; they roll them on the floor."

Strolling with me past more cheeses, she continues. "On smaller cheese—the Brie, the Camembert—this skin is part of the taste. It completes the package."

"Do you assemble your cheese plates here?" I ask.

"*Oui,*" she says, sorting through her options like a perky mother dressing her daughter. "On a good cheese plate you need a hard cheese like this Emmental, a flowery cheese—maybe Brie or Camembert, and a blue and a goat."

Across the street we pause at a table of duck, pigeons, quail, and rabbit. Marie-Alice sorts through the dead. With none of the tenderness shown in the cheese shop, she hoists a duck. Rubbing a thumb toughly on its rough and calloused feet, she says, "So. You see this? This is very good. He lived on a farm, not in an industrial kennel. This meat will be tasty on my menu tonight. Perhaps we will make the *canard a l'orange*."

We cross the street. Greeting the mom and pop of the butcher shop, Marie-Alice says, "They buy the veal only on the foot."

Walking in, she points to the red and gold medals that hang like a necklace across the ceiling. Hitting one with her umbrella, she says, "Each of these hung around the neck of a prizewinning little cow. When we see these, we know we get the top quality."

The ruddy-faced butcher, wearing a tiny plaid beret and dressed in a white apron over a fine shirt and silk tie, is busy chopping. A battalion of meat hooks hang in orderly lines from the ceiling. The white walls bring out the red in the different cuts of meat.

I say, "He's the best-dressed butcher I've seen."

Marie-Alice translates and shares his response. "His father dressed well. The customers expect this from him also. He changes his apron three times every day."

An equally well-dressed man comes in to pick up a steak, and Marie-Alice says he's from the British Embassy. Overhearing us, he tells us on his way out, "The meat here is more expensive, but the quality is always first rate."

A bent little old lady follows him, clutching dinner wrapped in waxy paper. Marie-Alice says, "She gets a fine cut of meat with the same service as the man from the embassy."

The butcher's wife, who operates the cash register, tells Marie-Alice that their 35th anniversary is this weekend. Marie-Alice relays their story to me. "Thirty-five years ago, the daughter of the rue Cler fish man married the son of the rue Cler butcher. She had shopped here with her mother. She saw the butcher's son chopping on that same table," Marie-Alice says, pointing to a well-worn but finely carved old work table. "She made an arrangement to see him, and, well, she left the fish shop."

Today she takes the money and he chops the meat. And the father—eighty-seven years old and still living upstairs—continues to come down, clean the knives, and make sure his son maintains the shop's tradition of quality.

As the postman flops a small pile of mail on the counter, the butcher's wife says, "But we have nobody to take the shop. Our children are not interested. I think we are the end of an age."

The dessert of our walk is the rue Cler *confiserie*. Marie-Alice introduces me to Corinne, who recently took over the shop from a woman who kept this neighborhood in fine chocolates for thirty years.

"Have you kept the old customers satisfied?" I ask.

"Of course," she says, giving a bag of pre-ordered chocolates to a pensioner. "The companies want you to take the new products, but I keep the old traditional candies, too. The old ladies, they want the same sweets they had eighty years ago."

Corinne takes us behind her tiny public shop area into the room where fancy chocolates are stuffed. Marie-Alice explains, "Until the last generation, the shopkeeper would live and produce back here and sell in the front. Most of these shops were like that."

After we leave the shop, Marie-Alice settles back down to her shopping. It's a Saturday, which means she'll need to stock her restaurant well for her many customers tonight. Before every purchase, she carefully assesses the quality of each item. Time doesn't seem to pass for her. I politely take her bags one by one, which only seems to encourage her to do more shopping. We make a couple of trips to her restaurant a few blocks away to drop off bags of food.

Hungry after eyeing so much food, I rub my stomach and say, "*Je suis femme.*"

"Oh, Rick," she says with a smile, "You just said that you are a woman. If you are hungry say, '*J'ai faim.*' Let's find Philippe."

Marie-Alice's husband is holding a table for us at the corner bistro. Our sidewalk perch is ideal for watching the constant flow of people.

Across from the *boulangerie*, above the "Boeuf-Cheval-Triperie" awning, a golden horse-head surveys the crowds. He knows that those toting daybags, fannypacks, and cameras eat the *boeuf*. Those with baguettes, dogs, and baby strollers eat the horse and tripe. And those with less than that wait for the end of the day when shops fill the rue Cler trash cans with day-old food.

Settling comfortably into her chair, Marie-Alice says, "This is a bistro, a real bistro. This is hard to find. Traditionally, a bistro is small. It's a family thing, the children work here, there is no hurry, and the food is good. Now, many bistro are too big. In these new places, the waiters don't care. It's rush, rush, rush."

She introduces me to our waiter, David (in France pronounced "Dah-VEED"). He hangs the day's chalkboard menu on the woven cane back of the extra chair at our table. David, who wears his white apron like a skirt and his black tie tucked into his white shirt, is interrupted by new arrivals. Judging from the number of cheeks he kisses, this is a local crowd.

David returns to help Philippe and Marie-Alice deal with the first topic: wine. The three of them discuss it, first like a chess move, then like a scandal, and finally like the suddenly obvious answer to a complex riddle.

The bottle arrives. Philippe, a rugged fifty with a classy suit jacket and an open collar, does the tasting formalities as if it really matters. He takes a slow sip. Cocks his head, frozen in thought. Then he comes to life and says *"superbe"* as only a Frenchman can.

While I thought I heard Chardonnay, the label reads Bordeaux. I take a sip and ask, "What grape is this made from?"

"Before I visit California, I would not understand this question," says Marie-Alice. "In Napa, I learned Americans consider wine by the name of the grape. A Chardonnay from Bordeaux and a Chardonnay from Burgundy is not the same at all. If you call this a Chardonnay and you don't like it, you won't know why. It is the sun and ground . . . not the grape. We are drinking Chardonnay grapes, yes, but this wine is a Bordeaux."

"This would confuse American buyers," I say.

"And the French understand this." says David. "There is a small town in the south, Minerve. The classic Minerve wine is a blend of three grapes. It is very popular with the French. But the Americans buy wine by the name of the grape. One Minerve wine maker is making wines not blended but labeled by the grape: Merlot, Cabernet, or Chardonnay. He sells the most. The other wine makers are fighting him. They say he has no pride in his region."

Philippe agrees, saying, "This is not right."

"You know your wine," I say.

"This is normal here," Philippe says. "We know to choose the right wine. We discussed the wine at home. I learned wine from nine years old."

Two Americans at the next table ask us how to order tap water. Philippe, with maximum flair and one hand in the air, says, "You ask for the Chateau Chirac."

Marie-Alice explains, "That is not a fine wine. It's our fine water. When Chirac was mayor of Paris he cleaned up our water. Now the water of Paris is very fine to drink."

Chatting about rue Cler's romantic ambience, the Americans tell me they conceived their daughter here two years ago and named her Paris. Now they're back—the first time away from their child—buying souvenirs with their baby's name on them.

Paris is a city loved by its residents as much as by its visitors. But the character of the city is changing. Over the years, developers have reshaped Paris. Small neighborhood shops have been steamrollered by sprawling office parks and shopping centers.

"There is no other street like rue Cler," says Marie-Alice with a sigh.

Philippe asks David how rue Cler survives. The waiter rolls up his sleeves, leans with both hands squarely on the back of the menu chair, and joins the conversation.

"Here in the seventh district, we had thirty years with one mayor, Monsieur Dupont. This is a very rich district. Very conservative. Monsieur Dupont stopped big investments and stores from coming in. Because of Monsieur Dupont, the seventh is a delight."

The cheery ambience we picked up on our stroll down rue Cler used to be commonplace in Paris. In the old days a child could be worthless in school but the shopkeepers knew he was a good kid. They'd find him a job. Neighborhoods were extended families.

Today, with the death of most
Parisian neighborhoods, cultural orphans abound.

*Marie-Alice toasts the art
of Parisian living.*

As I sip my Bordeaux,
Mimi from Hotel Leveque
walks by. Done with her shift
and heading home, she sees
me. She smiles and drags a
finger down her cheek like a
tear. I wave sadly, thinking
she's a victim of the times.
Then, as the parents of baby
Paris get up to leave—waving my guidebook at me—I realize
that, in a way, I fired Mimi. She's replaced by someone who can
speak English and communicate with the tourists I send. I'll
never see Mimi again after this trip.

In the new lean and mean capitalism, private schools give the
wealthy or gifted the skills necessary to succeed. Ariane will manage fine. Mimi will fade away.

"Today's economy has no heart," says Philippe.

"Rue Cler will survive," says Marie-Alice. "The 70s and 80s
were the time of *supermarchés*. Now we like our little shops
again."

"No," says Philippe. "In the last year only, twelve hundred
cafés in Paris closed. And in the countryside, traditional ways are
dying, too. On TV we see the 'SOS employment' announcements.
When a small village in the middle of nowhere is about to die, its
city hall advertises for a new owner to keep the vital shop or hotel
in business. But everybody comes to Paris. Twenty percent of all
the French are now here, in Paris. This is a problem. We are losing
the art of French living."

"Is that why French people drink so much wine?" I ask.

Philippe flags David back into the discussion and says, "No,
no. In fact, the French are drinking less alcohol. We sell no more
aperitifs in our restaurant. Even the French wine consumption is
down—this is a government fight against drunk driving."

David agrees. "Traditionally the French don't eat without wine. We drink wine with lunch and wine with dinner. In Russia people drink to escape. In America, it's for the stress. Here in France, it's the culture."

"Maybe traditionally," says Philippe. "But today, life in France is faster, too. There's more stress and many people have an alcohol problem. To deal with this, there is a new non-alcoholic trick: Prozac. Anti-depressants are very popular in France now. Fifty million French consume as much Prozac as 260 million Americans."

"My mother now takes this Prozac," David says.

"And now we don't have drunk drivers running off the road. We have sleeping drivers running off the road," says Marie-Alice.

As David dashes off to kiss the cheeks of a couple ready to leave, I comment on how confident, content, and self-assured this young man is with customers twice his age and economic standing. Europeans charm me with their ability to be proud of their position in life. Waiters and maids are professionals. An American might be apologetic about such a job, considering it a stepping stone to something of higher standing—even if it weren't. For the European, this is their place.

"Can this attitude survive?" I ask.

The ever-confident Marie-Alice responds, "Sure it can. If half your waking hours are spent at your job and you don't like your work, your life is a failure. Europe is not interested in what people do or how much they make.

"It is taboo to discuss money. We are interested in a person's art and intellectual value. A young man like David knows it is unrealistic to have a different life. He accepts this. Like the rue Cler shoemaker, he is respected not for the number of zeros in his paycheck, but for his work. He holds a . . ."

Philippe helps out, "Venerable?"

"Yes," Marie-Alice continues, "a venerable position in our community."

"That's French," I conclude.

"No," says Marie-Alice, looking out over rue Cler. "It is more than French, it's European."

Going Underground

With her trendy black sweater stretching to the tops of her fingers, Ariane looks like an artist waiting to be discovered. She leans against the hotel as if her father owns it.

"I love this street," I tell her. "There couldn't be a better urban home: big city options with village ambience."

Ariane agrees. "I could get a job tomorrow in New York. But I'd rather be unemployed in Paris."

"Shall we walk and talk?" I ask.

"Sure," she says. "Where would you like to go?"

"The Louvre." On every visit to Paris, I have a date with *Mona.*

Now that a plan is set, Ariane's eyes get even more intense, exuding a no-apologies directness. The small talk is over. "Tell me about your show," she says.

As we walk, I tell Ariane that it takes four of us—me, a cameraperson, a director, and an assistant—six days in Europe to shoot a thirty-minute show. It's a small crew and fast work. And that's just the start. Distilling the six hours of rough footage we bring home into a finished program is where most of the expense is. It takes about half-a-million dollars to make a thirteen-show season.

She's not impressed but does ask, "Who pays?"

I explain that the public television network loans us half of it. "Oregon Public Broadcasting, the patron station, kicks in the use of their studios. We borrow money we expect to get when the shows are sold to cable after their stint on public television. And we work for deferred wages."

"Is there any profit?" she asks.

"We sell videos with a plug at the end of each show," I explain. "Once the network loan is paid off, we pay our wages. Sales after that are split three ways— among our production company, the network, and Oregon Public Broadcasting. That's the profit."

"Why no underwriting?"

"We'd love some. But underwriting usually comes with strings attached. Visa almost gave us some. But at the last moment they said, 'And you will have to feature only hotels and restaurants that accept our credit cards and not American Express.'"

"And . . . ?" she asks.

"The deal died," I said.

Ariane looks at me like the child of a father who worked too hard and had no time for his family. "So, do you enjoy it?"

"If we were properly funded I would," I tell her. "But the financial pressure puts a strain on everyone involved. We survived producing fifty-two shows out of the love of making good TV and teaching good travel."

We round the corner and I point to the white outline of a dachshund stenciled onto the sidewalk with an arrow to the gutter.

"Cute," says Ariane, "but the dogs don't get it. Thank God for Chirac."

Hopscotching past a couple of turds, we leave behind the daylight and descend into Europe's greatest subway system. As we walk nearly a subterranean block, we pass some fifty posters advertising the new luxury Peugeot. I ask Ariane about the repetition.

"Advertisers buy Métro wall space by the meter and roll out their posters," she says. "You can psychoanalyze a neighborhood by its advertising. The seventh district is old and rich. The ads are expensive and promote luxury items."

Paris is not divided right bank and left bank but west—more sophisticated—and east—lowbrow.

On the train a tourist grabs my arm and says, "Hey, you're the travel guy. KUHT, right?" He sits down and invites himself into our conversation. "Do they censor you?" he asks.

"Well, not really," I answer. "But we censor ourselves. It's necessary to be sure we get good airplay. Programmers are responsive to viewer complaints. And we don't want to needlessly offend any potential sponsors."

Suddenly sounding like a detective, he says, "I thought so. You're more fun, less careful in your books. Why not on TV?"

Telling him again that self-censorship is a necessary evil reminds me of scriptwriting frustrations. Like a kid squirming in a dentist's chair, I endure the pain of careful reviewers scouring each script for problem-causing lines. They pull out playfulness like crooked teeth.

For example, my description of a portrait bust of Akhenaton

with "Mick Jagger lips" was nixed. To drive home the point that English is Europe's second language, I scripted, "When a Greek meets a Norwegian hiking in the Alps they communicate in English. What Greek speaks Norwegian?" Concerned that this might offend the seven Greeks who do speak Norwegian, the punch line was cut. Illustrating the changes you'll find as you near the Mediterranean by saying "People, like the towels and breakfasts, get smaller as you travel south" was potentially offensive. Groping for a way to adequately describe Norwegian nature, I wrote, "This cruise takes Norway's fjord beauty and lays it spread-eagle on a scenic platter"—much too suggestive. And a sentence that attempted to bring to life a vivid Viking exhibit—"You can almost hear the screams and smell the armpits of those redheads on the rampage"—was simply too gross.

In retrospect, I'm grateful that wiser television producers saved me from myself. Thankfully, writing allows for a little more recklessness.

As we change trains, Ariane rolls her imaginary camera from an escalator while I run up the steps. "Great dolly," she says at the top of the escalator.

"So smooth," I agree. "But for the first series my microphone was hard-wired to the camera and I couldn't do this fun stuff and talk at the same time. Finally, with a radio mic, I felt like a dog off his leash. And we could do more interesting stand-ups."

We glide along 300 meters of moving sidewalk. The Paris Métro is an inside world in constant motion. There's no sky, just a steady river of people. With an imaginary zoom lens, Ariane compresses the long, crowded tunnel into a mass of commuters, a sea of bobbing heads.

Riding the Métro makes me feel like a blood cell in an organism called Earth. Flowing from one artery to the next, we pass musicians pulling Brahms out of plugged-in cellos and talk-a-lot beggars with stringy hair pasted to their faces.

"Was the first series your first time in front of a camera?" she asks.

"Yes, and I had some problems," I reply. "I had this goony eye thing. When I was done saying my lines to the camera I'd look away as if I had glass eyes."

"Just blink after your last words," says Ariane.

"I know that now, but it took me thirteen shows to figure it out. I also had a habit of jumping into conversations before a sentence was finished and repeating lines people said to me."

Ariane shakes her head. "Stepping on lines. That makes editing the footage much more difficult."

This young Parisian woman has a way of making me feel defensive. I assure her that now, after fifty-two shows, we've really got our act together.

At first I thought that learning my lines was nothing more than memorizing words. Now I internalize the meaning of my lines—a huge difference. In early shows we recorded the voice track in a makeshift sound studio in a cheap hotel room. I'd stand sweating in a closet, blankets draped everywhere to deaden the acoustics. Recording each show was a four-hour ordeal. My diction was terrible. Now I know it's "get," not "git"; "any," not "iny"; "going to," not "gonna." We record the voice-overs in a Seattle studio, and I can do a show in a third the time.

I peer down the Métro tunnel and see a subterranean bubble shining in the distance: a hamlet of light with more people waiting for the same train. Nearly 300 such bubbles—some small, some virtual cities—fill that parallel world under the streets of the City of Light.

The platform fills with commuters. When our train finally arrives, three older women shove their way off. Battling her way onboard, Ariane looks back at them. As the door slams she hollers, "*Vous êtes si français.*"

Comfortably seated, Ariane says, "French people are never happy. It's part of our mentality. Self-critical. We insult each other by saying, 'You're so French.'"

"I thought the rude French person went out with de Gaulle," I remark.

"*Ooo la*, the rudeness survives," she counters. "Everybody knows the Parisians are famous to be really, really mean. We're not only rude to the tourists, we are rude to each other. The young generation maybe not so much. We have traveled and see how it is necessary to be more polite. But the older people have never traveled. This contributes to the problem."

Our train races, whistling, wheezing, and screeching around corners, to the next intersection. Gazing out the window into the darkness, I accidently make eye contact with the reflection of the old woman across from me. She doesn't look mean . . . only tired. By her side is a woman who must dress from the same mildewy closet. A long lifetime in Paris has made them weary. Much of their bodies has settled into their ankles. With nylon socks not quite reaching their modest knees, they jiggle in unison to the rhythm of the Métro rails.

We step off the Métro and our train vanishes, leaving only a big city wind. When on my own, I never leave the Métro without reviewing the Plan du Quartier—the neighborhood map posted on the Métro wall. Giddy as an economy traveler who's been bumped up to business class and is surveying the in-flight menu, I scan the map for unexpected sightseeing treats. But Parisians navigate their Métro with the emotions of robots. Ariane knows exactly which exit to take. I follow.

For Ariane, the Métro is a tool. For me it's a magic carpet. I don't just leave the Métro; riding the escalator in my best Louis XIV pose, I ascend. Outside is vividly outside when coming from the inside of all insides. Trees shimmer, backlit. The sun hits me like a phone call from an old friend.

Greatness is a matter of contrast. A good shower is great after a cold one. A noble city is royal after Belgrade. A cozy street is a slow-motion reunion of lovers after negotiating the Arc de Triomphe. And no museum is as great as the Louvre.

A Royal Perspective

Ariane and I join the line winding like a tail from the kite-like pyramid marking the entrance to Europe's top art gallery. If art nourishes the soul, the Louvre is a smorgasbord. Once inside, the vast glass pyramid serves as a skylight as mobs of hungry tourists choose their cultural bibs. Some take tours, others follow guidebooks. Joining those who slurp their art, we simply follow signs to *Mona Lisa*.

Of the thousands of pieces in this world's biggest museum, only *Mona Lisa* is signposted from the turnstile. Tourists slalom under the disappointed gaze of classical gods and past the forgiving eyes of Christian saints. Oblivious to Michelangelo's Slaves, yawning and stretching and waking up to the modern world, tourists trudge on to *Mona*.

"*Mona Lisa* is the only piece of art in the Louvre that you can hear," Ariane says.

She's right. Like a waterfall, its rushing commotion can be heard from two rooms away.

Barbarians belly up to the protective rail not to see *Mona*, but to photograph her. They're as illiterate as serfs when it comes to the "no flashes" sign. Hungrily squinting through cameras, they eye the painting. From behind her drool- and bullet-proof window she smirks at the crowd. I stand amid more tiptoes than anywhere in Paris. It's a Kodak pig-pile. Some pull several cameras from their bags. Japanese don't look at *Mona*, but they pose with her. From the rear of the crowd, video cameras held high like makeshift periscopes capture the scene.

Others, without cameras, come to really see the masterpiece. Solemnly, they wait their turn for a center spot. Like a lady on the prow of a ship, each stands strong, weathering the painting's stormy waves of beauty.

Stepping out of the commotion, I join Ariane on the sidelines, where she is looking not at the art but at the chaos it causes. I say, "People from all cultures look at her as if waiting for an explanation."

"Like the tourists—and you—look at us French," she says.

Titian's ignored portrait of François I, sporting his good-natured grin, watches the scene from three paintings over. He and *Mona* go way back. François brought Leonardo to France. And Leonardo brought *Mona*. When Leonardo died, *Mona* moved in with François.

Mona *Wannasees*

Mona and François seem forever still in their frames. But Veronese's giant *Wedding Feast of Cana* canvas, which fills the next wall with its frolicking cast of thousands, feels like a party aching to happen. Perhaps after hours, when moonlight pours through the skylight, Venetian nudes boogie, Veronese's string quartet comes to life . . . and Mona winks.

Ariane and I leave the Louvre. Pausing in its courtyard, we look toward the Arc de Triomphe. "What a great photograph this makes," Ariane says. "Paris was lucky to have kings and presidents who loved the city. Do you know the *perspective royale?*

"From the Louvre," she says, "looking in a straight line, you can see the obelisk in the place de la Concorde, the Arc de Triomphe, and far off in the distance, the Grande Arche de la Defense. This one view tells the history of Paris by century.

"Seventeenth century: the Louvre, the palace of France's kings," she says.

I jump in with, "Eighteenth century: the place de la Concorde, where Louis XVI lost his head at the guillotine and the old regime died with him."

Graciously accepting my contribution, she continues, "Nineteenth century: the Arc de Triomphe, celebrating Napoleon and his victories. This triumph was not just for Napoleon but for France."

"Twentieth century: the Grande Arch de la Defense, celebrating . . . " I pause, searching for the right word, " . . . the world."

The Grande Arche, built in 1989 on the 200th anniversary of the French Revolution, is a mega-structure that acknowledges a new age rising above nations. As if to bury the notion of six-story limits, the arch is surrounded by stiletto skyscrapers. Housing

30,000 office workers, it celebrates not the victories of a nation's armies but the triumph of international commerce. In the wake of this triumph, nationalism seems irrelevant and Paris looks quaint.

Ariane waves down a taxi and we ride up the Champs-Élysées toward Europe's wildest traffic circle. Our taxi waits to plunge into place Charles-de-Gaulle, a grand circle where a dozen boulevards converge on the Arc de Triomphe. Like referees at gladiator camp, traffic cops, stationed at each entrance to this ten-lane circus, let in bursts of eager cars.

While marble Lady Liberties scramble up Napoleon's arch—heroically thrusting their swords and shrieking at the traffic—all of Paris seems drawn into this whirlpool. Stirred by this call to arms, otherwise sedate tour bus drivers become daredevils. Egged on by applause from their suddenly bloodthirsty tour groups, they cut off six lanes at once as they charge to the inner lane.

It's a game of fender-bender chicken. This circle is the great equalizer. Tiny Deux Chevaux with their sardine-lid rooftops cranked open bring lumbering buses to a sudden cussing halt.

"In Paris a good driver gets only scratches, not dents," Arianne says.

Groping for the lost end of my seat belt, I say, "There must be an accident every few minutes here."

"When there is," says Ariane, "each driver is considered equally at fault. This is the only place where the accidents are not judged. No matter what the circumstances, insurance companies split the costs fifty-fifty."

We are momentarily stalled on the inside lane, giving me the chance to see the tomb of the unknown soldier. Marked by a quiet flame under the arch, it sits nearly unnoticed in the eye of this storm.

As if to make up for an excess of manners in the rest of its culture, Parisian traffic is anarchy. Throughout Paris, green lines—a quaint attempt to establish bike lanes—blink from under the wheels of the traffic.

In the 1980s, my friend Steve Smith (co-author of my France guidebook) and I shared ownership of a VW van in Europe. One day, Steve told me that when Parisians bump and grind in traffic, they generally don't even bother to stop. An hour later, a woman grazed our van. She gave me a not-quite-apologetic "we'll never be able to establish who's at fault" look and drove on.

"Vinnie van Go," as we called our van, was close to both Steve and me. Steve shipped Vinnie from Portland to Europe packed with his family's worldly belongings when they moved to France. My wife and I conceived our first-born under its pop-top. Vinnie served valiantly as a production wagon as we filmed our first thirteen public television shows. My publisher, Ken Luboff, who with John Muir published the cult-ish *How to Keep Your Volkswagen Alive: A Manual of Step by Step Procedures for the The Compleat Idiot*, vacationed with Vinnie. With Vinnie, I survived sudden Norwegian blizzards and corrupt Neapolitan cops. Once, while sleeping in Vinnie on a dark side street in Paris, I was jolted awake by voices of a gang of late night trouble-makers, who spent several minutes playing with the pronunciation of "Washington" on the license plate.

Along with its abundance of traffic cops, Paris seems to keep a bus barn filled with riot police. It's rare that some kind of *"manifestation"* isn't disrupting traffic somewhere in town. It was a *manifestation*—not traffic or thugs—that spelled the end of our handy Vanagon.

Vinnie was firebombed during a student riot, sacrificed for the cause of smaller classrooms. Steve, who was living in Paris at the time, sent me photographs of the blackened corpse of our van, which—along with about fifty other cars—burned in the riot. Vinnie van Gone.

Ariane and I survive our afternoon together without a hint of a *manifestation*, no fifty-fifty accidents, and no plans to make TV together. She gets out at her studio and I keep the cab for a ride to Montmartre.

Moonrise over Paris

By sundown, I'm wiping my feet on the steps of Sacre-Coeur. This neo-Byzantine church crowns Paris' only hill.

For years I'd finish tours here on Montmartre overlooking

Paris. While the group enjoyed views of the City of Light, I'd grab a prayerful moment in the Sacre-Coeur church. Marveling at the pitfalls we avoided, the lessons we learned, and the friends we made, I'd thank God for safe and happy travels.

Now I step inside without a group and warm my face over a tray of candles. Taking a seat in a pew, I remember how alone I was feeling when Paris gave me the most powerful religious experience of my life. It was early in my tour-guiding days. The tour was over. Seeing the last tourist off, I was overdue for some freedom. When I returned to my hotel room, a strange depression overcame me.

For three weeks I had been Mr. Travel, showing off Europe to the constant applause of shutter releases. Suddenly, no one in Paris even knew I was alive. Venturing outside the security of friends and the responsibility for followers, I stepped into solitude.

The long-awaited tomorrow was here. I was alone and free and expecting to be happy. But my small hotel room became tiny. A huge weight pushed me to the bed as my illusion of strength and power tumbled down on me like a Greek temple in an earthquake. God was telling me I couldn't be strong alone.

Good travel is more than counting blessings. It's understanding them. You appreciate the vintner and the land in the bouquet of a fine wine. You let a favorite artist share new beauties in times and places you've never been. You eat better ice cream than you thought possible. And you warm your spirit in the glow of a European who's found his niche in life. Good travel makes God obvious to me.

Stepping back outside the church, I join the gang sitting on the steps. From these steps lovers of Paris watch as the streetlights of each *arrondissement* pop on in a nightly electronic roll call, one district at a time.

I want to sit alone, but street vendors take turns with me, hawking their plastic gimmicks. First a soft-spoken young man flies his plastic wind-up bird. Next an older guy yanks on fluorescent yo-yos. Finally two boys bounce cigar-shaped balloons the size of small dirigibles between me and my view. Each wears a look of sincere curiosity, wondering why I will not buy their treasures.

A cruel local schoolgirl, more clever than I am, yells, "Police!" and the street merchants scatter. Those with retail displays laid out on a ground cloth pull a cord scrunching everything into a sack and vanish.

Suddenly only the romantics remain, loitering on the steps of Montmartre. Simon and Garfunkel wannabes sing energetically out of tune. At the base of this "mount of martyrs" the red sign of a cafeteria seems to introduce the hedonistic red light district by blinking "Self-Serve."

I walk downhill, grab a quick dinner at the self-serve restaurant, and then step into Paris' red light district, Pigalle. Six blocks of tour buses wait for their groups to finish their cancan evening.

In twenty-five years of Paris, I've never come close to buying a ticket to the cancan. But a red light district hits me like a surprise stoplight. Even if I were a customer, I'd be too nervous to get my money's worth, but looking is free and reasonably safe. Prostitutes decorate the bars they call their offices. I float by, swimming close, flirting but never touching.

I can't walk past Hotel de Douai without poking in. Back in the 1970s, this was my Parisian hotel of choice. It's just off Place Blanche. The "white place" got its name from its location at the base of the hill where the original plaster of Paris was quarried. Sloppily, it was loaded into wagons on Place Blanche.

Hotel de Douai was a carnival of character. The door man, Monsieur Millon, spoke no English but tried. When I'd say "thank you," he'd reply, "thank you YOU" with an enthusiasm that made it mean "you're welcome." When customers arrived and said, "Here's my luggage," he'd say, "Mine's over there." Thank you YOU. His boss was Jane Danic, a fat-ankled woman from Brittany. As if running a loving orphanage, she mothered her guests.

Jane was old enough to remember the days when a child would lose its French citizenship if given a Celtic name. In spite of her acceptable name, Jane had a secessionist fire that gave her a street evangelist's zeal. By day, she'd orient tourists with an entertaining lecture while scrawling instructions upside down on the free city map. By night, she was a fountain of red wine, breathing noisily, the hairs on her face rustling, and spouting stories about how Brittany was sick and tired of being ruled by Paris. A visit with Jane turned over cultural rocks the French tourist board didn't set out.

I loved Jane's hotel with its toilets—tiny detours off the spiral staircase between floors—strung together by a single pipe from a time when plumbing was humble. The WC lights went on only when the bathroom door was bolted.

Hotel de Douai's rooms came without right angles. I remember finishing a tour here with a particularly fun and hearty group. Gary was a favorite traveler from those days when I packed Valium to calm my customers after room assignments. He took me into his room and, as if defeated, admitted that he couldn't handle a room in which nothing was square. Knowing a good man cracking can set off an entire tour group, I found him a room with ninety-degree corners.

Slowly the Pigalle neighborhood spread. Reports came to me of high-heeled women checking into Hotel de Douai for less than a night. While for me, the charm of Hotel de Douai could survive a few prostitutes, I had to drop it from my tours. A couple of years later, it was sold, gutted, and went three stars.

Dropping by today, I ask about Jane and Monsieur Millon. The man at the desk says, "Who?"

When out late in Paris, I like to finish my day with a walk along the Seine. Floodlit cathedral, inky river. Full moon, lonely quay. Caryatid lovers, a walk with friends. Just enough red wine and then some. For years I've used the Seine riverbank walk under a floodlit Notre Dame as a finale for tours I've led. We saunter under trees, backlit by the moon and 2,000 years of history. With buttresses fingering its walls like a blind person "seeing" a close friend's face, the church glows. It's the way your last night in Paris should be.

Once, a few years ago, I was enjoying a last night in Paris with a particularly enthusiastic group of travelers. We had just broken out of a group hug and were still sharing stories about our trip. Suddenly, night became day as a barge at full throttle filled with flash-totin', Coke-guzzlin' tourists sprayed both banks of the river with searchlights. I lost it. It was the only time I've ever mooned anyone—and I wish it had come with a bullet. Looking through my legs at 400 tourists, I was blinded by the sweep of floodlights and a climax of flashes. If only I could circle the tiny white round thing in their scrapbooks. I'd autograph it.

St. Sulpice Grand-Orgue

It's the Sunday morning of my departure day. On the way to the airport I have time for Mass in a church with perhaps Europe's finest pipe organ. A cool wind blows down an empty rue Cler. The cheese man sleeps, so I have only strawberry jam for my breakfast baguette. Grabbing my bag, I kiss the air on either side of Mimi's big, happy face. On such a lovely morning, all troubles are forgotten. She yells *"bonne chance"* and cackles *"au revoir"* as the door to Hotel Leveque swings shut.

St. Sulpice has only twenty or thirty worshipers this morning. I grab a pew. Going to church anywhere south of the Rhine generally means going to Mass. Catholics claim that, since the Mass is the same everywhere, there's no language barrier. Maybe it's just the Lutheran in me, but I miss the alpha, the omega, and, except for communion, nearly everything in between.

When I make it to church in Europe, surrounded by huge buildings, statues of weary saints, and tiny congregations, it's the music that sends me.

The spiritual sails of St. Sulpice have been filled for two centuries by its 6,600-pipe organ. Organists from around the world come to Paris just to hear this organ.

As the first Mass of the morning finishes, half the crowd files quietly out but the rest, about a dozen, remain seated as the organist runs a musical victory lap. I happen to sit next to Lokrum, a young organist from Switzerland. He never comes to Paris without visiting St. Sulpice. When the organ stops, he whispers, "Follow me. You see nothing like this in America."

I follow Lokrum to the back of the church where the group gathers. A small churchmouse-of-a-man opens a tiny unmarked door and we scamper like sixteenth notes up a spiral staircase into the organ loft of our wildest fantasy. Organists are intimate with an obscure world. They have household words I've never encountered. They speak of masters from 200 years ago as if they just heard them in concert.

Lokrum stops me at a yellowed document. Dragging his finger down the glass frame, he says, "The twelve St. Sulpice organists. Most of them are famous in the evolution of pipe-organ music. With no break, they have made wonderful music in this church for over 200 years."

Like presidents or kings, the lineage is charted on the wall. Charles-Marie Widor played from 1870 to 1933. Marcel Dupre from 1934 to 1971. And now, Daniel Roth.

"Dupre started a tradition at St. Sulpice," Lokrum says. "Now people who love the organ are welcome here in the loft every Sunday."

The dozen gather around Daniel Roth. He knows he sits on a bench that organists the world over dream of warming. Maintaining Dupre's tradition of loft hospitality, Roth is friendly in four languages.

History is thumbtacked all around: dusty charts of the pipes, master organ builders, busts of previous organists, and a photo of Albert Schweitzer with Dupre. And overseeing all this is a bust of the god of organists, Johann Sebastian Bach.

Lokrum pulls me behind the organ into a dark room filled with what looks like eighteenth-century Stairmasters. "Before electricity, it took five men to power these bellows. And these powered the organ."

Suddenly, the music begins. Back at the organ, a commotion of music lovers crowds around a tower of keyboards in a forest of pipes.

In the middle of it all, under a dangling heat lamp, sits Daniel Roth. A slight, unassuming man who looks like an organist, he pushes back his flowing hair with graceful fingers. Then, with a boyish enthusiasm, he sinks his fingers into the organ.

With an assistant on either side of the long bench, and arms and legs stretched out like an angry cat, Roth plays all five keyboards. Supremely confident, he ignores the offbeat flashes of his adoring fellow organ lovers, follows the progress of the Mass via a tiny mirror, and makes glorious music.

The keyboards are stacked tall, surrounded by 110 stops—wooden knobs that turn the pipes off and on—in a multitude of tonal packages. In hurried conference, his assistants push and pull the stops after each musical phrase. They act quickly but as carefully as though God were listening.

Lokrum props a chair against the front wall of the organ, allowing me a commanding perch to oversee the musical action. On a well-worn wooden keyboard of footpedals spreading below the bench, Monsieur Roth's feet march with his fingers. A groupie flips over his cassette to catch the music as Roth cranes his neck to find the priest in his mirror.

I peer down at the busy keyboards and Roth's marching feet. Then, turning around, I peek through the pipes and down on a tiny congregation. Just as priests celebrate Mass in a church whether there are worshipers present or not, this organ must make music. I marvel at how the high culture of Europe persists. I'm thankful to experience it.

CHAPTER ELEVEN

HOME

"It's people that keep me
returning to Europe."

It's a jet lag morning. I awake to the dawning of dawn. Eyes still closed, I enjoy the moment of confusion that speedy travelers often wake to, wondering exactly where I am. I'm back in the world's coziest bed, next to my wife. Our kids are still sleeping—perhaps dreaming of travels to Chuckleslovakia.

I ponder the pillows I've warmed, the trains caught, spires climbed, and specialties *de la casa* nibbled. Most of all, I savor the fascinating parade of people I've met.

I've traveled in Europe long enough to see that people grow old faster than the buildings. The culture is changing. As Europe pulls itself into a higher standard of living, slices of its traditional culture slowly drop out of people's lives and into museums. The bent, black-clad widows with bad teeth are now standing straight, tinting their hair, and doing a lot less mourning. Prizes I once promoted as cultural treasures have been battered by an onslaught of good living. Many—from beerhall bands to cancan dances—seem to survive only as clichés kept alive for tourism.

But I've stopped fretting about that bulldozer of change. The essence of Europe, and the beauty of travel, remains its people.

This trip taught me that you can be alive or dead in a country—it all depends on how deeply you connect with the people you meet.

It's people that keep me returning to Europe: Piero cruising his alternative Venice, Petra revitalizing her Alp village hostel, and Paola singing of Rome's romantic wind. I remember Roberto declaring Fellini dead, Herr Jung sharing his World War II scars, and the Rhineland grandmother who brightened my morning with homemade marmalade. While generations pass, a steady stream of reinforcements flows in. Europe will continue to slap dance, yodel, and slurp escargot.

Travel broadens my perspective, sharpens my appreciation of things foreign, and adds more ingredients to the create-a-burger line of life. And each of these makes a plane ticket a good value. But above all, travel makes me happier to be home.

Propping myself up on my elbow, I give sleeping Anne a kiss on the cheek. I smile as I notice the small stack of cards on her bedside table . . . postcards from Europe.

POSTSCRIPT

The working title of this book was "Dancing with Europa." To write it, I planned on going to Europe to dance again with twenty years of favorite memories. I assumed that star moments of the past would pop up, ready for prime time. So I went to Europe, they popped up . . . and they were boring. Instead I found new magic moments. So I took what the storm brought in, along with a few favorite memories, and built this book.

Postcards from Europe chronicles a 3,000-mile circle through Europe. I did the loop three times in two years to write this book. On my first two trips I quarried raw material. A third trip was necessary to putty, sand, and polish. Even with a lifetime of experience, it was clear that I couldn't fill in the color without being there. For me, ideally, travel writing is writing while traveling.

As this book neared completion, I showed a particular section to my dad. His response after reading it: "Good writing, but it didn't happen that way." I did take some artistic liberties. I occasionally grafted real people, places, and experiences into travel "experiences" that are true in spirit. For instance, the account of my 1973 trip includes memories from my other early vagabond summers. In several cases—particularly in small town settings—I've changed the characters' names. Insignificant comments can become chain reactions that send small towns up in social flames.

Forgive the old girlfriend stories. My publisher recommended I cut back here. But they are some of my best memories and I strongly recommend seasoning European travel with romance.

I hope this book will have an interactive life. My Web site, www.ricksteves.com, has a "Postcards from Europe" corner with news on characters in the book; photos of featured people, places, and events; reader comments; and fun jetsam which—while interesting—didn't find a home in this book. Do drop in.

This book's table of contents makes a fine trip itinerary (it's the most popular of the tours we lead at Europe Through the Back Door). To do it on your own, my *Best of Europe* guidebook supplies the nitty-gritty, and my *Best of Travels in Europe* video covers the route, showing many of the people and places.

Of the more than three hundred long days I've spent filming *Travels in Europe*, very little is recounted in this book. Filming simply isn't much fun. I've been fortunate to have TV production partners whose commitment to teaching good travel has always overcome the frustrations that accompany producing a public television series almost entirely without corporate financing. I am thankful to the many people who helped produce *Travels in Europe*: especially John Givens, Pat Larson and Sandie Nisbet (my partners at Small World Productions), John Coney, photographer Tom Speer, Tom Doggett at Oregon Public Broadcasting, and the supportive folks at American Public Television, which distributes our series to public television.

The hardworking gang at John Muir Publications in Santa Fe is forever supportive and wise in keeping my books selling. And my friend and in-house editor Risa Laib (who knows and cares for my books as much as I do) brings clarity and consistency to my writing.

This book would not exist without the support of many talented people at Europe Through the Back Door. Our hardworking staff of thirty travelers (in our Edmonds office just north of Seattle) and about as many tour guides (who lead the 130 tours we operate each year) keep ETBD running smoothly when I'm off writing postcards. Our free quarterly travel newsletter explains our work (tel. 425/771-8303 or www.ricksteves.com).

While I wouldn't trade my job for any other, it's tough to find enough time for my wonderful family. For this reason, I dedicated this book to my supportive wife and our less patient kids. I've traveled with Anne, Andy, and Jackie every year since the kids were born. Our eleven-year-old Andy has been to Europe that many times. As I wrote this book, I came up with no family stories. The truth is, I enjoy my family most at home. Maybe that's because for me, Europe is undeniably work. And when I'm home, I'm not Rick Steves the travel guy . . . but just Dad.

Happy travels!
Rick Steves

Rick Steves' guidebooks cover all your travel needs!

Learn the essential travel skills before you go.
Rick Steves' Europe Through the Back Door
Rick Steves' Europe 101: History and Art for the Traveler

Take along guidebooks for country specifics.
Rick Steves' Best of Europe
Rick Steves' France, Belgium & the Netherlands
Rick Steves' Germany, Austria & Switzerland
Rick Steves' Great Britain
Rick Steves' Ireland
Rick Steves' Italy
Rick Steves' Scandinavia
Rick Steves' Spain & Portugal

Explore!
Rick Steves' Florence
Rick Steves' London
Rick Steves' Paris
Rick Steves' Rome
Rick Steves' Venice

Communicate!
Rick Steves'
   French Phrase Book
   German Phrase Book
   Italian Phrase Book
   French/Italian/German
     3-in-1 Phrase Book
   Spanish/Portuguese
     2-in-1 Phrase Book

Enjoy!
Rick Steves' Mona Winks

Dream!
Rick Steves' Postcards from Europe: 25 Years of Travel Tales from America's Favorite Guidebook Writer

---

AVALON TRAVEL

Rick Steves' books are available at your local bookstore. To get Rick's free newsletter and learn more about Europe Through the Back Door call (425) 771-8303 or visit www.ricksteves.com.

For more information about Avalon Travel Publishing, visit www.travelmatters.com

About the Author

Ellen L. Frost is Director, Government Programs, U.S.-Japan Relations, in the Washington, D.C. office of Westinghouse Electric Corporation. In that capacity she advises both her company and a high-technology industry group on U.S.-Japan relations and their impact on business activities. In the field of U.S.-Japan relations she specializes in technology transfer, trade and investment, research and development, and defense issues.

Before joining Westinghouse in 1981, Dr. Frost was Deputy Assistant Secretary for International Economic and Technology Affairs at the Department of Defense. In that capacity she was responsible for policy decisions on international economic issues of interest to the Department of Defense, including technology transfer, export controls, coproduction, and foreign aid. Prior to that, she worked in the U.S. Treasury Department (1974–77), the U.S. Senate (1972–74), and the U.S. Department of State (1963).

Dr. Frost is a member of the Council on Foreign Relations in New York and the International Institute of Strategic Studies in London. She is Vice Chairman of the Executive Committee of the Japan-America Society of Washington and Chairman of the Technology Cooperation Committee of the Aerospace Industries Association.

Dr. Frost has published several articles on technology transfer as an issue in U.S. relations with Japan, China, and Western Europe.

She holds a Ph.D. from Harvard University, an M.A. from the Fletcher School of Law and Diplomacy, and a B.A. from Radcliffe College, where she was elected to Phi Beta Kappa. She is married to William F. Pedersen, Jr., an environmental lawyer. They have two children.